Management of Turfgrass Diseases

J. M. Vargas, Jr.

Michigan State University
East Lansing, Michigan

Burgess Publishing Company
Minneapolis, Minnesota

Editorial: Gerhard Brahms, Elisabeth Sovik
Art: Adelaide Trettel, Lynn Guilfoyle Dwyer
Production: Morris Lundin, Pat Barnes

Cover designed by Adelaide Trettel

Burgess Publishing Company
7108 Ohms Lane
Minneapolis, Minnesota 55435

H   G   F   E   D   C   B   A

PREFACE

This book is meant primarily for undergraduates in turfgrass management or turfgrass pathology and for turfgrass managers in the field (e.g., golf course superintendents, lawn-care operators, landscapers, and garden store operators). It contains the technical information necessary for decision making in all areas of turfgrass management, as well as practical information useful in the day-to-day operation of turfgrass management programs.

Although the emphasis is on diseases, all aspects of turfgrass culture are touched upon. In addition to helping readers solve the riddle of which grasses are resistant and which are susceptible to various diseases, this book presents cultural programs designed to keep the incidence of disease to a minimum on susceptible grasses, and fungicide programs for diseases that require such management. The recommendations that are made take into account all the cultural aspects of turf management (e.g., diseases, cultivation, fertilization, mowing). The aim is to provide the densest turf for the longest period of time, not the greenest, lushest turf (which is usually the shortest lived).

This book differs from most books on turfgrass management in that it is not simply a compilation of facts which the reader must evaluate. (Such an approach is fine for the experienced turfgrass manager but does little for the novice, who obviously needs the most help.) Turfgrass management is an art based on sound scientific knowledge. Not everyone can manage turf successfully, even with all the facts, for the facts must be interpreted and integrated into the management program. Interpretation and integration are what this book aims at. New discoveries will, of course, be made, but this book is an up-to-date account of the current state of the art and science of turfgrass disease management.

I sincerely thank James B. Beard, George W. Bird, Don Blasingame, Herb Cole, Phil Colbaugh, T. E. Freeman, Charles Gould, Bobby G. Joyner, W. A. Meyer, Noel Jackson, George Kozelnicky, Charles Laughlin, Bob E. Partyka, Kenyon T. Payne, Paul E. Rieke, Pat Sanders, Robert Sherman, Richard Smiley, Ward Stienstra, and A. J. Turgeon for editing various portions of the manuscript and for their excellent suggestions. Carolyn Brown, Sarah Pounder, and Chris Weiler gave valuable technical assistance, as did Hope Shepard, who also helped type the manuscript. Linda Swain spent long hours typing and organizing the book, and Ron Detweiler conducted my research program so I could devote the necessary time to writing the book. A special thanks to Julia Roesler for the fine artwork she prepared.

I am also grateful to Frank Howard, for having faith in me; Harry Young, for taking a chance on me and convincing me to stand up for what I believe in; Roy Wilcoxson, for teaching me to deal harmoniously with fellow scientists and employees; and Gene Saari, who convinced me that to be anything less in this life than a plant pathologist would be to fail. Others who inspired me are Mike Prescott, Bob Kroll, Ed Klos, Jim Percich, Chuck Laughlin, Bill Fields, Don Benham, and Gordon La Fontaine.

A special thanks to Mary Ann, Jay-Jay, Michael, and Katie, who were patient and understanding during the long hours I neglected them while writing this book.

CONTENTS

To the one I love

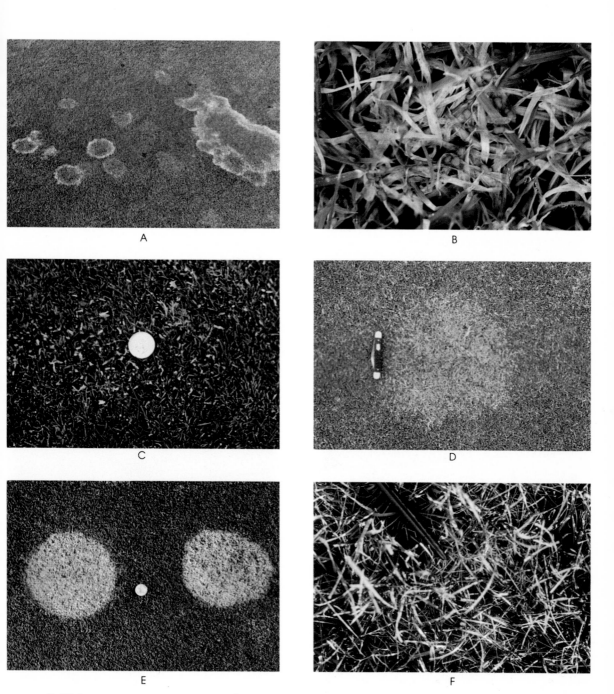

PLATE 1

(A) *Typhula* blight (gray snow mold) showing the grayish colored mycelium of the fungus in a Penncross creeping bentgrass turf
(B) Sclerotia of *Typhula incarnata* in Penncross creeping bentgrass immediately after the snow has melted
(C) Basidiocarps of *Typhula incarnata* which arose in the fall from sclerotia that were produced the previous spring and oversummered in the thatch
(D) *Fusarium* patch in a Penncross creeping bentgrass turf during the fall
(E) *Fusarium* patch (pink snow mold) in a Penncross creeping bentgrass turf in the spring after the snow has melted
(F) *Corticium* red thread in a fine-leaf fescue turf

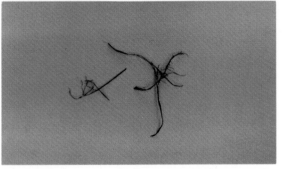

G

H

(G) Closeup of *Corticium* red thread on Pennlawn spreading fescue
(H) Typical "frog-eye" symptoms of *Fusarium* blight

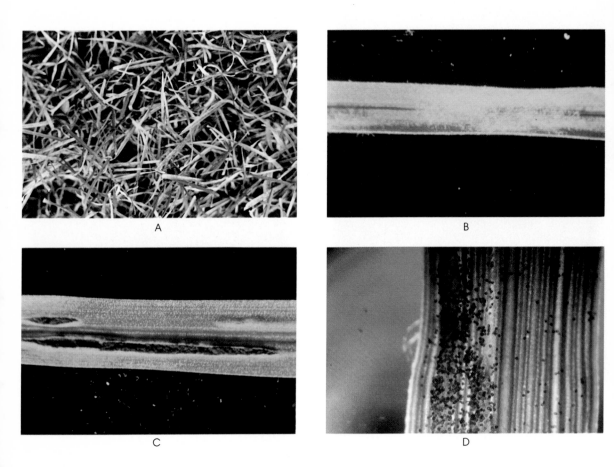

A

B

C

D

PLATE 2

(A) Powdery mildew on blades of Merion Kentucky bluegrass
(B) Closeup of powdery mildew on Merion Kentucky bluegrass blade
(C) Closeup of stripe smut on Merion Kentucky bluegrass blade; note the brown teliospores erupting through the epidermis
(D) Rust-colored urediospores of bermudagrass rust on a Sunturf bermudagrass leaf

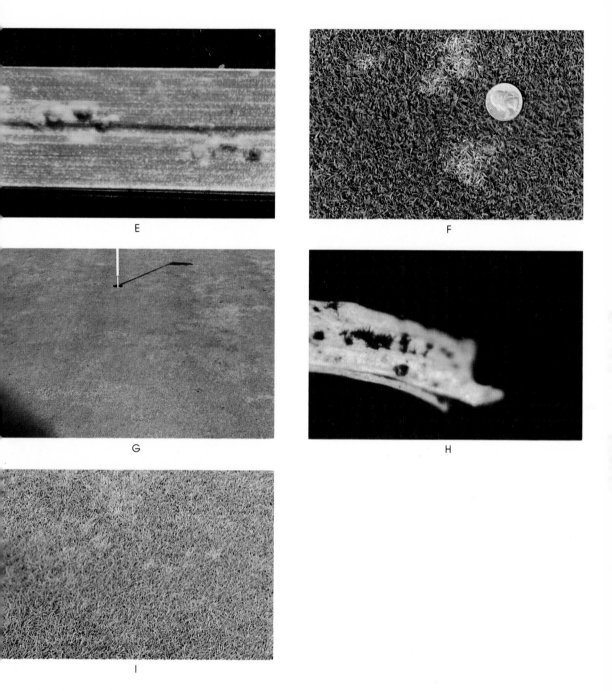

(E)   Closeup of rust pustules on Merion Kentucky bluegrass
(F)   Closeup of *Sclerotinia* dollar spot on a Toronto creeping bentgrass
(G)   Anthracnose damage on an annual bluegrass-creeping bentgrass green; the annual bluegrass has been severely thinned and yellowed while the creeping bentgrass remains unaffected
(H)   Closeup of anthracnose acervuli on a leaf of annual bluegrass
(I)   Yellow tuft in a Penncross creeping bentgrass turf

PLATE 3

(A) *Pythium* blight in overseeded ryegrass (Photograph courtesy of Dr. Don Blasingame)
(B) Foliar symptoms of gray leaf spot on St. Augustinegrass (Photograph courtesy of Dr. Don Blasingame)
(C) Closeup of St. Augustine decline symptoms on turfgrass blades (Photograph courtesy of Dr. Bobby G. Joyner)
(D) Spring dead spot in a bermudagrass turf (Photograph courtesy of Dr. Don Blasingame)
(E) Closeup of *Ophiobolus* patch in Kentucky bluegrass
(F) *Rhizoctonia* brown patch in St. Augustinegrass (Photograph courtesy of Dr. Don Blasingame)

chapter one

INTRODUCTION TO TURFGRASS DISEASES

CAUSES OF TURFGRASS DISEASES

There are five groups of organisms that cause plant diseases—fungi, bacteria, viruses, nematodes, and mycoplasma. Fungi are the most important cause of turfgrass diseases; they are followed in importance by the nematodes and the viruses. There is only one major viral disease of turfgrass, St. Augustine decline. No economically important turfgrass diseases caused by bacteria or mycoplasma are known at present, but it is possible that some will be discovered.

A *disease* is an abnormality in structure or function that is caused by an infectious agent and that kills the plant or destroys its aesthetic value. Diseases are sometimes classified into two categories, infectious and noninfectious (or physiological), but I prefer to consider noninfectious diseases as injuries. *Injury* is damage to a plant that is caused by a noninfectious agent and that kills the plant or destroys its aesthetic value. Hail, lightning, nutrient deficiencies, and fertilizer or pesticide burn are noninfectious agents that can injure plants.

A *pathogen* is an agent that causes a disease. Most pathogens are parasites as well. A *parasite* is an organism that obtains some or all of its nutrients from a living host. (The organism a parasite lives on is called its *host*.) Some pathogens are *obligate parasites*; they can obtain their nutrients only from a live host or living tissue. Rust, powdery mildew, and all viruses are obligate parasites. Organisms that live only on dead organic matter are called *saprophytes* (slime molds are an example). Organisms that are mostly parasitic but that can, under certain conditions, live as saprophytes are called *facultative saprophytes* (for example, *Typhula*, *Sclerotinia*, and *Helminthosporium*). Organisms that live most of the time as saprophytes but that can, on occasion, become parasites are called *facultative parasites* (for example, *Fusarium*, *Rhizoctonia*, and *Pythium*). Table 1-1 shows the classification of some organisms that are known to cause disease in turfgrass, and figures 1-1 and 1-2 illustrate the developmental stages of the facultative saprophytes *Helminthosporium* spp.

In order for disease to occur, three conditions are necessary: a susceptible host, a virulent pathogen, and a favorable environment. These three conditions are called the plant disease triangle. If any one of them is missing, disease will not develop.

The disease process usually involves four steps. They are infection, incubation, symptom development, and inoculum production. *Infection* is the process by which a disease-producing organism (pathogen) enters the plant. *Incubation* is the period during

1

Table 1-1.   A Classification of Organisms That Cause Turfgrass Diseases

Obligate Parasites	Facultative Saprophytes	Facultative Parasites	Saprophytes
Erysiphe graminis	*Corticium fuciforme*	*Colletotrichum*	Fairy ring fungi*
Parasitic nematodes	*Fusarium nivale*	*graminicola*	*Mucilago spongiosa*
Puccinia spp.	*Gloecercospora sorghi*	*Fusarium roseum*	*Physarum cinereum*
St. Augustine decline	*Helminthosporium* spp.	*Fusarium tricinctum*	
virus	*Ophiobolus graminis*	*Pythium* spp.	
	Piricularia grisea	*Rhizoctonia solani*	
	Sclerophthora macrospora	*Alternaria* spp.	
	Sclerotinia homoeocarpa	*Curvalaria* spp.	
	Typhula spp.		
	Urocystis agropyri		
	Ustilago striiformis		

*There is evidence that some fairy rings may be weak parasites.

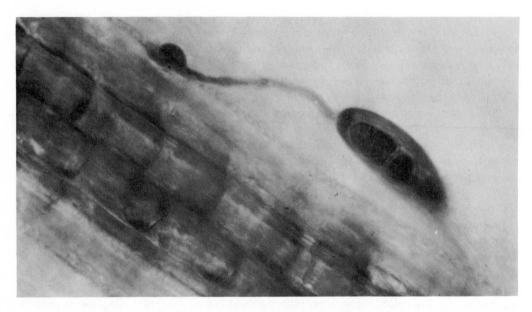

Figure 1-1.   Conidiospore of *Helminthosporium sorokinianum* on a fescue leaf. The germ tube has produced an appressorium.

which the pathogen inhabits its host without producing visible symptoms. The interaction between the pathogen and its host results in *symptom development. Inoculum production* is the process whereby the pathogen reproduces propagules for self-preservation. The inoculum can be simply the spore of a fungus, or it can be the entire organism, as it is in the case of a virus or a bacterium.

IMPORTANCE OF TURFGRASS DISEASES

Disease plays a major role in determining the success or failure of a turfgrass stand. It is often the single most important factor limiting the successful growth of a cultivar or

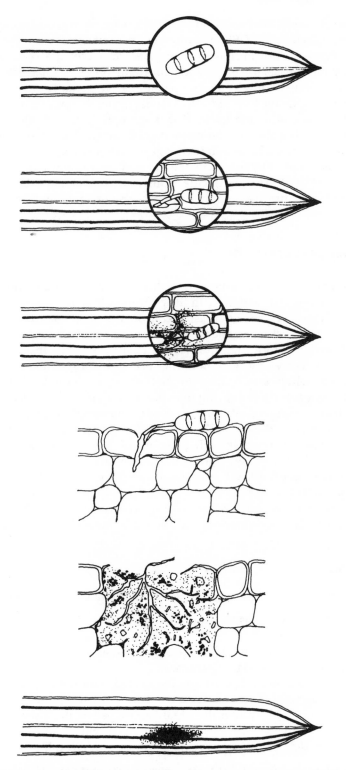

Figure 1-2. Germination of a *Helminthosporium* conidiospore and subsequent penetration, incubation, and development of symptoms on a turfgrass blade

species, a fact that you must keep in mind when selecting a turfgrass species or cultivar. For example, spring dead spot (SDS) on bermudagrass limits its widespread use as a fairway grass, especially in the northern regions of the warm-season grassbelt; St. Augustine decline (SAD), a viral disease, has eliminated St. Augustinegrass as a desirable turfgrass in many areas; and *Fusarium* blight and stripe smut have made it impractical to plant Kentucky bluegrass cultivars like Merion, Windsor, and Fylking. The best-textured, nicest-colored, fastest-germinating grass, if it is susceptible to a major pathogen, will turn into the worst-looking and poorest-colored grass imaginable when it becomes decimated by a disease, and you will wish it hadn't germinated at all.

Turfgrass diseases caused by fungi are of great economic importance. It is difficult to get exact figures, but the turfgrass fungicide industry was estimated to be 22 million dollars in 1976. More fungicides are used on turfgrass than on any other single crop in the United States.

IDENTIFYING TURFGRASS DISEASES

A little knowledge is said to be a dangerous thing—and it is! Often samples of dead or dying grass are collected and mailed, with little information, to a diagnostic laboratory. At the laboratory, disease organisms are isolated from the plant material and a diagnosis is made. Under such circumstances a disease may be diagnosed as "Helminth" or as *Fusarium* blight when it is neither. Or what appear to be black *Helminthosporium* lesions are observed on dying turf, and it is assumed that Helminth is causing the problem, which may or may not be the case. It would be difficult to find a patch of Kentucky bluegrass in the spring that didn't have *Helminthosporium* lesions, or to make isolations from turfgrass roots and not find *Fusarium* species, but does that mean these organisms are causing the disease? Maybe. Before you jump to conclusions, look at the other symptoms in the area. Ask such questions as: Were there many black lesions? Were they large? Did the grass show a general, all-over thinning? If the answers are yes, then *Helminthosporium* is probably the cause. Were "frog-eye" patterns present? Was there evidence of wilt inside the "frog-eyes"? Did hillsides and southern exposures get the disease first and most severely? When wilting occurred did syringing seem to help? If the answer to all of these questions is yes, then it is likely that *Fusarium* blight is the problem.

Koch's Postulates

Koch's postulates provide a basis for establishing the cause of a disease.

1. *Association*—The organism suspected of causing the disease must always be present when the disease occurs.
2. *Isolation*—It must be possible to isolate the suspect organism and grow it in a pure culture (except in the case of obligate parasites).
3. *Inoculation*—When a disease-free host is inoculated with the organism, it must exhibit the same symptoms observed when the disease occurs spontaneously.
4. *Reisolation and comparison*—When the organism suspected of causing the disease is reisolated from the inoculated plants, grown in a pure culture, and then compared to the first organism isolated, the two organisms must be identical.

It is often difficult to satisfy all of Koch's postulates. For example, the first research that showed *Fusarium roseum* and *F. Tricinctum* to be the causal agents of *Fusarium* blight failed to demonstrate "frog-eye" symptoms, and therefore Koch's postulates were not completely satisfied, leaving the exact cause of the disease still open to question. Spring dead spot provides a contrasting example. Many pathogenic fungi have been isolated from bermudagrass, but since no one has produced dead spots by inoculating turf with these organisms, researchers have felt it best not to name any of the pathogenic organisms associated with the disease as the causal agent until such time as postulates 3 and 4 are satisfied.

Taking Samples

When you take samples of diseased grass, follow these instructions:

1. Look for an area that has just begun to show symptoms. Older areas may be contaminated with saprophytic organisms living on the dead tissue.
2. Take a large enough sample. You need at least a 6-inch plug, not just a couple of leaves. Include the root system of the plant in your sample.
3. If the sample is to be mailed, wrap it in paper. Never put it in a plastic bag, because the saprophytic fungi, bacteria, and nematodes will turn the sample to mush before it arrives. The one exception is soil samples for nematode analysis, which should be placed in a plastic bag to keep them from drying out. Samples should be mailed immediately after they are taken and early in the week, so that they don't sit in the post office over the weekend.

Include the following information with your samples:

1. Species and cultivar of turfgrass
2. Age of the grass stand
3. Symptoms (wilt, yellowing, stunting, leaf spots, thinning, etc.)
   a. Initial symptoms
   b. Current symptoms
4. Prevalence of the disease (a few spots, large areas, all greens, one green, etc.)
5. Severity of the disease (moderate, severe)
6. Location of the disease (high spots, low spots, edges of greens, near house, under tree, etc.)
7. Soil type (clay, sand, loam, heavy soil, etc.)
8. Recent treatments
   a. Fertilizer (date of last application)
   b. Pesticides (not just fungicides) applied in last month
   c. Cultivation (give dates)
      (1) Coring (aerifying)
      (2) Spiking
      (3) Vertical mowing
9. Weather
   a. Just before symptoms developed
   b. At the time symptoms developed
10. Date the problem was first observed

Interpreting Research

It is often difficult for laypersons to interpret the data supplied by researchers. The researcher may tell only half the story or may not relate laboratory findings to what actually happens in the field. For example, Fylking is still reported to be resistant to *Helminthosporium* melting-out, which it is, and which sounds good since *Helminthosporium* melting-out is a major disease. But if the researcher fails to mention that Fylking is susceptible to *Fusarium* blight (fig. 1-3), as a matter of fact so susceptible that *Fusarium* blight will completely destroy the Fylking turf in a matter of a few years, you will be surprised and disappointed when your stand of grass becomes decimated. Yet I have seen this happen. Sometimes, after expounding a variety's good points for 10 minutes, a scientist will end by saying "Of course it has some other problems" or "It is, of course, susceptible to *Fusarium* blight." Unless you know how susceptible it is to *Fusarium* blight, or how serious a disease *Fusarium* blight is, you will probably plant it thinking "Well, it only has one problem compared to so many good points." It would be like buying a car that was perfect except for a defective motor. In both cases you waste a lot of money on something that won't work.

Figure 1-3. *Fusarium* blight on Fylking Kentucky bluegrass

The same thing happens with data on disease. Researchers publish results and give talks stating that Kentucky bluegrass is more susceptible to rust and *Corticium* red thread at high nitrogen levels. It is true, too—in the greenhouse or laboratory, where grass is grown in pots, fertilized, and artificially inoculated and readings are taken before the grass is mowed or clipped. But in the field nitrogen will help control rust and red thread on Kentucky bluegrass. Why? The difference is that in the field the grass is mowed at least once a week. Since rust and red thread take from 10 to 14 days to develop after the grass is infected, and both are foliar pathogens, weekly mowing will ensure that the infection is mowed off before the disease develops. Such laboratory data do increase our understanding of the disease, but they belong in scientific journals and at scientific meetings, not in journals read by lay people and not at turfgrass conferences and other grower meetings. Why explain laboratory results to a person whose livelihood is growing grass in the field, if what happens in the laboratory has no correlation with what happens in the field? Be wary of laboratory data that are not accompanied by good field data.

This brings up another point. Each year new ideas come forth, some with good data to back them up, others with no supporting data or one year's experimental results, or merely some random observations. Before you rush headlong into trying a new product or cultural practice that may cost you your job, ask to see the data. If you have trouble understanding the data, ask your local turf expert for an evaluation. If a cultural practice or chemical control could result in the loss of turf, try it on a small area first to see how it works under your conditions, regardless of the advice you have been given.

DISEASE MANAGEMENT

The word *management* is used in this book in preference to the word *control*. Control implies the eradication of a disease problem. In reality, however, the problem will occur season after season or recur many times during a single growing season. Therefore, diseases actually are managed rather than controlled, and an approach that stresses management should prove more illuminating and useful to the turfgrass grower than one that assumes control is possible.

Too often turfgrass pathologists have dealt with single diseases as though they occurred in a vacuum. Too often chemical and cultural recommendations or cultivar selection are based on consideration of only one disease. However, a single species or cultivar may be attacked by many diseases throughout the growing season, and therefore the total picture must be evaluated. Recommendations of cultivars, cultural practices, and chemical agents must reflect a knowledge of all the diseases that can occur on a given species or cultivar throughout the season.

Plant pathologists also need to stop talking about diseases as though they occur on just any green vegetation. Diseases attack specific grass species, or, in some cases, specific cultivars. Turfgrass diseases should be thought of in relation to the specific cultivar or species they afflict.

Strategies for dealing with turfgrass diseases include planting cultivars that are resistant to the major diseases and employing appropriate cultural practices and fungicide programs. Chapters 11 through 13 discuss such strategies.

chapter two

FUNGUS DISEASES OF TURFGRASSES, I

Disease: Anthracnose

Pathogen: *Colletotrichum graminicola* (Ces.) Wils. (syn. *C. cereale* Manns)

Hosts: Annual bluegrass, creeping bentgrass, Kentucky bluegrass, fineleaf fescue, perennial ryegrass

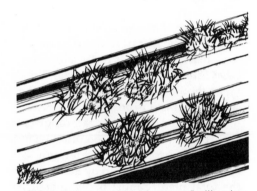

Colletotrichum graminicola acervuli with setae

Anthracnose has been described as a minor disease of annual bluegrass and several other turfgrasses in England [72, 121]. In the United States it has been reported to be one of the key factors causing death of annual bluegrass during warm weather [149] (HAS decline of annual bluegrass, see pp. 26-27). It appears to be one of the factors that limit the successful growth of fine-leaf fescues in the warmer areas of the cool-season grassbelt, and Duell and Schmit [31] have reported that anthracnose eliminates perennial ryegrass in roadside turfs.

Symptoms

Anthracnose is characterized by irregularly shaped patches of yellow-bronze turf ranging in size from a few inches to several feet. Leaf lesions initially appear as elongate reddish brown spots on the leaves. These spots may enlarge, eventually encompassing the entire leaf blade. Numerous black fruiting bodies (acervuli) of the fungus can be seen on the foliage as the disease progresses. The acervuli have black spines (setae) protruding from them.

Occurrence

C. graminicola can overwinter as a saprophyte in the plant debris or as a pathogen in infected tissue. Its life cycle is illustrated in figure 2-1. It appears to be a weak pathogen

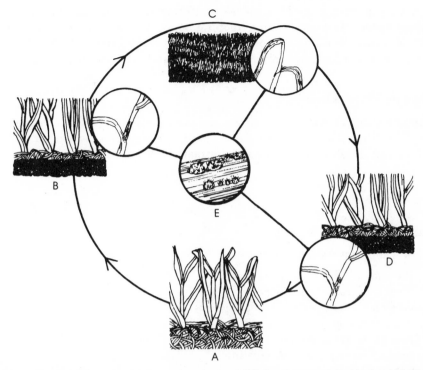

Figure 2-1. Life cycle of *Colletotrichum graminicola. A,* the fungus overwinters in dead plant tissue in the thatch and on stems beneath the leaf sheath. *B,* visual infections in the spring are confined mostly to the stems beneath the leaf sheaths. The main symptom is yellowing of the plant. *C,* when the weather becomes hot the plants turn bronze and die. Acervuli are evident on the leaves. *D,* Acervuli disappear from leaf blades as cool weather returns, but are present on stems beneath the leaf sheath. Yellowing of the plant occurs again. *E,* closeup of acervuli on an infected plant.

which attacks turf growing under conditions of low soil fertility, high temperature stress, or both. It can show up on the roots, stolons, or leaves, but is most commonly found on the foliage of the grass plant. *C. graminicola* usually infects grass blades from the tip down, especially grass that has been freshly mowed. The serious damage to the turf occurs during periods of high temperature and humidity when the turf is under severe stress. The disease is most severe in areas of compaction, heavy traffic, and poor soil drainage. In addition, anthracnose seems to be one of the key factors in HAS decline of annual bluegrass (pp. 26-27).

Management

Cultural Practices

Anthracnose can be managed with light nitrogen application (½ pound per 1000 square feet) when it occurs during cool weather. The same light nitrogen applications will help to reduce the severity of the disease during warm weather, but fungicide treatments will also be necessary to prevent severe turf loss.

Resistant Cultivars

Creeping bentgrass appears to be resistant to anthracnose in the northern region of the cool-season grassbelt, but it is reported to be susceptible in the southern regions, the Kentucky bluegrass–bermudagrass transition zone, and the warm-season grassbelt.

Even in the northern region of the cool-season grassbelt, a wide range of resistance and susceptibility probably exists among creeping bentgrass cultivars. Furthermore, while Kentucky bluegrass, perennial ryegrass, and the fine-leaf fescues are listed as susceptible, there is undoubtedly a great range of resistance and susceptibility among their many cultivars.

Chemical Management

Anthracnose can be managed with benzimidazole systemic fungicides like benomyl, thiophanate-methyl, and thiophanate-ethyl applied every 2 to 3 weeks, or with contact fungicides like chlorothalonil, mancozeb, or maneb plus zinc sulfate applied every 7 to 10 days.

Disease: *Rhizoctonia* brown patch

Pathogen: *Rhizoctonia solani* Kuhn

Hosts: Annual bluegrass, bahiagrass, bermudagrass, centipedegrass, colonial bentgrass, creeping bentgrass, fine-leaf fescues, Kentucky bluegrass, meadow fescue, perennial ryegrass, St. Augustinegrass, tall fescue, velvet bentgrass, zoysiagrass

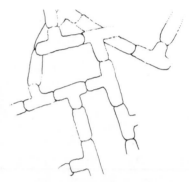

Rhizoctonia solani mycelium

Rhizoctonia brown patch is the most widespread disease of turfgrass. It occurs in all areas where turf is grown except for the cool, humid Pacific Northwest, and it attacks all known turfgrasses. *Rhizoctonia solani* has one of the widest host ranges of agricultural crops of any plant pathogen, in part because it is a soil inhabitor; that is, it lives on organic matter present in the soil and competes well with the other saprophytic microorganisms. It is thus distinguished from a soil invader, which does not compete well with saprophytic microorganisms and usually disappears after the host tissue decomposes.

Symptoms

The disease occurs as circular brown patches in the turf, from a few inches up to several feet in diameter. The infected leaves first appear water-soaked and dark, eventually drying, withering, and turning dark brown. Brown to black sclerotia are sometimes found beneath the leaf sheath or on the stolons. When the humidity is high a "smoke ring," which consists of the mycelium of the fungus, surrounds the outer margins of the diseased area (fig. 2-2). The "smoke ring" will disappear as the foliage dries. It is *not* necessary to have a "smoke ring" in order to have *Rhizoctonia* brown patch. Too often superintendents say, "I have what looks like brown patch but it can't be because there is no smoke ring." While the "smoke ring" aids in identifying brown patch, it is not essential.

In the early stages of *Rhizoctonia* brown patch only a few leaves and grass plants are destroyed, but if the disease is not checked immediately many more grass plants will be

Figure 2-2. *Rhizoctonia* brown patch with "smoke ring" evident on a golf course green (Photograph courtesy of Dr. Bill Daniels)

lost, especially on low-cut turf such as golf course greens. If warm weather continues and treatment is not applied, algae can cover the turf area infected by brown patch, eventually forming a hard crust which makes recovery even more difficult.

Another identifying characteristic of brown patch is a musky odor perceptible 12 to 24 hours before the disease appears and sometimes persisting after the disease appears. Some old-time superintendents spray "as needed," using the musky smell as an indicator of when to spray.

The disease takes quite a different form in the Pacific southwestern United States. Madison [90] reports *Rhizoctonia* brown patch as being primarily a disease of the roots and crowns. The damage to the grass is in the form of a ring, with the grass in the center remaining fairly healthy. The outer ring of grass turns brown and dies, usually from desiccation due to its damaged root system.

Occurrence

R. solani survives adverse periods as sclerotia or as mycelium in plant debris. It can also survive as a saprophyte in the thatch. When the soil temperature rises into the 60s the sclerotia begin to germinate and the fungus begins to grow. The fungus grows in a circular pattern, as most fungi do, but it apparently does not parasitize the grass plant until the air temperature rises into the mid-80s with high humidity and nighttime temperatures in the 70s or higher. *R. solani* is basically a weak parasite. At low temperatures it grows as a saprophyte or causes minute infections that do not seriously damage grass plants which are in good growing condition. It is only after a grass plant suffers heat stress and high-temperature growth stoppage begins that the balance switches to favor the fungus and disease development. One thing is certain, the fungus doesn't grow 6 inches or 3 feet overnight, as some plant pathologists suggest. *R. solani* simply cannot grow that fast. If it did, the entire area would be covered with mycelium instead of just having a "smoke ring" around the outside.

In laboratory experiments, Rowell found the cut leaf tip to be the primary site of entrance of *R. solani* [110]. However, the fungus can also enter through the stomates or by direct penetration of the grass blade. Hearn [59] reported that with the arrival of warm weather the fungus infects roots first, then stolons, and finally leaves.

Joyner et al. [73] report brown patch occurring on Kentucky bluegrass during cool weather with symptoms similar to the "frog eye" of *Fusarium* blight. The organism isolated from the spots appeared to be *R. solani*. Another isolated fungus was similar to *Rhizoctonia* but appeared to belong to the *Ceratobasidium* Rogers group. Detweiler and I (unpublished data) observed a similar disease in creeping bentgrass during the cool weather of the fall and isolated what appears to be a species of *Rhizoctonia*. Thus *Rhizoctonia* can no longer be considered strictly a warm-weather pathogen, or brown patch strictly a warm-weather disease. The genetic variability within the artificially grouped collection of organisms called *Rhizoctonia* is apparently great enough that *Rhizoctonia* can be a pathogen over a wide temperature range.

Management

Cultural Practices

Bloom and Couch [10] reported that in the greenhouse *Rhizoctonia* brown patch was least severe when the nitrogen level was low and levels of phosphorus and potassium were normal. The importance of several factors in contributing to the severity of the disease decreased in the following order: high nitrogen > normal phosphorus and potassium > low NPK > a balanced NPK program. High levels of nitrogen in the field during or just prior to the onset of hot humid weather will increase the severity of the disease; therefore minimum amounts of nitrogen, no more than ½ pound per 1000 square feet (actual), should be used as hot humid weather approaches. Normal levels of phosphorus and potassium should always be maintained except where *Poa annua* eradication programs or other special treatments are going on. As with *Sclerotinia* dollar spot, removal of the guttation water (dew) as early as possible in the morning will help to reduce the severity of the disease.

Resistant Cultivars

There appear to be no resistant species or varieties.

Chemical Management

There are many contact and systemic fungicides for managing brown patch; however, to be effective they must be used! *Rhizoctonia* brown patch is a disease in which infection takes place long before symptoms are evident, and when the symptoms do occur, large areas of turf are involved. If the disease is not treated right away and if the weather stays hot and humid, a considerable amount of grass may be lost and recovery may not take place until cool weather returns. Those who rely on a curative program and spray when they smell the musky odor should pray they don't develop hayfever. By and large, a preventive fungicide program is the best treatment.

Disease: *Sclerotinia* dollar spot

Pathogen: *Sclerotinia homoeocarpa* F. T.
Bennett

Hosts: Annual bluegrass, bahiagrass,
bermudagrass, centipedegrass,
chewings fescue, colonial bentgrass, creeping bentgrass, perennial ryegrass, Kentucky bluegrass, creeping and spreading
fescue, St. Augustinegrass, velvet
bentgrass, zoysiagrass

Dollar spot symptoms on a grass blade

Most golf course superintendents consider *Pythium* blight the most important
turfgrass disease, yet they spend more money trying to manage *Sclerotinia* dollar spot.
This is true throughout most of the temperate and hot humid regions of the United
States. On golf courses across the nation more money is spent to manage dollar spot than
is spent on any other turfgrass disease.

Symptoms

Sclerotinia dollar spot is found throughout the United States except in the arid regions
of the West. The disease is characterized by round, bleached-out or straw-colored spots
ranging from the size of a quarter to the size of a silver dollar (hence the name dollar
spot). The spots appear as sunken areas in the turf, especially in turf mowed to half an
inch or shorter. Individual spots may coalesce and destroy the turf in large undefined
areas (fig. 2-3). If the fresh spots are observed in the morning while the grass is still wet,
the grayish white fluffy mycelium of the fungus can be seen. The disease is spread primarily by mowers and other maintenance equipment carrying the infected plant tissue.
Infected plant tissue is also carried by golf shoes and carts. When the disease is controlled
only on the greens, its recurrence will usually be noticed first on the side of the green
that gets traffic from the infected approaches and fairway.

Sclerotinia dollar spot symptoms on individual grass blades appear as bleached-out or
light tan lesions the entire width of the blade, with reddish brown bands on the ends in
bentgrass, Kentucky bluegrass, red fescue, zoysiagrass, and bermudagrass. The reddish
brown banding does not occur on annual bluegrass.

Occurrence

Dollar spot occurs when the temperature is between 60 and 90 °F. There appear to be
at least two strains, one which occurs during cool weather (when the temperature is below 75 °F) and one which is favored by high humidity, warm days, and cool nights. Endo
et al. [38], and Endo and Malca [37] found a toxin associated with discoloration and deterioration (stunting and necrosis) of bentgrass roots. Endo [35] was able to associate the
lack of pathogenicity at 50 and 90 °F (10 and 32 °C) with lack of toxin production. Toxin
production occurred at temperatures between 60 and 80 °F (15.5 and 26.8 °C), and so did
stunting and browning of the roots and the invasion of foliar tissue by the pathogen.
Stunting, browning, and necrosis also occurred when the plant roots were separated
from the fungus by a cellophane bag that allowed diffusion of the water-soluble toxin
only, and the fungus could not subsequently be isolated from the affected root tissue.

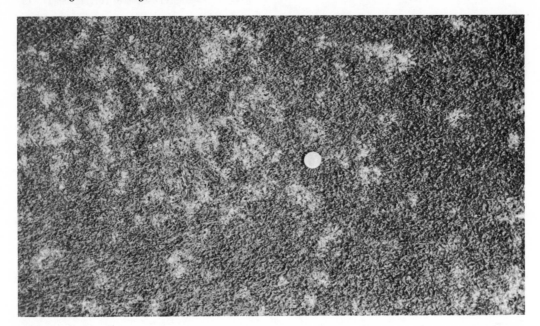

Figure 2–3. Closeup of *Sclerotinia* dollar spot on bermudagrass. (Photograph courtesy of Dr. Don Blasingame)

Management

Cultural Practices

Cultural management of dollar spot involves regulating the nitrogen level in the soil. According to one school of thought, the number of infections will be greater at high nitrogen levels, but the damage will be less severe than if nitrogen levels are low, because although fewer spots appear in the latter case, they tend to be larger and the damage is more severe. From a practical point of view, during periods of severe infection by *Sclerotinia* dollar spot the nitrogen level must be kept up in order to reduce the severity of the disease and to make the fungicide program more effective. Light and frequent application of nitrogen (½ pound per 1000 square feet) is best, both for managing the disease and for general growth of the grass plant, especially during periods of warm weather.

Couch and Bloom [20] found low soil moisture, not nitrogen level, to be important in the development of dollar spot. Their laboratory experiments showed foliar blighting in Kentucky bluegrass grown under conditions of low soil moisture to be more than double that in plants grown at field capacity. Howard et al. [68] and Smith [122] have reported more dollar spot in seasons with low rainfall. Therefore, the turf area should be kept near field capacity and adequate nitrogen provided when *Sclerotinia* dollar spot is a problem. The greatest benefit can be obtained from a good fungicide program when it is combined with these cultural practices.

"Removing the dew" to prevent *Sclerotinia* dollar spot is a common practice on golf course greens. It involves "poling" or "wiping" the dew with a bamboo pole, dragging a hose over the area, or washing the dew off with water. The latter practice may seem to defeat the purpose, since you are trying to dry off the green, but what you really want to do is remove the guttation water which makes up a large portion of what is referred to as dew. Guttation water is a fluid rich in carbohydrates and amino acids that is exuded from the tip of the grass blade through a structure called a hydrothode. This fluid supplies a nutrient-rich medium for the fungus to grow in as it spreads from leaf to leaf. Therefore, anything that will remove guttation water, such as diluting it with irrigation water or breaking up the droplets so the foliage will dry faster, will help reduce the severity of the disease.

Resistant Cultivars

There are no varieties of creeping bentgrass that are resistant to *Sclerotinia* dollar spot, and no resistant varieties of annual bluegrass are known. There are references which list one variety of creeping bentgrass as being moderately resistant or moderately suscepti-ble, but from a practical point of view all are susceptible, and a fungicide treatment will be required to prevent serious damage to the turf.

For the other grasses, it is simpler to name the most susceptible varieties so they can be avoided where *Sclerotinia* dollar spot is a major problem.

Turfgrass Species	Cultivar
Kentucky bluegrass	Nugget, Sydsport
Red fescue	Dawson
Perennial ryegrass	Manhattan
Bermudagrass	Ormond, Tifway, Sunturf
Zoysiagrass	Emerald
Bahiagrass	Pensacola

Chemical Management

Sclerotinia dollar spot can be managed by many contact and systemic fungicides. For specific chemicals, see chapter 6 and the appendix, and for a treatment schedule for specific turfgrasses, see chapters 11 and 12.

Disease: Fading-out, *Helminthosporium–Curvularia* complex

Pathogens: *Curvularia lunata* (Wakker) Boedijn, *C. geniculata* (Tracy and Earle) Boedijn, *C. intermedia* Boedijn, *C. protuberata* Nelson and Hodges

Hosts: Annual bluegrass, Kentucky bluegrass, creeping bentgrass, fine-leaf fescue, *Poa trivialis* L., Canada bluegrass

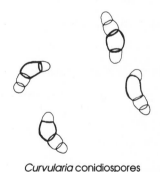

Curvularia conidiospores

Plant pathologists are still debating whether *Curvularia* causes a disease of turf or whether it is simply a secondary organism (saprophyte) invading an old *Helmintho-sporium* lesion. Couch [18] and Madison [90] have tended to discount *Curvularia* as a pathogen, while Howard [66] has supported the idea of *Curvularia* as a pathogen either alone or as part of a *Helminthosporium–Curvularia* complex. Brown et al. [13] showed that four species of *Curvularia* are pathogenic on Kentucky bluegrass, spreading fescue, and creeping bentgrass. Hodges and Madsen [63] concluded that *Curvularia geniculata* was a weak pathogen on Kentucky bluegrass under high temperature conditions (25 to 35 °C), but that it is part of a true disease complex with *Helminthosporium sorokinianum* at 30 °C. Lesions are initiated by *H. sorokinianum* and then necrotic tissue is invaded by *C. geniculata*, which is extremely aggressive at high temperatures. The occurrence of both pathogens results in a more severe disease than either is capable of causing alone. While the debate will probably go on forever, the evidence put forth by Brown et al. [13] and Hodges and Madsen [63] leaves little doubt that under proper conditions *Curvularia* species, either alone or in conjunction with *H. sorokinianum*, can be important turfgrass pathogens.

Symptoms

On Kentucky bluegrass and spreading fescue the grass blades turn yellow from the tip back, eventually becoming brown and then gray, until finally the whole blade looks shriveled. On creeping bentgrass the blades go from yellow to tan to shriveled. Leaf spots with tan centers and red or brown margins are sometimes observed on red fescue and Kentucky bluegrass but never on creeping bentgrass [13].

Occurrence

Fading-out is a warm-temperature disease (above 85 °F). Like anthracnose, it appears to attack grass plants that are experiencing heat stress or high-temperature growth stoppage. The disease is favored also by high humidity. Since *Curvularia* is a good saprophyte like *Rhizoctonia*, it can survive quite well in the plant debris until the ideal conditions are present, and then it becomes pathogenic.

Management

Cultural Practices

Syringing to cool the microclimate temperature will help reduce the severity of fading-out in open areas, but in areas with poor air circulation it may worsen the disease by raising the humidity [13].

Resistant Cultivars

No information is available on cultivars resistant to fading-out.

Chemical Management

Chemicals that can be used to treat fading-out include chlorothalonil, cycloheximide, cycloheximide-PCNB, and cycloheximide-thiram.

Disease: Copper spot

Pathogen: *Gloeocercospora sorghi* Bain and Edgerton

Host: Bentgrass (especially low-cut creeping bentgrass)

Gloeocercospora sorghi conidiospores

Copper spot, unlike *Sclerotinia* dollar spot and *Rhizoctonia* brown patch, is not a widespread disease on golf course greens. But it can be important when it does occur. It is usually a warm-weather disease (80 °F or higher), although it may begin when temperatures are in the low 70s [18]. It is not unusual to see grass infected simultaneously with dollar spot and copper spot.

Symptoms and Occurrence

Gloeocercospora sorghi survives periods away from the host as sclerotia in the mat and thatch. Infection can take place rapidly (within 24 hours) and considerable turf may be lost with heavy infections. The lesions are small and reddish at first. They enlarge to cover the entire width of the blade and can eventually destroy the entire leaf blade. The spots that develop in the turf are usually 1 to 3 inches in diameter and are copper to reddish pink. The pink color is due to the pink spore masses of the fungus, which are gelatinous when observed in the early morning "dew."

Management

Cultural Practices

No information is available on cultural practices for managing copper spot.

Resistant Cultivars

No information is available on cultivars resistant to copper spot.

Chemical Management

Cycloheximide, chlorothalonil, and anilazine will manage copper spot if it occurs. Since fungicides are normally part of a good preventive program, a special spray program for copper spot should not be necessary. However, the timing of fungicide application may have to be altered where copper spot is a problem.

Disease: Fairy rings

Pathogen: Many fungi, mostly in the class Basidiomycetes

Hosts: All turfgrasses

Fairy rings are caused by many soil-inhabiting fungi of the class Basidiomycetes. For a list of the different species associated with this disease see the book by Couch [18]. For identification of the specific fungus causing a particular ring, you will need to consult an expert who is experienced in identifying basidiomycete fungi. In general, identification of the species involved is not really necessary if control is your prime concern. If fairy rings appear, you can do one of three things: fumigate, excavate, or try to enjoy them for their aesthetic beauty. When fairy rings occur on greens, however, the third solution is not recommended for golf course superintendents who want to keep their jobs.

Symptoms

Fairy ring fungi tend to grow in a circle through the organic matter in the soil, mat, and thatch, breaking down organic matter as they grow and releasing nitrogen (ammonia) that eventually is reduced by other soil microorganisms to nitrates. This nitrogen stimulates turfgrass growth ahead of the dead or dying turf and sometimes behind it as well (see fig. 2-4). The area of increased growth—known as the zone of stimulation or the activity zone—is where the turf may die. Sometimes, however, instead of dying, the grass plants in the zone of activity simply turn yellow (chlorotic) or become stunted. The yellow grass in the zone of activity may die if heat or drought stress is applied, but usually if the turf is watered it will recover from the yellow, although it may still be stunted.

Figure 2–4.   Fairy ring on a bowling green

What causes the yellowing, stunting, or dying in the zone of activity? The yellowing and stunting certainly suggest some type of parasitic activity. Filer [40] demonstrated penetration and death of the cortical cells by the fairy-ring-producing fungus *Marasmius oreodes*. Filer [40, 41] also suggests that hydrogen cyanide production by *M. oreodes* is a possible explanation for the pathogenicity of the fairy ring fungi. The presence of the mycelium of the fungus in the thatch and soil could also account for the death of the grass plant. Mycelium is hydrophobic and consequently is impervious to water, creating a desert below it. Once the soil under the fungus mycelium becomes dry, it is difficult to wet again by artificial irrigation unless a wetting agent is added. A cross-sectional diagram of a fairy ring in a turfgrass profile is shown in figure 2-5.

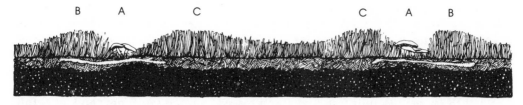

Figure 2–5. Cross section of a fairy ring in a turfgrass profile. The structure is typical of a *Tricholoma*-type fairy ring, which very seldom causes death of the turf. The mycelium (main body) of the fungus usually forms a thin layer that is confined to the thatch. *A*, stunted turfgrass with mycelium evident in the thatch; *B*, outer zone of stimulation; *C*, inner zone of stimulation.

Occurrence

By and large, fairy rings are caused by fungi that live or survive by spores or other means in dead organic matter in the soil or thatch. Areas that previously were forested, or ones in which stumps or logs have been used as fill, are prime candidates for the development of fairy rings. Many of the fungi that cause fairy rings are wood-decaying fungi. They also flourish in soils that are high in organic matter (for example, muck and peat).

It is still unclear what causes the regrowth of dormant mycelium or initiates spore germination, but it is undoubtedly related to the phenomenon of fungistasis. Beard et al. [7] showed that 3 or more pounds of nitrogen initiated the development of *Tricholoma* fairy ring, with an indication that the form of nitrogen might be important since the fairy ring development started after the nitrogen source was changed from ammonium nitrate to urea. Pesticides may also cause the development of fairy rings by destroying saprophytic bacteria and fungi that normally remove exogenous nutrient sources. The nutrients that build up can serve as food for germinating spores of fairy ring fungi.

Management

Management or removal of fairy rings is difficult and expensive, and you should study the total situation carefully before making a decision. If the fairy rings are on a putting green they definitely should be removed. But if they are in the fairway they should generally be ignored, with the possible exception of a large concentration in a critical land zone or on the approach to a green, in which case the entire area should be fumigated and reseeded. Fairy rings should be removed by fumigation from sod fields for obvious reasons. On areas used for athletics, on commercial areas, or on home lawns they should be ignored or turned into a conversation piece, unless they are numerous or really unsightly. If almost the entire area is covered with them, or if they are bothering you, have the sod removed and the entire area fumigated. If you have only a few small ones you may wish to dig them out.

Cultural Practices

The cultural practice most often recommended is fertilization with nitrogen to stimulate growth of the surrounding grass so that it will mask the tall dark green grass in the zone of stimulation. This is where identification of the fairy ring fungus becomes important. Adding nitrogen to mask fairy ring symptoms caused by *Tricholoma* species may only result in more fairy rings [7], and the same is probably true for many of the other species of fungi that cause fairy ring.

Another method consists of trying to drown the fairy ring by supersaturating the area with water for 48 or more hours. This treatment has not been effective in all cases and the fairy rings always return later that season or the next. In other words, you can't drown them.

The best way to manage fairy rings is to dig them out. Go a foot beyond the ring, square it off, remove the sod, and then remove the soil within the square to a depth of 1 foot. Fill the hole with uninfested soil, and reseed or resod (with new and, hopefully, fairy-ring-free sod).

Resistant Cultivars

Since fairy ring fungi are basically saprophytic, the concept of resistant cultivars is not applicable.

Chemical Management

You must learn to like fairy rings or else fumigate them or dig them out. The information about drilling holes and pouring fungicides down them to eradicate fairy rings isn't worth the paper it is written on. The result of such a management procedure is usually replacement of the original fairy ring with several new ones, which develop from the unkilled portion of the first ring. If you have put on a few pounds over the winter this may be good exercise, but it won't get rid of your fairy rings.

Disease: *Fusarium* blight

Pathogens: *Fusarium roseum* f. sp. *cerealis* (Cke.) Snyder and Hansen, *Fusarium tricinctum* f. sp. *poae* (Pk.) Snyder and Hansen (both sometimes in combination with nematodes or soil fungi)

Hosts: Kentucky bluegrass, centipede-grass

Fusarium fungi

As turfgrass diseases go, *Fusarium* blight is a newcomer. It was identified as a turfgrass problem on Kentucky bluegrass by Couch and Bedford in 1966 [19] and as a problem on centipedegrass in Alabama in 1972 by Subirats and Self [132]. *Fusarium* blight also has been reported to be a problem on red fescue and creeping bentgrass [19].

Symptoms

The disease appears as circular spots in the turf, ranging in diameter from 6 to 24 inches. The grass in the center of the spots appears healthy, but is surrounded by a band of dead turf. This symptom is commonly referred to as a "frog-eye." However, under severe conditions, or on such supersusceptible varieties as Pennstar or Fylking, the entire circle of grass will be killed. Where temperatures exceed 90 °F and the humidity is high, the disease can be seen as a foliar blight, but in most of the northern United States and in California it occurs as a root and crown rot [36].

Plants infected with *Fusarium* blight have shortened root systems which are poorly developed, and even when the grass begins to recover, the roots and shoots remain stunted. The spots first appear as wilted turf (dark blue to purple) and, if not treated, will turn straw colored to light tan (also known as dead). See figure 2-6.

On centipedegrass the primary symptoms are blighting at the cut ends of the blades and midblade discoloration, sometimes accompanied by tissue collapse. The root systems of infected plants are brown. Most of the injury to centipedegrass occurs in the early spring. The grass either fails to initiate new growth or else the new growth soon deteriorates. There is both a leaf-blight and a root-rot stage [132].

Occurrence

The *Fusarium* blight fungus can overwinter in the thatch and in infected plants. It is also a good saprophyte and is often found in plant debris. In the southern part of its range, the high temperature and humidity are sufficient stress to cause development of *Fusarium* blight. In northern or arid regions, additional stress is necessary for the disease to develop. Nematodes are one of the most common stresses. The stunt nematode *Tylenchorhynchus dubius* has been shown to play a key role in the development of *Fusarium* blight [30]. It weakens the turf and possibly changes the metabolism of the grass plant, making it more susceptible to what is generally regarded as a weak pathogen, *Fusarium roseum*. Almost anything that contributes to drought stress (e.g., sod laid on compacted soil, compacted soil, excessive nitrogen) will predispose the plants to infection by *Fusarium*.

Figure 2–6. Kentucky bluegrass turf infected with *Fusarium* blight. Note the wilted turf.

Recent evidence suggests that *Fusarium roseum* and *Fusarium tricinctum* may not be the primary cause of *Fusarium* blight [112, 118, 119]. In field trials, Smiley and Craven found that plots treated with the fungicide iprodione showed significantly less *Fusarium* blight than the untreated control plots [116, 117, 118, 119]. Examination of Kentucky bluegrass crowns from the experimental plots revealed higher percentages of *F. roseum* in the treated plots. In laboratory experiments iprodione either had no effect on the growth of *F. roseum* or was slightly stimulatory [116]. Similar results have been reported by Sanders et al. [112].

Smiley and Craven [119] now believe that the disease may be abiotic and that fungicides and cultural management procedures affect thatch oxidation. They believe the fungicides may have a hormonal effect which alleviates physiological drought stresses induced by poor oxidation, by drought *per se*, by high temperatures, and by excess radiation.

Smiley (personal communication) also has evidence that treatment with nemacur reduces both nematode populations and *Fusarium* blight symptoms. As with iprodione-treated plots, the percentage of crowns infected with *F. roseum* was higher in the treated plots than in the untreated controls. However, his observations that the crowns were infected and that *Fusarium* blight symptoms did not occur in iprodione-treated plots where nematode populations were high, led him to conclude that nematodes are not involved in the development of *Fusarium* blight.

Sanders [111] had similar results with the experimental fungicide triadimefon (Bayleton, BC 6447). Triadimefon completely suppressed *Fusarium* blight field symptoms when applied as a preventive but was not effective when applied as a curative. In laboratory studies, however, Triadimefon was not fungitoxic against *F. roseum* and *F. tricinctum*. Sanders and his coworkers suggest that triadimefon may be acting on other sensitive organisms that are involved in the development of *Fusarium* blight field symptoms [112]. They hypothesize that certain soil fungi are capable of making soil hydrophobic, causing drought stress and a high negative water potential in the grass plant and leading to an explosive colonization of the turfgrass plant by the fusaria. They suggest that soil fungi could be predisposing turfgrass plants to attack by fusaria and that triadimefon may act on the fungi that cause the predisposition.

In view of all the evidence, both new and old, it seems to be time for a new hypothesis about what causes the disease called *Fusarium* blight. I think it can be best explained by figure 2-7.

Scientists always want to find a single cause for a disease, even though diseases are usually the result of many factors. It is probable that *Fusarium* blight has multiple causes. First, there are four kinds of predisposition–parasite factors—environmental, cultural, host, and soil biotic. Then there is the colonizing factor, which may be nothing more than a saprophyte or weak parasite colonizing dead or dying tissue. The four kinds of predisposition factors plus the colonizer factor cause *Fusarium* blight. In figure 2-7 each type of predisposition factor is given the number 1 and the colonizer is also given the number 1; together they add up to 5, the number assigned to *Fusarium* blight. If one type of factor is controlled, *Fusarium* blight will not develop, just as, if one number is subtracted, the sum will no longer be 5.

More specifically, the environmental factors of high temperature and high humidity can be partially eliminated by syringing and improving air drainage. The cultural factors of drought stress, nitrogen fertility, and compacted soils can be eliminated by supplemental irrigation, proper timing of application, and cultivation, respectively. Plants that serve as hosts to *Fusarium*, nematodes, or soil fungi can be replaced by plants resistant to

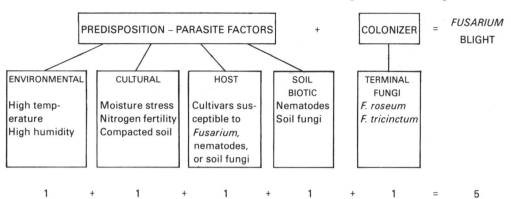

Figure 2–7. Factors that may be involved in the development of *Fusarium* blight. Only one predisposition factor from each category need be present for the development of *Fusarium* blight to occur, although more than one factor from a given category may be involved. Elimination, by cultural or chemical means, of all the factors that are present from any one category is sufficient to prevent occurrence of the disease.

any one of the three. Soil biotic factors (nematodes and soil fungi) can be eliminated by nematicides and fungicides (e.g., triadimefon). And, finally, the pathogen or colonizer can be eliminated by fungicides effective against *F. roseum* or *F. tricinctum* (e.g., benomyl, thiophanate-ethyl, thiophanate-methyl).

Management

Cultural Practices

High nitrogen levels early in the season will increase the severity of *Fusarium* blight [141]. Where the disease is a problem, it is a good idea to fertilize in the early fall and then after top growth has stopped (dormant application), following up with frequent light applications throughout the summer.

Correct watering is the key to treating symptoms of *Fusarium* blight in the North. Healthy turf should be watered once a week to a depth of 6 inches to encourage deep root development. But turfgrass plants infected with *Fusarium* blight have short root systems, and irrigating to a depth of 6 inches serves no purpose. What is needed is frequent light watering to keep the top inch or half inch of soil or thatch moist, because that is where the roots of the infected turfgrass are. Infected plants may still wilt and die on days when the temperature is above 80 °F, but if the turf is syringed during the warmest part of the day turf loss should be minimal.

Resistant Cultivars

The following Kentucky bluegrass cultivars appear to be resistant to *Fusarium* blight, although they certainly are not immune: Adelphi, Majestic, Parade, Touchdown, Brunswick, Baron, and Cheri. Kentucky bluegrass cultivars that are especially susceptible are Fylking and Pennstar, with Merion not far behind. This may surprise you, because *Fusarium* blight of Merion Kentucky bluegrass has received the most attention, but Fylking and Pennstar are even more susceptible. There are indications that certain cultivars may be susceptible in some regions but resistant in others. For example, Nugget has good resistance in the northern region of the cool-season grass belt, and Bensun appears to have good resistance in more southerly regions.

Chemical Management

Fusarium blight can be managed chemically with high concentrations (4 to 8 ounces per 1000 square feet) of the benzimidazole systemic fungicides applied as drenches. To be effective the fungicide must be drenched into the root zone before it dries on the foliage, and the results are better if the area has been irrigated the night before. The benzimidazole systemic fungicides not only manage the *Fusarium* fungi but also reduce nematode populations [81]. Resistance to the benzimidazole systemic fungicides by the *Fusarium* fungi has been observed [120]. Probably a 3- to 5-year management program with these fungicides is the maximum that you can expect. If they become EPA-approved, iprodione and triadimefon can also be used to manage *Fusarium* blight, but remember that triadimefon needs to be applied as a preventive.

For commercial turf areas where there is an interaction between the fungus and the nematodes, nematicides also will manage the disease. Even with chemical management (which can be expensive) a good fertilizing and watering program should be continued. In the long run, overseeding with resistant cultivars may be the best solution.

Disease: Gray leaf spot

Pathogen: *Piricularia grisea* (Cke.) Sacc.

Host: St. Augustinegrass

Conidiophore and conidiospores of *Piricularia grisea*

Gray leaf spot is a problem primarily on St. Augustinegrass, although it has been found on bermudagrass, crabgrass, foxtailgrass, and barnyardgrass as well as on many other turf and nonturf grasses [137]. The disease is most severe during warm, humid weather [45]. It also occurs along coastal areas in the South, in southern California, and in shaded areas in the northern St. Augustinegrass growing region.

Symptoms

The lesions first appear as tiny brown spots that enlarge and become oval or elongated. The mature spots usually have depressed gray centers with irregular brown margins surrounded by a ring of chlorotic tissue. If foliar infection is severe, the leaves may appear burned or scorched. Lesions also are found on the leaf sheath, spike, and stems. Diseased areas on the leaf sheaths and spikes are similar to those found on the leaf blades, whereas those found on the stem are often brown to black. These symptoms are illustrated in figure 2-8.

Occurrence

Piricularia grisea overwinters as spores and dormant mycelium in the lower leaves of infected plants and in the thatch. As the temperature rises, the spores are blown by the

Figure 2-8. Closeup of foliar symptoms of gray leaf spot (Photograph courtesy of Dr. Bobby G. Joyner)

wind and splashed by water to healthy plants, which they can infect. Under conditions of high humidity and high temperature (80 to 90 °F) the disease can develop rapidly [45]. Newly sprigged, rapidly growing grass is more susceptible to gray leaf spot than are well-established St. Augustinegrass turfs [137].

Management

Cultural Practices

Avoid excessive nitrogen levels or apply nitrogen just before and during the time of year when gray leaf spot is a problem. Irrigation in the middle of the day will allow foliage to dry quickly and thus help reduce the severity of the disease.

Resistant Cultivars

The yellow-green types of St. Augustinegrass, such as Roselawn and Floratam, are more resistant than the blue-green types, such as Bitter Blue and Floratine (T. E. Freeman, personal communication).

Chemical Management

Gray leaf spot can be managed by weekly applications of one of the fungicides recommended in chapter 6 and in the appendix.

Disease: HAS decline of annual bluegrass

Pathogens: *Helminthosporium sorokinianum, Colletotrichum graminicola,* along with physiological factors

Host: Annual bluegrass

Before 1975 the dying of *Poa annua* (annual bluegrass) was attributed to "wilting" (direct high-temperature kill) or the natural dying of a winter annual. Vargas and Detweiler [149] showed that fungicide treatments would prevent annual bluegrass from dying during summer stress periods. They showed that annual bluegrass was not dying from heat stress, drought stress, or the natural dying of a winter annual, but from other causes that could be mitigated by fungicides. The summer die-off was originally all attributed to the fungus *Colletotrichum graminicola,* the causal agent of the disease anthracnose. Subsequent research disclosed that other factors are involved, mainly *Helminthosporium sorokinianum* and senescence. The name proposed for this malady of annual bluegrass is HAS decline of annual bluegrass (Helminthosporium-Anthracnose-Senescence). Management of this disease complex during the summer stress period through the use of fungicides will allow the successful growth of annual bluegrass, which is the major component of golf course fairways and greens in the cool-season grassbelt. It is no longer necessary to try to eliminate annual bluegrass through expensive, time-consuming overseeding programs, which seldom work anyway.

Symptoms

The initial characteristic symptom of HAS decline is yellow-bronze coloring of the turf. Later, the turf takes on a more bronze appearance, with irregular brown to purplish black lesions on the leaf blades. The lesions are caused by *Helminthosporium sorokinianum* and *Colletotrichum graminicola.*

In cool weather, the turf will remain yellow, with little thinning or dying. But when temperatures climb into the 80s, especially if the humidity is high, the bronze-yellow turf will turn bronze within 48 hours unless fungicides are applied. HAS decline may initially appear as irregular spots 1 to 2 feet in diameter, but large areas, even an entire fairway, can be thinned and lost overnight. The affected plants turn bronze-yellow, an indication of senescence, not dark blue or purple as occurs with wilt. It is at this time that the black fruiting structures (acervuli) of the anthracnose fungus can be seen in chlorotic tissue or, more commonly, in newly killed tissue. The black spines (setae) protruding from the acervulus distinguish *C. graminicola* from most of the other fruiting bodies produced by saprophytic fungi. The acervuli can be seen with the aid of a hand lens or a dissecting scope.

Occurrence

HAS decline begins to occur after a week or more of daytime temperatures in the 80s. The disease is most severe when nighttime temperatures stay above 70 °F for three or more nights in a row. HAS decline is most severe on annual bluegrass under stress, for example, compacted areas and areas subjected to heavy traffic and poor soil drainage. The disease will also be severe if nitrogen levels are too high or too low.

Management

Cultural Practices

In years of moderate temperature, HAS decline can be prevented by the application of nitrogen. A nitrogen program of ½ pound of actual nitrogen per 1000 square feet in June, July, and August should prevent the disease. This program should be supplemented by applications of 1 pound of actual nitrogen per 1000 square feet in early September and dormantly (after vertical plant growth has stopped).

Chemical Management

Before discussing chemical prevention, let's consider the other problems that were mistaken for HAS decline. The first of these was wilting of annual bluegrass. What color does grass turn when it wilts? It turns blue or purple, not yellow! (Yet many people say, "Look at my grass turning yellow and wilting.") HAS decline has been mistakenly identified also as *Pythium* blight, but in the northern United States *Pythium* blight is a spot disease. *Pythium* blight spots start out about the size of dollar spot and may grow very rapidly, eventually coalescing to cover large areas. *Pythium* blight is not a disease that kills large areas in irregular patches, as people often think. It kills large areas of turf only where water is standing.

The use of benzimidazole systemic fungicides (benomyl, thiophanate-methyl, or thiophanate-ethyl) applied as a drench at a concentration of 2 ounces per 1000 square feet has caused the recovery of badly diseased areas in about 10 days [149]. This suggests that, although the turf appeared dead, the crowns must still have been alive for recovery to have occurred so quickly.

One-ounce rates and nondrench applications also worked, but recovery took much longer [149]. Recovery took place when the temperature was in the high 80s or low 90s. The root systems of annual bluegrass were observed to be dense and 1 to 1½ inches long in the treated areas, and very sparse and short in the untreated areas, again suggesting that HAS decline is responsible for much of what has previously been called wilting of annual bluegrass. Contact fungicides such as chlorothalonil and mancozeb applied every 7 to 10 days will also prevent HAS decline [150].

chapter three

FUNGUS DISEASES OF TURFGRASSES, II

The *Helminthosporium* Diseases

The *Helminthosporium* diseases are the most widespread and serious of all diseases of the cool-season turfgrass species. The common names of the *Helminthosporium* diseases and the species which they affect are listed in table 3-1.

Table 3-1. The *Helminthosporium* Diseases and Their Hosts

Common Name	Pathogen	Turfgrasses Affected
Leaf Spot	*Helminthosporium sorokinianum* (Drechslera sorokinianum) (syn. H. sativum)	Annual bluegrass, Kentucky bluegrass, colonial bentgrass, creeping bentgrass, perennial ryegrass, fine-leaf fescue, meadow fescue, tall fescue
Melting-out	*Helminthosporium vagans* (Drechslera vagans) (syn. D. poae)	Kentucky bluegrass
Net-blotch	*Helminthosporium dictyoides* (Drechslera dictyoides)	Fine-leaf fescues, tall fescue
Red leaf spot	*Helminthosporium erythrospilum* (Drechslera erythrospila)	Creeping bentgrass
Brown blight	*Helminthosporium siccans* (Drechslera siccans)	Ryegrass
Leaf blotch	*Helminthosporium cynodontis* (Drechslera cynodontis)	Bermudagrass
Zonate eyespot	*Helminthosporium giganteum* (Drechslera gigantea)	Bermudagrass
Stem and crown necrosis	*Helminthosporium spiciferum* (Drechslera spicifer)	Bermudagrass
Other bermudagrass helminthosporiums	*Helminthosporium rostratum* (Drechslera rostratum) *Helminthosporium stenospilum* (Drechslera stenosipila) *Helminthosporium triseptatum* (Drechslera triseptatae)	Bermudagrass
Leaf blight and crown rot	*Helminthosporium catenaria* (syn. Drechslera catenaria)	Creeping bentgrass

Disease: *Helminthosporium* leaf spot

Pathogen: *Helminthosporium sorokinianum* Sacc. ex Sorokin (syn. *H. sativum* P. K. B.; *Drechslera sativus* Drechsler ex Dastur)

Hosts: Annual bluegrass, Kentucky bluegrass, fine-leaf fescues, colonial bentgrass, creeping bentgrass, perennial ryegrass

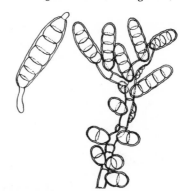

Helminthosporium sorokinianum conidiophore and conidiospores (one germinating)

Helminthosporium sorokinianum is the most widely occurring of the helminthosporiums. It attacks Kentucky bluegrass, fine-leaf fescues, colonial bentgrass, creeping bentgrass, annual bluegrass, and perennial ryegrass.

Symptoms

The first symptoms are small dark purple to black spots on the leaf blade (fig. 3-1). As the spots enlarge, their centers often turn light tan. At temperatures exceeding 85 °F, distinct spots are often absent and the entire blade appears dry and straw colored. The disease usually is confined to the leaf blades during cool weather. Leaf sheaths, crowns, and roots will become infected during hot, humid weather, and severe thinning of a turfgrass stand can occur in a short period of time.

Occurrence

Helminthosporium leaf spot is a warm-weather disease like red leaf spot (net-blotch, brown blight, and melting-out are cool-weather diseases). *H. sorokinianum* overwinters as dormant mycelium in infected plants and in the dead grass plant which makes up the mat. When the temperature reaches 70 °F or more, the leaf-spot phase of the disease becomes evident. At 85 °F the leaf-blighting stage begins and becomes progressively worse as the temperature rises. The disease is most severe when the temperature reaches 95 °F and the humidity is high [158]. Colbaugh and Endo [16] showed the disease to be most severe under conditions of drought stress followed by rewetting. They believed that the germination of *H. sorokinianum* spores increased during the period of drought, owing to the absence of a volatile inhibitor which is present when the mat remains moist. The inhibitor will return an hour after rewetting.

Management

Cultural Practices

Little, if any, nitrogen should be applied during warm weather, when *Helminthosporium* leaf spot is active. Potassium and phosphorus should be maintained at adequate levels as determined by soil tests. The work of Colbaugh and Endo [16] suggests that keeping the turf damp during periods when *H. sorokinianum* is active should help to reduce or even prevent development of the disease.

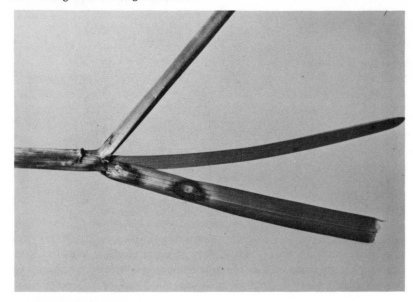

Figure 3-1. Close-up of a *Helminthosporium* lesion on a grass blade

Resistant Cultivars

There is very little data on the resistance to *Helminthosporium* leaf spot of Kentucky bluegrass, colonial bentgrass, creeping bentgrass, fine-leaf fescues, Italian ryegrass, and perennial ryegrass. That is not to say that there are no resistant cultivars. There may well be some, especially among the new improved Kentucky bluegrasses and perennial ryegrasses, but none has been identified yet.

Chemical Management of *Helminthosporium* Diseases

Several fungicides can be used to manage the various *Helminthosporium* diseases. All of them are contact fungicides, and most must be applied every 7 to 10 days to be effective (iprodione is the exception). For the best results, apply the fungicides as preventives just before the disease season begins. For example, to prevent melting-out in Kentucky bluegrass, apply fungicide when the grass begins to green up; to prevent leaf spot on the fine-leaf fescues, apply fungicide just before the weather turns warm. For more information on the fungicides available to treat *Helminthosporium* diseases, see chapter 6 and the appendix; for appropriate times to apply them, see chapters 11 and 12.

Disease: *Helminthosporium* blight (net-blotch)

Pathogen: *Helminthosporium dictyoides* Dreschler (syn. *Drechslera dictyoides* Paul and Parberry)

Hosts: Fine-leaf fescues, tall fescue, meadow fescue

Helminthosporium dictyoides conidiospores

Helminthosporium blight, or net-blotch, is a disease that occurs during the cool weather of spring and fall. It is often called leaf spot, but leaf spot is caused by *Helminthosporium sorokinianum*. Since the primary *Helminthosporium* problem on fine-leaf fescues occurs in the warm weather of summer, perhaps a lot of what was thought to be "leaf spot" caused by *Helminthosporium dictyoides* is actually leaf spot caused by *H. sorokinianum*. Numerous isolations of *Helminthosporium* lesions have been made for Michigan State University's fine-leaf-fescue breeding program, and over 90 percent of them have been *H. sorokinianum*, regardless of the time of year [153]. Data from the southern half of Michigan obviously do not imply that this is the case everywhere, but our findings do suggest that leaf spot, not net-blotch, may be the important disease on the fine-leaf fescues.

Symptoms

The initial symptoms are similar to the other *Helminthosporium* diseases—tiny purplish to black spots on the leaf blade that eventually enlarge. On the fine-leaf fescues the enlarged spots usually extend the entire width of the blade. On the broad-leaf species, like the tall fescues and meadow fescue, the disease initially occurs as irregular dark purple to black transverse strands, resembling dark threads drawn across the leaf. These strands look like a net—hence the name net-blotch.

Occurrence

The development of *Helminthosporium* blight, or net-blotch, is described in the literature as similar to *Helminthosporium* melting-out in Kentucky bluegrass. The fungus survives the dormant period as mycelium in infected tissue on the living host and in the mat. In the spring conidiospores are produced in infected plant parts and are water splashed or wind blown to healthy plant tissue. The leaf-spot phase of the disease is supposedly inconspicuous in the spring. Crown and root infection are thought to take place during this time, although the symptoms are not expressed until the warm dry weather of summer. In actual fact, both the leaf-spot and the crown-and-root-rot phases take place during the cool weather of spring and fall. The decline of fine-leaf fescue during the warm weather is due to *H. sorokinianum*, which is readily isolated from the fine-leaf fescues during the warm weather of summer. Whichever of them it is, and it may be both of them, it limits the widespread use of fine-leaf fescues. Finding varieties resistant to these pathogens should allow much wider use of the fine-leaf fescues and extend their range to the warmer areas of the cool-season grassbelt.

Management

Cultural Practices

The fine-leaf fescues are grasses that grow best with low maintenance. Using minimal amounts of nitrogen with normal levels of phosphorus (P_2O_5) and potassium (K_2O) will help fine-leaf fescue stands survive. Minimal amounts of water should also be used. The fine-leaf fescues can withstand a tremendous amount of drought stress, but they cannot stand overwatering. The tall and meadow fescues also require benign neglect for their survival.

Resistant Cultivars

There are no varieties of fine-leaf fescue or any other fescue species that are truly resistant to either *H. sorokinianum* or *H. dictyoides*. The variety C-26, which is a hard fescue, has about the best resistance of any fine-leaf fescue. To repeat an earlier statement, since *Helminthosporium* is primarily a problem during the warm weather of summer, and since *H. sorokinianum* is a warm-weather pathogen, I believe *H. sorokinianum*, not *H. dictyoides*, is the major pathogen on fine-leaf fescues.

Chemical Management

See chapter 6, the appendix, and page 30.

Disease: *Helminthosporium*   brown blight

Pathogen: *Helminthosporium   siccans* Drechsler (syn. *Drechslera siccans* Shoemaker)

Hosts: Italian ryegrass, perennial ryegrass

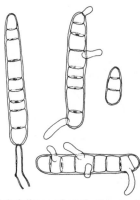

Helminthosporium siccans conidiospores (two germinating)

Helminthosporium brown blight is a serious problem on ryegrass during the cool weather of spring and fall. It is becoming one of the factors limiting the successful adaptation of some of the new perennial ryegrasses, most of which were selected for their finer texture, better mowability, and other agronomic characteristics, with little regard for potential disease problems.

Symptoms

The first symptoms are small brown spots, which appear on the grass blades. The spots enlarge and may develop white centers. A second foliar symptom consists of dark brown streaks on the leaf blade. Both symptoms may occur simultaneously on the same blade. The entire blade of susceptible varieties can be destroyed if the infection is severe. Turf that is heavily infected with brown blight may show extensive thinning.

Occurrence

Like the other helminthosporiums, *Helminthosporium siccans* survives the dormant period in the infected tissue of living plants and in the dead tissue making up the mat. In the spring, conidiospores are produced in the infected tissue and are wind blown and water splashed to healthy tissue. Brown blight is supposed to have a leaf-spot stage in the spring, followed by rotting of the root and crown in the summer and another leaf-spot stage in the fall. But, much as in melting-out in Kentucky bluegrass (pp.37–39), what actually happens is that the whole process (leaf-spot stage, crown-and-root-rot stage) occurs during the cool weather of the spring and fall, with few signs of disease evident during the warm summer months.

Management

Cultural Practices

Excess nitrogen during cool weather increases the severity of brown blight. Reducing nitrogen during the spring and fall and maintaining adequate levels of phosphorus (P_2O_5) and potassium (K_2O) will help to manage the disease. Unfortunately, red thread and crown rust are also a problem during cool weather, and management of these two diseases requires high levels of nitrogen. Moreover, the time of year when brown blight is a problem is also the time of year when the plant can best utilize nitrogen for its growth and development. A management decision obviously will have to be made. (This problem is discussed at length in chapter 11.)

Resistant Cultivars

There are varieties of perennial ryegrass that are resistant to brown blight, and they should be used in preference to the susceptible varieties. Yorktown II, Diplomat, and Omega are probably the best. There are other resistant varieties, but they are susceptible to other serious diseases like *Rhizoctonia* brown patch and *Corticium* red thread. The situation is similar to that in Kentucky bluegrasses: many varieties are resistant to melting-out, but they shouldn't be used because of their susceptibility to *Fusarium* blight or stripe smut. (For a more detailed discussion, see chapter 11.) The resistance and susceptibility of the perennial ryegrasses to various diseases are discussed in chapter 9.

Chemical Management

See page 30.

Disease: *Helminthosporium* leaf blotch

Pathogen: *Helminthosporium cynodontis* Marig. (syn. *Drechslera cynodontis* Nelson). *H. giganteum* Heald and Wolf, *H. rostratum* Drechsl., *H. spiciferum* (Bain) Nicot., *H. stenospilum* Drechsl., and *H. triseptatum* Drechsl. are all known pathogens of bermudagrass

Host: Bermudagrass

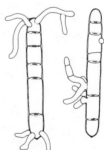

Helminthosporium giganteum
conidiospores germinating

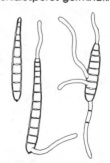

Helminthosporium cynodontis
conidiospores (one germinating)

Helminthosporium rostratum
conidiospores (two germinating)

Leaf blotch is caused by *Helminthosporium cynodontis*. The other pathogens listed may cause diseases that are just as damaging, but there is not sufficient information to warrant separate discussions of them. Therefore, leaf blotch will be discussed as an example of a *Helminthosporium* disease on bermudagrass. Keep in mind, however, that other *Helminthosporium* diseases of bermudagrass may be equally important. Leaf blotch can be a serious problem, especially in humid areas and during years of frequent spring and fall rains.

Symptoms

The first symptoms are small olive-green spots that appear on the leaves. The spots later grow into big brownish green to black blotches (fig. 3-2). If the infection is severe, the leaves eventually wither and become light tan. Turf infected by *H. cynodontis* is straw colored. The affected area may be small at first and then spread.

Occurrence

The fungus overwinters and summers as dormant mycelium in the infected tissue on the host and in the mat. With the advent of wet weather in the late winter and early spring and the breaking of dormancy in the bermudagrass, the fungus begins to sporulate and produce conidia. The conidia are then wind blown and water splashed to healthy tissue, which they infect. Leaf blotch tends to disappear with warm weather, much like melting-out of Kentucky bluegrass, but it may return with the cool wet

Figure 3–2.   *Helminthosporium* on bermudagrass (Photograph courtesy of Dr. Don Blasingame)

weather in late summer and early fall. Thus bermudagrass may enter the dormant period in a weakened condition and die during the winter.

Management

Cultural Practices

Reducing nitrogen in the early spring and early fall will help to manage leaf blotch. A balanced program of phosphorus and potassium should be maintained. Avoid excess watering during the early spring and fall, or water in the daytime so the foliage has a chance to dry.

Resistant Cultivars

No information is available on the resistance of bermudagrass cultivars to leaf blotch.

Chemical Management

See chapter 6, the appendix, and page 30.

Disease: *Helminthosporium* leaf blight and crown rot (formerly C-15 problem and red leaf spot)

Pathogen: *Helminthosporium catenaria* (syn. *Drechslera catenaria*)

Host: Toronto creeping bentgrass (C-15)

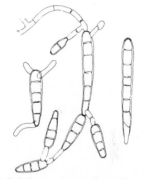

Helminthosporium catenaria conidiospores (some germinating)

Helminthosporium leaf blight and crown rot is a disease that has become important since 1968. It seems to attack only Toronto creeping bentgrass, also known as C-15. There appear to be two distinct strains of Toronto, one susceptible to *Helminthosporium* leaf blight and crown rot and the other susceptible to and contaminated with stripe smut. These two diseases have made Toronto, or C-15, totally unacceptable as a turfgrass. The disease was identified by Meyer and Turgeon [92] as *Helminthosporium* red leaf spot (caused by *Helminthosporium erythospilum*); however, recent data of Larsen [79] show the disease to be *Helminthosporium* leaf blight and crown rot caused by *Helminthosporium catenaria*.

Symptoms

Toronto creeping bentgrass is used primarily on golf course greens, and therefore the problem is usually found on closely mowed turf. A green infected with the disease looks undernourished, as though it lacks nitrogen. The entire turf area is severely thinned. A closer examination reveals grass growing in areas the size of quarters, surrounded by straw-colored dead or dying areas of similar size. The grass blades on infected plants look withered (fig. 3-3). Individual annual bluegrass plants can be seen invading the bare areas, and there may also be patches of off-type creeping bentgrass (usually Washington or a closely related cultivar). If the disease is not checked, the entire Toronto creeping bentgrass green will be converted into an annual bluegrass green within a few years. This is the point at which the superintendent says, "The disease has disappeared," or else, "I finally have it under control!"

Occurrence

Helminthosporium leaf blight and crown rot is noticeable almost as soon as the grass begins to green up in the spring, and it will get worse as long as cool weather persists. The turf will begin to recover somewhat with the advent of warm summer weather, but it will decline again as the cool nights of late summer or early fall arrive.

Management

Cultural Practices

Meyer and Turgeon [92] have reported that an increased nitrogen level in conjunction with a good fungicide program has reduced the severity of *Helminthosporium* leaf blight and crown rot (they referred to it as red leaf spot). Raising the height of cut to half an inch or more will also make the disease less severe, but it won't make you popular with golfers.

Figure 3–3.   *Helminthosporium* leaf blight and crown rot thinning a Toronto creeping bentgrass green. Note the patch of annual bluegrass that is beginning to invade the green.

Resistant Cultivars

Since most creeping bentgrass except Toronto appears to be resistant to *Helminthosporium* leaf blight and crown rot, you can prevent the disease by avoiding Toronto.

Chemical Management

Meyer and Turgeon [92] demonstrated management of *Helminthosporium* leaf blight and crown rot by applications of Daconil 2787 in concentrations of 6 ounces per 1000 square feet every week from the beginning of the growing season until the end, in conjunction with high levels of nitrogen in the spring. Turgeon (personal communication) has found that applications of 3 ounces of Daconil 2787 per 1000 square feet every week all season long also will manage the disease. If you are thinking of stretching the spray interval to every 2 weeks, or spraying only until the grass looks good, I can tell you from personal experience that it won't work. Larsen [79] found that two 4-ounce applications of iprodione per 1000 square feet in the spring provide excellent control throughout the entire growing season. He recommends an additional fall application, just to be on the safe side.

Disease: *Helminthosporium* melting-out

Pathogen: *Helminthosporium vagans* Drechsler (syn. *Drechslera poae* Shoemaker)

Host: Kentucky bluegrass

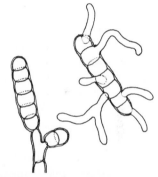

Helminthosporium vagans conidiophore and conidiospores (one germinating)

Helminthosporium melting-out is potentially the most important disease of Kentucky bluegrass. This may surprise many people who think of *Fusarium* blight as the most serious disease affecting Kentucky bluegrass turf. The reason *Fusarium* blight is so important today is because there are now so many Kentucky bluegrass cultivars resistant to melting-out. Merion was the first; hence, its popularity. Before Merion was developed, the main drawback of Kentucky bluegrass was its susceptibility to melting-out. In other words, if there were no cultivars resistant to melting-out (e.g., Merion, Fylking, Pennstar, and Nugget), *Fusarium* blight would not be a problem, because melting-out would destroy the turf long before *Fusarium* blight appeared.

This brings up an important aspect of selecting or breeding for resistance to a particular pathogen or disease. The introduction of varieties resistant to a major disease often results in the emergence of diseases previously minor or unknown in that crop species. For example, before the selection of Merion, *Fusarium* blight was unknown and stripe smut and rust were unimportant in Kentucky bluegrass. Red thread was unknown as a disease of perennial ryegrass before the introduction of Manhattan.

Helminthosporium diseases of Kentucky bluegrass are usually referred to as either "melting-out" or "leaf spot." The pathogens responsible for these diseases are *Helminthosporium vagans* and *Helminthosporium sorokinianum* (syn. *H. sativum*), respectively. *H. vagans* is a cool-weather pathogen, whereas *H. sorokinianum* is a warm-weather pathogen.

Symptoms

The first symptoms of melting-out are black to purple spots on the leaf blades. Spots eventually appear on the leaf sheaths and move down and invade the crowns and roots of the grass plant. From a distance the turf will appear either yellow or blackish brown. These colors are a reflection of the nitrogen level of the turf during infection. At low nitrogen levels, infected turf turns yellow; with high nitrogen levels, it turns blackish brown. As the disease progresses, the infected area becomes thin and brown, similar in appearance to wilted turf. Unless a fungicide is applied, what was once a Kentucky bluegrass turf will die and be replaced by broadleaf weeds and weedy grasses.

Occurrence

Helminthosporium melting-out is described by Couch [18] and Britton [12] as a disease that has a leaf-spot stage in the cool, wet period of spring or fall, followed by a melting-out, or crown-and-root-rot, stage in the warm weather of summer. In my opinion, it is a cool-weather disease, and Monteith and Dahl [94] agree. Why the discrepancies? I believe we are dealing with two separate diseases: (1) melting-out, caused by *H. vagans*, which is a problem during cool weather, and (2) leaf spot, caused by *H. sorokinianum*, which also has a melting-out stage that occurs during warm weather.

The leaf-spot stage begins early in the spring with the coming of cool wet weather and temperatures between 55 and 70 °F. If the cool wet weather (especially nice, slow drizzle) continues, the melting-out, or crown-and root-rot, stage of the disease will occur and the infected Kentucky bluegrass will begin to thin and die. Severe loss of turf can occur within a 3-week period. Then, with the coming of warm dry weather (temperatures above 70 °F), the infected turf will begin to recover and fill in. The degree of recovery depends on several factors, including the severity of the infection, the varieties of Kentucky bluegrass, the nitrogen level, and the irrigation practices. The life cycle of *H. vagans* is illustrated in figure 3-4.

Fall infection with *H. vagans* should also be mentioned. Such infections do occur, but the melting-out stage is rarely seen. However, this does not mean that fall infection should be ignored or considered unimportant, since it can give rise to early loss of turf in the spring, sometimes before any fungicide applications can be made.

Management

Cultural Practices

Raising the height of cut during the cool wet weather of spring and fall will help the turfgrass stand to survive an attack by melting-out. Avoiding high nitrogen levels dur-

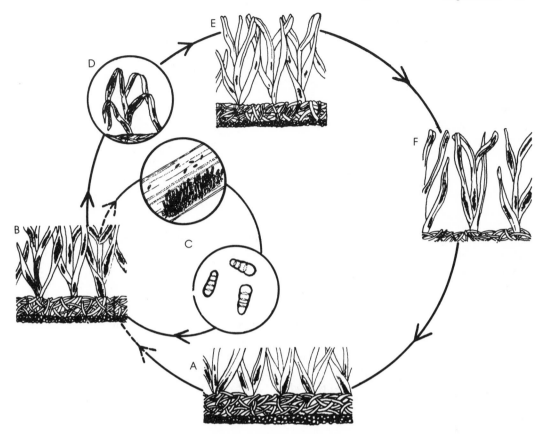

Figure 3–4.   Melting-out of Kentucky bluegrass caused by *Helminthosporium vagans. A, Helminthosporium vagans* overwintering on the lower portions of the plants and on dead plant material in the thatch; *B*, severe infection of the foliage during the cool wet weather of early spring; *C*, sporulation and reinfection continue as long as the cool wet weather persists. The crowns and root are affected also; *D*, severe thinning of the turf and death of the grass plant result in susceptible cultivars if the cool weather persists for more than 2 weeks; *E*, grass plants that are still alive recover with the arrival of warm weather. *H. vagans* oversummers mainly in the surface layer of the thatch and on the lower parts of the plants; *F*, foliar infection begins again with the advent of cool, wet, fall weather. Severe thinning usually does not occur at this time, but infections can lead to severe loss of turf under snow cover in the spring, or to severe epidemics when the turf greens up.

ing the cool weather of spring and fall will help to reduce the severity of the disease. Applications of nitrogen in the fall, after the grass plants become dormant, will supply needed nitrogen without causing lush spring growth.

Resistant Cultivars

See chapter 8 for a discussion of the subject.

Chemical Management

See chapter 6, the appendix, and page 30.

Disease: *Helminthosporium* red leaf spot

Pathogen: *Helminthosporium erythro-spilum* Drechsler (syn. *Drechslera erythrospila* Shoemaker)

Hosts: Redtop, colonial bentgrass, creeping bentgrass, velvet bentgrass

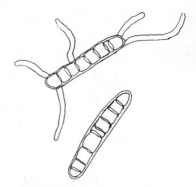

Helminthosporium erythrospilum conidiospores (one germinating)

Red leaf spot is a disease of the bentgrasses and redtop that usually occurs during warm wet weather. Meyer and Turgeon [92] have reported it as a severe problem on Toronto creeping bentgrass in Illinois all season long.

Symptoms

The lesions start out similar to other *Helminthosporium* lesions, as small, dark reddish brown spots on the leaf blade. As the spots grow, they develop straw-colored centers surrounded by reddish brown borders. If warm wet weather continues, the entire blade may wither, giving the stand of turf a drought-stricken appearance. Severe thinning of creeping bentgrass may be caused by red leaf spot infections.

Occurrence

The fungus survives the dormant period in the infected tissue of living plants and in the infected dead tissue in the mat. In the late spring, conidiospores are produced in these infected areas and wind blown or water splashed to healthy bentgrass plants. During periods of wet warm weather, red leaf spot can cause severe thinning of bentgrass turfs. On creeping bentgrass greens even moderate thinning can be a serious problem. Thirty-percent thinning of a home lawn or a fairway is sometimes tolerable, but on a putting green that amount of thinning is disastrous.

Management

Cultural Practices

Couch reports that reducing the nitrogen level during warm weather greatly reduces the severity of red leaf spot [18]. Meyer and Turgeon [92], on the other hand, report that high levels of nitrogen in conjunction with fungicide treatment provide the best control. Whichever nitrogen program you use, adequate levels of P_2O_5 and K_2O should be maintained.

Cultivars

There are no cultivars known to be resistant to red leaf spot.

Chemical Management

See chapter 6, the appendix, and page 30.

Diseases: *Pythium* blight (grease spot, cottony blight)

Pathogens: *Pythium aphanidermatum* (Edson) Fitzpatrick (syn. *P. butleri* subrm.) and *Pythium ultimum* Trow

Hosts: Annual bluegrass, Kentucky bluegrass, bermudagrass, colonial bentgrass, creeping bentgrass, tall fescue, fine-leaf fescues, rough bluegrass, perennial ryegrass, annual ryegrass, redtop

Oogonia of *Pythium*

Pythium blight can be devastating. When the temperature and humidity are high, it can destroy large areas of turf overnight. *Pythium* blight is the only turfgrass disease you can actually see spreading. No wonder many superintendents consider it the most important disease of golf course turfs—it can kill a lot of grass in a very short time.

Symptoms

The first symptoms of *Pythium* blight are circular reddish brown spots in the turf, ranging in diameter from 1 to 6 inches. In the morning dew, infected leaf blades appear water soaked and dark and may feel slimy. As they dry, the blades shrivel and turn reddish brown. When the spots are wet with dew, you can see the active mycelia of the fungi (purplish gray or white and cottony, depending on the species of *Pythium*) on the outer margins of the spots.

The infected grass plants collapse quickly. If the temperature and humidity remain high, the spots may coalesce and large areas of turf can be lost in as little as 24 hours. *Pythium* blight follows drainage patterns and it can be spread by equipment; hence, it often appears in streaks.

Pythium blight is a spot disease. If you notice large irregular dead patches in your turf without having seen spots first, the problem is not *Pythium* blight, and you must look for a different cause.

Occurrence

Like *Rhizoctonia* and *Fusarium*, *Pythium* is a good saprophyte. It is usually present in the thatch or the soil or both and requires only the proper conditions to become pathogenic. *Pythium* is also a "water mold" and can survive quite well under water-logged conditions and in the debris of ponds. Ponds are an important source of inoculum, especially in southern areas where pond water is used for irrigation. Each time a golf course is watered with infested pond water, the green, tee, or fairway is reinoculated with *Pythium* and the disease becomes harder to control.

Although *Pythium* blight is a warm-weather disease that is most destructive when the temperature is between 85 and 95 °F, it is primarily a disease of cool-season grasses. It will attack bermudagrass, especially common bermudagrass, but the damage is less than when it infects cool-season grasses. *Pythium* blight is a problem mainly in the South, where greens, tees, and fairways of dormant bermudagrass are overseeded in the fall with annual ryegrass or perennial ryegrass, which are very susceptible (see fig. 3-5). And

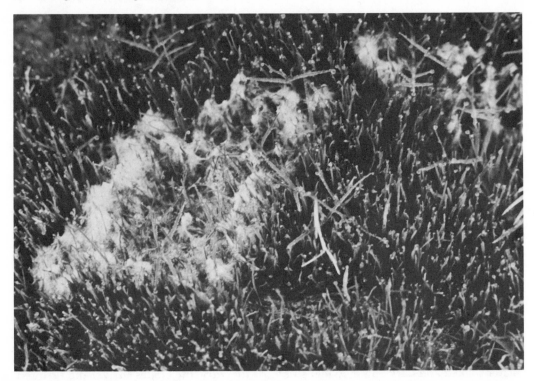

Figure 3-5.   *Pythium* blight with mycelium present on overseeded annual ryegrass (Photograph courtesy of Dr. Don Blasingame)

it is also a serious summertime problem on bentgrass greens in the South. Bentgrasses need constant moisture and, as mentioned above, watering with infested pond water reinfects the grass.

Management

Cultural Practices

Good soil drainage is essential for effective management of *Pythium* blight. Turfgrasses growing in poorly drained or compacted soil have short root systems and in warm weather require a great deal of water to prevent wilting. Frequent watering usually results in standing water, so that instead of dying from wilt the grass dies from *Pythium* blight. Where it is too expensive to rebuild the greens or the tees, or if large parts of the fairways are affected, light watering after sunrise and syringing at midday will help to manage *Pythium* blight. There is, however, no substitute for good soil drainage. In its northern range, where it is a problem for just a couple of weeks a year (and not every year), *Pythium* blight occurs only in poorly drained areas. Rebuilding greens in those areas is well worth the time and money. Good air drainage also helps to manage the disease.

High nitrogen levels cause lush growth and make *Pythium* blight worse. No special program of nitrogen fertilization is necessary, since low to moderate nitrogen is normally recommended for turfgrass during hot humid weather.

Resistant Cultivars

There are no varieties of creeping bentgrass, colonial bentgrass, annual ryegrass, or perennial ryegrass that are resistant to *Pythium* blight, and no data are available on the resistance of the new Kentucky bluegrass cultivars. Most of the improved bermudagrass cultivars are tolerant of or resistant to *Pythium* blight.

Chemical Management

In spite of the fact that *Pythium* blight is a severe disease that spreads rapidly, many superintendents in prime *Pythium* blight areas, such as the bermudagrass–Kentucky bluegrass transition zone, still refuse to institute preventive fungicide programs, even during hot humid weather. It must be the gambling spirit in them, because they know *Pythium* blight will come when the weather gets hot. Betting against *Pythium* is like playing Russian roulette with five chambers loaded and one empty. Before chloroneb and terrazole became available, fenaminosulf (Dexon) was the only chemical that controlled *Pythium* blight. It was expensive and it breaks down quickly in sunlight, so there was once a valid excuse for not instituting a preventive fungicide program. Today there is no excuse.

Disease: *Ophiobolus* patch

Pathogen: *Ophiobolus graminis* Sacc.

Hosts: Annual bluegrass, Kentucky bluegrass, colonial bentgrass, creeping bentgrass, velvet bentgrass, tall fescue

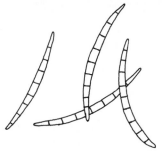

Ophiobolus graminis conidiospores

Ophiobolus patch is not a widespread disease. It occurs in England, northern Europe, and the coastal areas of the Pacific Northwest in America. (In the Pacific Northwest it is considered the second most important turfgrass after *Fusarium* patch.) It was first described as a turfgrass disease in 1937 by Schoevers [113] in Holland, and Gould et al. were the first to describe it in North America [53]. *Ophiobolus* patch resembles *Fusarium* blight and spring dead spot in being a circular disease (i.e., the center of the diseased turf tends to fill in) and a disease that is hard to control.

Symptoms

Ophiobolus patch appears first as a patch of bronzed or bleached turf. The grass in the center eventually dies and is replaced by broadleaf weeds or more often, by annual bluegrass (fig. 3-6). At first the spots are 4 to 6 inches in diameter, but they may grow to a diameter of several feet over a period of years. The plants in these patches have poorly developed roots and are easily pulled out. The black hyphae of the fungus can be seen under the base of the leaf sheath.

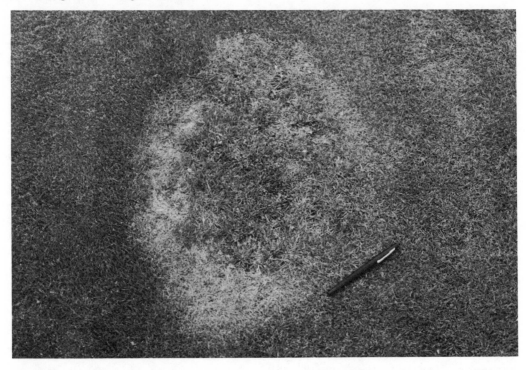

Figure 3–6.   *Ophiobolus* patch in a Kentucky bluegrass turf with annual bluegrass invading the center (Photograph courtesy of Dr. Bill Daniels)

Occurrence

Ophiobolus graminis can survive as a saprophyte in the thatch and as dormant mycelium in the perennial parts of the grass plant. It is a fungus that attacks primarily the crown and root of the plant, usually during the cool wet weather of the spring and fall. According to Smith [123] the disease is favored by applications of lime and by high pH, but Davidson and Goss [26] found that the incidence was no greater in lime–treated plots than in untreated control plots. The difference may be due to a difference in the initial pH of the soils used in the two experiments. Smith [123] demonstrated that fertilizers which raise the pH also increase the incidence of the disease.

Management

Cultural Practices

Adequate levels of phosphorus and potassium should be maintained. Obviously, liming should be avoided in areas where *Ophiobolus* patch is a problem. Similarly, an acidic fertilizer such as ammonium sulfate [26, 52], rather than a fertilizer that could make the soil basic, should be used. Sulfur [26, 52], phosphorus [26], or a combination of the two will help to manage the disease.

Resistant Cultivars

Creeping bentgrass appears to be the species of turfgrass most susceptible to *Ophiobolus* patch. Kentucky bluegrass and annual bluegrass are listed as susceptible, yet it is very common to see these species growing in patches where *O. graminis* has destroyed the creeping bentgrass. The fine-leaf fescues and the perennial ryegrasses seem to be the most resistant of all the cool-season turfgrasses.

Chemical Management

Gould suggests applying high concentrations of chlordane [52]; however, the Environmental Protection Agency has restricted the use of that pesticide. Davidson and Goss showed that multiple applications of Fore managed the disease, but attributed the effectiveness of this fungicide partly to the sulfur it contains [26]. Until a more satisfactory chemical treatment is found, the best way to deal with *Ophiobolus* patch is to employ the recommended cultural practices.

Disease: Powdery mildew

Pathogen: *Erysiphe graminis* D. C.

Hosts: Bermudagrass, Kentucky bluegrass, fine-leaf fescues, redtop

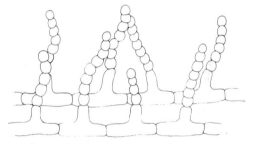

Erysiphe graminis conidispores

Powdery mildew is a classic example of a disease which attacks turfgrass plants that are growing under suboptimal environmental conditions. When bermudagrass, Kentucky bluegrass, redtop, and fine-leaf fescues are grown under the sunlight conditions that are optimal for them, they are resistant to powdery mildew. They become susceptible only when they are grown under low light intensity. For example, most tests say that Merion Kentucky bluegrass is susceptible to powdery mildew and resistant to *Helminthosporium* melting-out. Yet when Merion is grown in full sunlight it is resistant to both diseases, and when it is grown in the shade it loses its resistance to them. What ought to be said is that Merion is resistant to both powdery mildew and melting-out when grown in full sunlight and susceptible to both when grown in the shade.

Symptoms

Turf infected with mildew has a grayish white cast and looks as though it has been dusted with flour. The first symptoms are individual white patches on the leaf blade, but eventually the whole blade becomes covered with one white mass. As the disease progresses the leaves turn yellow, wither, and die (see fig. 3-7). When the leaves begin to deteriorate, brown to black cleistothecia may be found.

Occurrence

Erysiphe graminis overwinters as ascospores in cleistothecia. The ascospores are released in the spring, germinate, and infect turf in the late spring or early summer. In about 4 days the primary infection produces numerous conidiospores (secondary inoculum), which reinfect the grass, and the cycle continues throughout the season as long as there is some turf left.

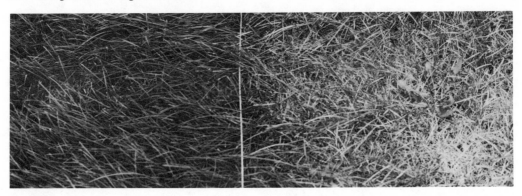

Figure 3-7. Powdery mildew thinning a Kentucky bluegrass stand where no chemical treatment has been applied (right) and a plot treated with an experimental fungicide that was denied registration (left)

The conidiospores are hyaline, with thin cell walls, and can germinate in about 2 hours. Although most fungi that infect turfgrass require free water for their spores to germinate, this is not true of *E. graminis*, which can germinate if the humidity is high enough.

The interesting thing about the infection caused by *E. graminis* is that only the epidermal layer of leaf cells is invaded by the fungus. By means of a haustorium, a specialized feeding structure, the powdery mildew fungus can extract the nutrition it needs from the living cell. Most fungi that are obligate parasites have haustoria.

Management

Cultural Practices

The obvious way to manage powdery mildew culturally is to remove the shade. But you are not going to cut down your favorite tree just to grow a little grass, and no matter how hard you try, you cannot eliminate the north side of your house. In the case of the tree, however, pruning the low branches will increase air circulation and let in a little more light.

Resistant Cultivars

Spreading fescue and the other fine-leaf fescues are the grasses usually recommended for shady places. The fine-leaf fescues do fine in open shade but not in dense shade, because they are susceptible to *Helminthosporium* leaf spot and powdery mildew. *Poa trivialis* and *Poa annua* are the only other species that grow well in the shade and both are considered weeds, but you can mow them, and they both look better than bare ground. In northern areas of the cool-season grassbelt both Nugget and Bensun Kentucky bluegrass have been grown successfully in shaded areas.

Chemical Management

Chemical management of powdery mildew is an exercise in futility. It was once hoped that systemic fungicides would manage powdery mildew for 6 to 8 weeks, but resistance to them in a season and a half destroyed that dream. Dinocap and cycloheximide are impractical because they have to be applied frequently and in dense shade, and even if you use them you still have the problem of *Helminthosporium*, which will have to be treated too. No one wants to spray every week for an eternity just to have a little grass in the shade. If you don't like *P. trivialis* or *P. annua*, try ornamental plantings.

Disease: *Corticium* red thread (pink patch)

Pathogen: *Corticium fuciforme* (Berk.) Wakef.

Hosts: Annual bluegrass, creeping bentgrass, Kentucky bluegrass, perennial ryegrass, fine-leaf fescue, bermudagrass

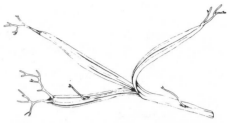

Corticium fuciforme stroma on infected leaves

Corticium red thread is a disease of slow-growing turf, whether the slow growth is caused by lack of nitrogen or by cold temperatures. It is a problem especially in the northern part of the United States and in Canada, Great Britain, and the north coastal areas of Europe, where the cool weather that often slows turf growth is accompanied by frequent drizzle or fog.

Red thread has become a greater problem since the energy crisis caused a sharp rise in fertilizer prices. Even before the cost of fertilizer went up it was fairly common to see *Corticium* red thread thinning roughs, which often were maintained with low levels of nitrogen. Now that prices are high, nitrogen fertilization has been reduced or eliminated on many golf course fairways, and it is not uncommon to find *Corticium* red thread there.

Symptoms

Corticium red thread is easily recognized by the red to coral pink stroma produced on the leaf blade and sheath. Early in the morning when the dew is still present, or on rainy days, the stroma looks gelatinous and fleshy. As the grass dries the stroma also dries and becomes thin and threadlike. When seen from a distance, infected turf often appears to be suffering from lack of water; from a little closer, it looks as though it has *Helminthosporium* leaf spot; and from directly above, especially in red fescue, the disease resembles *Sclerotinia* dollar spot. A close examination of the grass blades, however, reveals red to coral pink stromata. A *Corticium* red thread infection of a fine-leaf fescue turf is pictured in figure 3-8.

Occurrence

Corticium fuciforme survives periods away from the host as stroma and dormant mycelium in host tissue. Development of the disease is favored by temperatures below 75 °F and by wet weather. The cool drizzly days of spring and fall are ideal for the development of *Corticium* red thread, and the disease spreads from plant to plant by the growth of the stroma. When they break up, the stromata can be carried long distances by the wind. They are often cut off by mowing, and then spread by both the wind and the mowing equipment.

Management

Cultural Practices

The obvious cultural practice is fertilization with nitrogen. This is a good solution in springtime, provided the slow growth is due to lack of nitrogen and not cold weather. In the fall, the answer is not so simple. The areas of the cool-season grassbelt in which *Corticium* red thread is most severe are the same areas in which *Fusarium* patch is most se-

Figure 3-8.   *Corticium* red thread in a fine-leaf fescue turf

rious, and the nitrogen treatment that alleviates the *Corticium* red thread problem will aggravate *Fusarium* patch. In addition, *Typhula* blight and desiccation can be a problem in these areas and increasing the nitrogen level will make the turf more succulent and consequently more susceptible to *Typhula* blight and desiccation.

What should be done? Since *Corticium* red thread is neither as severe a disease as *Fusarium* patch or *Typhula* blight nor as destructive as desiccation, a good nitrogen fertilization program should be followed in the late summer. The date of the last application will vary, but it should be early enough to allow the turf to harden off before the permanent snowfall. Then an appropriate fungicide can be used to manage *Corticium* red thread. Fortunately, there are many fungicides that are effective.

Resistant Cultivars

No conclusive data are available yet on cultivars resistant to *Corticium* red thread. Because it is a minor disease that can be managed relatively easily by cultural practices and fungicides, selecting a cultivar solely for its resistance to *Corticium* red thread is generally not practical. Cultivars should be chosen for their resistance to the turfgrass disease that is likely to be the most serious threat, and in most areas that is not *Corticium* red thread. Although turfgrass cultivars that are resistant to *Corticium* red thread and *Fusarium* patch might be very important in the Pacific Northwest and in parts of Europe, they would be of minor importance in most other areas of the world.

As mentioned above, data on varietal reaction of *Corticium* red thread are inconclusive. However, Manhattan perennial ryegrass should not be grown in localities where *Corticium* red thread is a problem. Manhattan is another example of a cultivar chosen for an agronomic characteristic (winter hardiness and mowability) with little or no regard for potential disease problems. In the northern coastal regions of the United States and Europe, Manhattan is attacked by *Corticium* red thread, and in the midsouthern and southern United States it is subject to stem rust. Therefore it is probably inadvisable to plant Manhattan in those areas.

Chemical Management

High-maintenance turf will require some type of chemical management in the fall and winter. This is necessary because late-season nitrogen applications that might alleviate the *Corticium* red thread problem will increase the severity of the more serious diseases *Fusarium* patch and *Typhula* blight. Fall nitrogen applications that cause the turf to be lush before the advent of freezing weather can also cause serious turf loss from desiccation during open winters. In cool climates, several weeks of cool fall weather, especially of cold rain, can lower the soil temperature to a point where grass growth is minimal even when daytime temperatures are adequate for growth. Under these conditions, sufficient or even excess nitrogen does little to stimulate top growth, and fungicide treatments are necessary to prevent severe turf loss. Some fungicides that can be used on *Corticium* red thread are chlorothalonil, cycloheximide, and cycloheximide–thiram.

Disease: Rusts

Pathogen: *Puccinia* spp.

Hosts: *Puccinia graminis* Per. f. sp. *agrostidis* Erikss.—Stem rust, Kentucky bluegrass
Puccinia striiformis West.—Stripe rust, Kentucky bluegrass
Puccinia coronata Corda f. sp. *agropyri* Erikss.—Crown rust, perennial ryegrass, tall fescue
Puccinia cynodontis Lacroix—Bermudagrass rust
Puccinia zoysiae Diet.—Zoysiagrass rust
Puccinia brachypodii Otth. var. *poae* nemoralis (Otth.) Cummins and H. C. Green—Leaf rust, Kentucky bluegrass

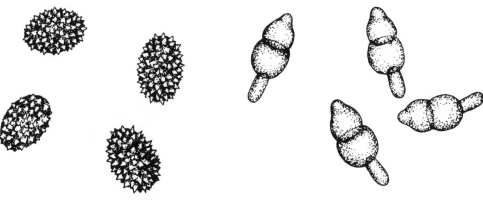

Puccinia graminis urediospores   *Puccinia graminis* teliospores

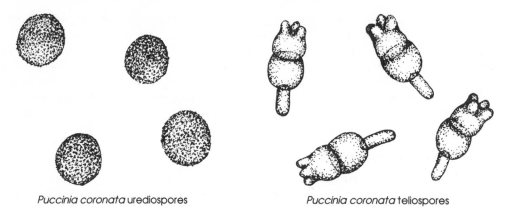

Puccinia coronata urediospores   Puccinia coronata teliospores

The rusts are, in general, minor diseases on mowed turf; the one exception is stripe rust. On adequately fertilized turf that is mowed once a week, rust is not a problem. It can become a problem, however, when the grass stops growing in the fall because of cool weather. If cool weather comes early in the fall, rust can become serious enough to warrant the application of fungicides. Stem rust on Kentucky bluegrass and crown rust on perennial ryegrass are serious problems in seed fields in the Pacific Northwest; such fields do require fungicide treatments.

Symptoms

The rust diseases are characterized by the yellow to dark brown uredospores that protrude through the ruptured epidermis of the grass plant. At a distance rust-infected turf looks yellow, but close examination will reveal rust-colored uredospores protruding through the epidermis of the grass plant.

Occurrence

Stem Rust

Rusts have different spore stages which occur on different hosts. *Puccinia graminis* has five spore stages: the uredial and telial, which occur on the grass; the basidiospores, which are produced on the teliospores and then infect the barberry, the pycnial stage, which occurs on the barberry and during which mating takes place; and the aecial stage, when aecial spores are produced and then carried by the wind back to the grass host. All this is interesting, but has very little practical value in the epidemiology of the disease.

In the southern part of the Kentucky bluegrass belt, the fungus can overwinter as mycelium or active uredospores in infected plants. (Britton [11] found stem rust surviving as far north as Lafayette, Indiana.) In the spring uredospores are produced on overwintering plants and are carried northward on the prevailing southerly winds of summertime. They land on susceptible Kentucky bluegrass plants, germinate, and infect the plants. It takes 10 to 14 days from the time of infection until spores erupt through the epidermis. Each infecting uredospore can produce hundreds of new uredospores, and it doesn't take long for an epidemic to develop.

Leaf Rust

Leaf rust can overwinter in northern areas in Kentucky bluegrass plants. It is not as widespread or as important as stem rust.

Stripe Rust

Lawns severely infected with stripe rust look orange or brown. The pustules in the leaves are yellow and run lengthwise up the sheath and leaf blade between the vein. On the West Coast, stripe rust is active during the winter months [34, 54] and is most severe during cool moist periods in the early spring and late fall. It can cause serious loss of turf in the western United States.

Zoysiagrass Rust

The rust on zoysiagrass was first described by Kreitlow et al. in 1965 [77]. It can be a serious problem because zoysiagrass grows slowly and consequently is mowed less frequently than are other turfgrass species. Zoysiagrass lawns infected with *Puccinia zoysia* have an orange discoloration and may be severely thinned. The disease is most serious during periods of cool moist weather and in shaded areas [77, 44, 76]. Emerald and Meyer are the most susceptible cultivars [76, 44]. Severe rust infection on zoysiagrass usually requires fungicide treatment. Maneb and sulfur both control the disease when applied at 5-day intervals.

Crown Rust

Crown rust, caused by *Puccinia coronata*, is a common disease on perennial ryegrass and tall fescue. The pustule is yellow and the disease will turn the turf the same color. The disease gets its name from the crownlike appearance of the teliospores. Pennfine and Manhattan are very susceptible and crown rust is becoming a limiting factor in their use, expecially in the southern range and coastal areas of the United States. One of the main uses of perennial ryegrass is for athletic turfs, notably football fields. The rusts are worst when the grass is growing the slowest, which is exactly the time that football is played. Where rust is a problem, both Pennfine and Manhattan should be avoided.

Bermudagrass Rust

Puccinia cynodontis can cause a serious rust problem on some of the improved bermudagrass cultivars, although it seldom is severe enough to destroy a bermudagrass turf. In nurseries where bermudagrass cultivars are grown to be harvested and sold as sprigs for propagation, *P. cynodontis* can do a lot of damage. In nurseries the bermudagrass is not mowed, and consequently the rust has a chance to go through many infection cycles. The cultivar Sunturf is one of the most susceptible bermudagrasses , but the common types are resistant [156]. Infected grass blades have pustules that contain cinnamon-brown uredospores and black teliospores, but the general appearance of rust-infected bermudagrass turf is yellow.

Management

Cultural Practices

In many cases proper use of nitrogen can eliminate rust as a problem. If the turf can be mowed at least every 7 days, rust should not be severe. Zoysiagrass, which is slow growing, is an exception. Fungicide treatments may be necessary on other turfgrass species as well in areas where the turf grows slowly because the spring and fall are prolonged, cool, and wet. Bear in mind that applying excessive nitrogen in the fall to control rust could lead to more serious problems with snow molds or desiccation. During this time of year, fungicides are a better treatment for minor rust problems than is nitrogen, since high levels of nitrogen encourage other diseases that are more damaging than rust.

Resistant Cultivars

The rusts are most severe on improved cultivars and almost nonexistent on the common types of grasses. More explicitly, cultivars like Merion Kentucky bluegrass, Emerald and Meyer zoysiagrass, Sunturf bermudagrass, and Manhattan perennial ryegrass, which each consist of a single genotype, are very susceptible, while the cultivars known as common type (e.g., common bermudagrass, common perennial ryegrass, common Kentucky bluegrass) are natural blends of different genotypes of the same species. Rusts produce specific races that attack specific grass varieties [156] (see section on physiologic races in chapter 1). If a turf is made up of grass of a single genotype, a race of rust specific to that genotype can destroy the entire turf. On the other hand, if a turf is a blend of grass plants of differing genotypes, a specific race of rust that attacks one genotype probably will not harm the others. Instead of the whole turf being destroyed, the worst that might happen would be loss of one of the grasses making up the blend.

Blending some of the improved varieties would be a way to avoid severe outbreaks of rust. But why not simply plant a common type? Because the most important disease must be managed first and by the most efficient means. In the case of Kentucky bluegrass that means managing *Helminthosporium* melting-out, *Fusarium* blight, and stripe smut. Planting common, Newport, or Park Kentucky bluegrass instead of a cultivar resistant to all three of these major diseases, just to avoid rust, would be like catching smallpox to avoid cowpox! It is far easier to manage mild diseases like rust than devastating ones like melting-out, *Fusarium* blight, and stripe smut. Planting blends of some of the newer Kentucky bluegrass cultivars that are resistant to all three diseases should reduce the rust problem. So far there are no conclusive data on the resistance or susceptibility of the new improved Kentucky bluegrasses to rust. Knowing the rust fungus, with its numerous races, I would guess that all cultivars eventually become susceptible. For a further discussion of blending, see chapter 8.

Chemical Management

As explained before, chemical management of rusts may be necessary on slow-growing turf. Chemical management is also needed on grasses grown for seed production, because they are not mowed, and on cultivars propagated vegatatively (e.g., some varieties of bermudagrass and zoysiagrass), which are not mowed either. Fungicides that are effective are cycloheximide, chlorothalonil, mancozeb, maneb plus zinc sulfate, and zineb. They should be applied at intervals of 10 to 14 days for as long as the disease remains active.

Disease: Slime mold

Pathogens: *Mucilago spongiosa* (Leyss.) Morg., *Physarium cinereum* (Batsch) Pers.

Hosts: All grasses

Slime molds are not pathogenic on turf, although they may strike fear into the heart of the novice turfgrass manager. These saprophytes usually do nothing more than cause an unsightly appearance. If they persist for several days on the foliage they may cause chlorosis, but serious permanent damage seldom occurs.

Physarium cinereum is more common than *Mucilago spongiosa* [18]. The fruiting bodies can be observed on the foliage of the grass, on clover and other weeds, and on the soil or thatch. They consist of grayish white fruiting structures encompassing purple spores and often resemble cigarette ashes. Spots in the turf are usually irregular circles a few inches to a few feet across. If wet cool weather persists, large irregular areas may become covered with slime mold. A typical slime mold infestation is illustrated in figure 3-9.

Figure 3-9.   Slime mold on turf and weed foliage (Photograph courtesy of Dr. Don Blasingame)

Management

Chemical management is not necessary; in fact it is a waste of time and money. If the infestation is heavy, poling, brushing, or a sharp spray of water from a hose will remove the slime mold from the leaf.

chapter four

FUNGUS DISEASES OF TURFGRASSES, III

Disease: Spring dead spot

Pathogen: Unknown

Host: Bermudagrass

Spring dead spot (SDS) causes more damage to bermudagrass, particularly in the cooler parts of the warm-season grass regions, than any other single disease. Bermudagrass is probably the finest fairway grass from a golfer's point of view. It is an upright-growing turf which gives the ball an excellent, firm lie. But it is discouraging to have beautiful lush green bermudagrass fairways, greens, and home lawns in the fall, before the bermudagrass becomes dormant, only to find large areas that fail to green up in the spring because they have been destroyed by spring dead spot.

Symptoms

Spring dead spot is first evident in the spring after the bermudagrass breaks dormancy and begins to green up. It appears as brown, more or less circular spots in the turf, ranging in diameter from a few inches to 3 or 4 feet (fig. 4-1). Except for the well-defined circular spots so typical of fungus diseases, the grass looks as though it has simply failed to break dormancy; the foliage has the typical straw color of dormant bermudagrass. Examination of the stolons and root, however, reveals black discoloration. In late spring the dead spots may have green centers. The green centers are often the result of invasion by broadleaf weeds and weed grass, especially in the northern regions of the bermudagrass belt. In the southern part of the bermudagrass belt, where good broadleaf weed management is practiced, the spots will be covered over by bermudagrass stolons growing in from the periphery of the spots. However, the roots produced at the nodes are short and dark and do not "root down," suggesting the presence of a toxin [89] or a high concentration of the pathogen. Kozelnicky [75] found that seedings of common bermudagrass, Pennfine perennial ryegrass, Penncross creeping bentgrass, and some nonturf grass species that were grown in soil from spring dead spots showed stimulated growth for about the first 2 weeks. The same kinds of grasses, when seeded in soil taken from areas adjacent to the dead spots, showed no stimulated growth during the first 2 weeks. After 2 weeks, however, the growth of plants in soil from the dead spots was retarded, while the plants in soil that had been adjacent to the dead spots continued to grow normally. Stolons of Tifway, Tifgreen, Tidwarf, Tufcote, and common bermuda-

Figure 4–1. Spring dead spot in a home lawn turf (Photograph courtesy of Bill Small)

grasses, Meyer and Emerald zoysiagrasses, and Penncross creeping bentgrass that were sprigged into soil from spring dead spots all showed retarded growth compared to stolons of the same varieties that were sprigged into soils that had not come from dead spots. These results suggest that a toxic substance is present in soil where spring dead spot symptoms have appeared. The notable exception was volunteer *Poa annua*, which grew much better in the soil from the dead spots.

Occurrence

The cause of spring dead spot is unknown, even though many types of fungi, including helminthosporiums, curvularias, pythiums, fusaria, and *Ophiobolus graminis*, have been isolated from diseased tissue. But all attempts to reinoculate and produce spring dead spot symptoms have failed. Therefore it is likely that more than one organism is involved—perhaps a nematode interacting with a fungus, or a warm-temperature fungus predisposing the grass to injury by a cool-temperature fungus, or the interaction of several different fungi. It is also possible that SDS is caused by a soil fungus of the fairy ring type that, while not itself parasitic on bermudagrass, predisposes the turf to infection by other fungi or to winter injury.

Although the cause of spring dead spot it still a mystery, several facts about the disease are known. It is more prevalent in bermudagrass turfs that receive high maintenance than in those under low-maintenance programs. Since highly maintained turfs are given more nitrogen, it is possible that nitrogen is a direct cause of spring dead spot. But the effect of nitrogen might be indirect rather than direct, because turfs that get more nitrogen tend to have more thatch, and heavy thatch also appears to be associated with the disease. Another factor associated with the development and severity of spring dead spot is the length of dormancy: the longer the period of dormancy, the more severe the disease. But bermudagrass is known to be susceptible to cold-temperature kill. Although the dormant period is longer in the northern part of the bermudagrass belt, the winters are also more severe, and therefore the greater severity of the disease may be due to weakening of the grass plants by cold weather rather than to dormancy per se. Kozelnicky [75] found that bermudagrass actually dies in Georgia during January and February and that the incidence of death depends on the severity of the winter.

Another important question is, When does infection occur—in the spring, summer, fall, or winter? Of course the answer is tied up with the cause of the disease. Several investigators may have shed some light on the matter. Wilcoxen [159] found that fungicide applied any time during the growing season helped reduce the severity of spring dead spot the following spring. Sturgeon and Jackson [131] demonstrated that when high rates of PCNB + ethazole were applied as soil drenches, the dead spot would fill in during the second year after application. By applying large amounts of several fungicides as soil drenches in October and November, Lucas [87] was able to prevent the occurrence of spring dead spot the following spring.

Management

Cultural Practices

Cultural practices that reduce thatch, such as vertical mowing and topdressing, also help manage spring dead spot, presumably because they lessen the amount of thatch. Lucas [87] showed that extra applications of nitrogen during August and September made spring dead spot worse and resulted in lower-quality turf the following spring.

Resistant Cultivars

At this time there do not appear to be any truly resistant varieties. The improved varieties like Tiffine, Tifgreen, and Sunturf are reported to be more susceptible than common bermudagrass, but their "susceptibility" may simply be due to the fact that they usually receive more maintenance (i.e., more nitrogen) than common bermudagrass does.

Chemical Management

Wilcoxen's work [159] has shown that fungicides applied to bermudagrass turfs during the growing season will reduce the severity of spring dead spot. The fungicide used in the study was chlorothalonil, which was applied biweekly at a concentration of 3 ounces per 1000 square feet. One test area received treatment during April and May, a second area was treated during June and July, a third during August and September, and a fourth from April through September. There was, of course, an untreated control plot. The April-May area received only three treatments because the study was not begun until late April. When the plots were read the following spring, all the treatments had either reduced spring dead spot or maintained it at the same level. The untreated control plot, on the other hand, had too many spots even to be read. Sturgeon and Jackson [131], working with large amounts of PCNB + ethazole applied as a drench, showed that a single application may provide control for more than one season. Lucas [87] managed spring dead spot in the spring of 1974 with six monthly applications of benomyl from July through December 1973 in an area that had severe spring dead spot in the spring of 1973. Lucas [87] also investigated the effect on disease management of the timing of fungicide application. He was able to prevent the occurrence of spring dead spot by applying benomyl at monthly intervals during the fall (October, November, December), but he found that applications of benomyl at other times of the year did not control the disease. Moreover, the effective application rates were too high to be economical for use on golf course fairways. Further experiments in the next few years should tell us more.

While the exact cause of this devastating disease is not known, at least a program for managing it seems to have been found. You may want to try Wilcoxen's [159] or Lucas's [87] approach on your fairways on an experimental basis to see which one is best for you. The cost of treating golf course greens is certainly within most budgets. Whether or not such a program is economical for fairways is another question, but you should keep in mind that 7000 or 8000 dollars a year for a fungicide program is cheaper than resprigging the fairway every 4 to 5 years, not to mention the inconvenience caused by the reestablishment operation or by not reestablishing and having to settle for something less than bermudagrass fairways.

Disease: *Typhula* blight (gray snow mold)

Pathogens: *Typhula incarnata* Lasch ex Fr., (syn. *Typhula itoana* Imai), *Typhula idahoensis* Remsb., *Typhula ishikariensis* Imai

Hosts: Annual bluegrass, colonial bentgrass, creeping bentgrass, fine-leaf fescues, Kentucky bluegrass, perennial ryegrass, tall fescue, velvet bentgrass

Typhula blight is an important disease in the northern areas of the Northern Hemisphere where snow stays on the ground for extended periods. It is most important in regions where snow cover remains on the ground for 3 months or more without a thaw. It may be found in combination with *Fusarium* patch (pink snow mold) but its range does not extend as far south as that of *Fusarium* patch. Unlike *Fusarium* patch, which occurs with or without snow cover, it does require some type of cover to be pathogenic. The cover is usually provided by snow, but leaves, straw mulch, and desiccation covers will also suffice.

Typhula incarnata is the most significant pathogen of gray snow mold in the eastern United States and Canada, whereas *Typhula ishikariensis* prevails from Wisconsin west. *Typhula idahoensis* appears to be a minor pathogen in both areas, at least for now. *T. ishikariensis* was reported by Vaartnous and Elliott to be the most important pathogen causing snow mold on red fescue and Kentucky bluegrass turfs in northwestern Canada in 1968 [143]. J. D. Smith [125] also reported widespread occurrence of the fungus in western Canada, and Stiensra [130] has reported that *T. ishikariensis* is an important pathogen in Minnesota.

Symptoms

At temperatures between 30 and 55 °F the *Typhula* fungus grows and infects. As the snow melts, circular grayish straw-colored to dark brown spots appear in the turf. The spots range from 3 inches to 2 feet in diameter, but most are between 6 and 12 inches across (fig. 4-2). Immediately after the snow melts, the grayish white mycelium of the fungus can be seen, especially in the outer margins of the spots. The disease gets its common name, gray snow mold, from the color of the mycelium. *Typhula* blight is worse in winter when the snow falls on unfrozen turf or on turf that has not been hardened off by frost. Often when snow falls on frozen ground the disease develops only in the spring when the snow begins to melt.

Figure 4-2. Fungicide-treated golf course green (top) compared to heavily *Typhula*-blight-infected creeping bentgrass fairway. Both green and fairway are Fencross creeping bentgrass; the uninfected grass around the trap is Kentucky bluegrass.

Occurrence

The life cycle of *Typhula* blight caused by *T. incarnata* is illustrated in figure 4-3. The *Typhula* fungi oversummer as sclerotia. In early spring, when the snow is melting, the sclerotia may be as large as 3/16 of an inch and can easily be seen with the naked eye. Later on they dry and shrink and become invisible (or at least hard to detect). As sclerotia the fungus can survive unfavorable warm temperatures and the fungicides that may be part of a summer program of disease control. With the arrival of cool wet fall weather and in the presence of ultraviolet light, the sclerotia swell and germinate, producing pink, club-shaped sphorophores [103] from which basidia and basidiospores arise. The basidiospores are carried by the wind to new places or to areas where the disease was eradicated last season. When conditions are right, the spores germinate and infect the grass plants. But if the fall remains warm or dry or both, the sclerotia may not germinate to form basidia. Instead, they will germinate directly as mycelium under the snow and cause infection that way. In the latter case, management by eradication would be possible, for reinfestation would be a slow process. Nonetheless, *Typhula* blight is a serious annual problem in northern areas.

Management

Cultural Practices

It is important that the turf not be lush going into the winter; if it is, *Typhula* blight will be much worse. It is very difficult to give a date for the last application of nitrogen to actively growing turf because dates for the first lasting snowfall vary so much. Depending on the area, the last nitrogen application should be sometime between mid-

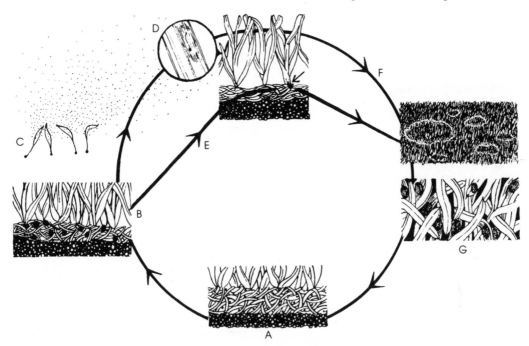

Figure 4–3. Life cycle of *Typhula* blight caused by *T. incarnata. A, Typhula* oversummers as sclerotia in the thatch or mat; *B,* sclerotia swell with the advent of cool weather and germinate, producing basidiocarps, when exposed to ultraviolet light; *C,* basidiocarps produce many basidiospores, which are disseminated by the wind; *D,* basidiospores germinate and infect turfgrass; *E,* some sclerotia germinate and infect turfgrass directly, without production of basidiocarps; *F, Typhula* infects the turf under snow cover or in the melting margins of the snow during the spring thaw; *G,* close examination of the turf immediately after the snow has melted reveals the presence of light brown to reddish brown sclerotia.

August and mid-September. This is not to be confused with dormant nitrogen feeding, that is, applying nitrogen after the top growth has stopped. Dormant feedings promote early greening-up in the spring and quick recovery of turf damaged by snow mold. Whenever possible, effective fungicides should be applied to turf receiving dormant nitrogen feedings.

Resistant Cultivars

Beard [3] reported that creeping bentgrass cultivars exhibit varying degrees of susceptibility to *Typhula* blight, but from a practical point of view they all require fungicide treatment.

Vargas et al. [148] reported on the resistance of Kentucky bluegrass cultivars to *Typhula itoana.* Adorno, Monopoly, P-114, Bonnie Blue and Galaxie were the most resistant, while Fylking, Pennstar, Campus, South Dakota Certified, and Prato were the most susceptible. Because Kentucky bluegrass is not as severely damaged as annual bluegrass and the bentgrasses, it may be possible to alleviate the snow mold problem by using more resistant cultivars in areas where the infestation is severe. Vaartnous and Elliott [143] found Park to be the most resistant to *T. ishikariensis* and Merion and Nugget the most susceptible. The data of Vargas et al. [148] support their findings, although Park had a heavy infestation of *Fusarium* patch. This information may be useful in areas where *Typhula* blight is the most serious disease and *Helminthosporium* melting-out, *Fusarium* blight, and stripe smut are not a problem. (See the section on Kentucky bluegrass varieties in chapter 9 and the section on interpreting data in chapter 1.)

The red fescues are, in general, more resistant to snow mold than are the Kentucky bluegrasses and the bentgrasses. According to Vaartnous and Elliott [143], Boreal and Reptans are the most resistant to *T. ishikariensis*. But use of the fine-leaf fescues is limited by their susceptibility to *Helminthosporium* diseases.

Chemical Management

Chemical management of snow molds is necessary on putting greens, whether they consist of annual bluegrass or creeping bentgrass. Often money is spent on spraying to manage summer diseases on creeping bentgrass fairways, but snow mold management is forgotten. *Typhula* blight will then infect and kill creeping bentgrass fairways unless fungicides are used, and annual bluegrass will begin to fill in the bare places during the spring. I am not opposed to annual bluegrass fairways, but those who are should realize that a good preventive fungicide program is necessary to prevent creeping bentgrass fairways from turning into annual bluegrass fairways. I disagree with the idea that it is possible to maintain creeping bentgrass fairways without a fungicide program to manage snow molds. Fungicides are needed even in southern areas where people say, "Oh, I only get about twenty percent snow mold a year, so it's hardly worth spraying." But 20 percent a year times 5 years is 100 percent. While all the creeping bentgrass will not be destroyed in 5 years, most of it will, and *Poa annua* will replace it.

The mercury fungicides have for many years been the standard for snow mold management. Although fungicides containing PCNB and chloroneb are also being used now, they are not without problems. PCNB is phytotoxic to some bentgrasses, among them Cohanse (C-7). Toronto (C-15) and Penncross, however, appear to tolerate PCNB. Chloroneb is not effective against *Fusarium* patch, and in areas where both *Typhula* blight and *Fusarium* patch occur or where *Fusarium* patch is the major problem, other fungicides must be used in combination with chloroneb. Furthermore, chloroneb appears to be species specific, for though it controls *Typhula* blight caused by *T. incarnata*, it is not very effective against *T. ishikariensis*. Vargas and Turgeon [154] showed that chloroneb is a slow systemic fungicide, which may account for some of the erratic results reported by various researchers, although it is effective as a contact fungicide as well. Stienstra [130] has found that in many areas (and particularly in Minnesota), combinations of two or three fungicides are necessary for snow mold management. This is because many different species of fungi are involved in the snow mold complex.

Disease: *Fusarium* patch (pink snow mold)

Pathogen: *Fusarium nivale* (Fr.) Snyder and Hansen

Hosts: Annual bluegrass, Kentucky bluegrass, rough bluegrass, colonial bentgrass, velvet bentgrass, creeping bentgrass, perennial ryegrass, fine-leaf fescues, tall fescue

Fusarium nivale

In the Pacific Northwest, the British Isles, and northern Europe, *Fusarium* patch is the most important turfgrass disease. This is mainly because all these areas have extended periods of cool wet weather without snow cover. *Fusarium* patch is also a problem in any area with a cool wet spring or fall or snow cover in the winter months. If annual bluegrass, creeping bentgrass, velvet bentgrass, colonial bentgrass, and perennial ryegrass are infected with *Fusarium* patch, the grass plants may be destroyed. Kentucky bluegrass and red fescue, while susceptible to the disease, are not as seriously affected and the grass plants usually do not die.

Symptoms

Without snow cover, *Fusarium* patch occurs as reddish brown spots in the turf. The spots range in diameter from less than 1 inch to about 8 inches, although larger ones are sometimes found. When there is snow cover, the circular spots are usually from 2 or 3 inches to 1 or 2 feet in diameter and are tan to whitish gray or reddish brown (see fig. 4-4). Shortly after the snow has melted, the pink mycelium of the fungus can be seen at the advancing edge of the spot, hence the common name "pink snow mold."

Occurrence

Fusarium nivale can survive as mycelium and conidia in the thatch and will actively grow on the grass residue. Infection takes place when the temperature is below 60 °F, even though in culture the fungus grows best at temperatures between 60 and 77 °F [12]. This is probably because when the temperature is below 60 °F the plant grows more slowly and is therefore more vulnerable to attack by the fungus (also, the fungus has less

Figure 4–4. *Fusarium* patch on a golf course green after the snow has melted

competition from other antagonistic microorganisms at this temperature). *F. nivale* and other snow molds are examples of pathogens that have found ecological niches where they can survive with less competition from other saprophytic and pathogenic microorganisms.

Management

Cultural Practices

Fertilizing with nitrogen causes lush growth going into the snow mold season and will make the turf more susceptible to *Fusarium* patch. It will also make management with fungicides more difficult. It is hard to recommend a specific date for the last application of nitrogen, since temperatures and seasons vary so much. It should be early enough to give the turfgrass a chance to harden off before the onslaught of snow or frost or, in areas of mild winters, before the grass becomes dormant. Also, if the turf is lush and there is an open winter (i.e., one without snow cover), large areas of grass can be lost to desiccation.

Resistant Cultivars

There is no creeping bentgrass that is truly resistant to *Fusarium* patch; all require preventive chemical treatment. Annual bluegrass also requires chemical treatment. Kentucky bluegrass and annual bluegrass appear to be more susceptible to *Fusarium* patch than is creeping bentgrass. In fact, *Fusarium* patch has been observed to select the annual bluegrass patches on greens that are predominately creeping bentgrass.

Chemical Management

There are many contact fungicides that can be used to manage *Fusarium* patch where there is no lasting snow cover. If there is permanent snow cover for 3 months or longer, either the mercury or the systemic fungicides must be used. Although the benzimidazole systemic fungicides do manage *Fusarium* patch, they also predispose the grass to an invasion of *Helminthosporium* and must be used in combination with contact fungicides like mancozeb. Also, strains of *F. nivale* resistant to the benzimidazole systemic fungicides have been reported in the Pacific Northwest.

Other Snow Molds

Sclerotinia borealis, the low-temperature basidiomycetes (LTB), and a white isolate of *Rhizoctonia solani* are also known to cause snow mold disease. In Canada the distribution of the snow mold fungi is *Sclerotinia borealis* in the colder regions, *Typhula* species in the intermediate temperature zone, and *Fusarium nivale* in the warmer regions [84, 85].

The symptoms of LTB are similar to those of gray snow mold except that there are no sclerotia and many isolates produce hydrogen cyanide. LTB can attack Kentucky bluegrass, red fescue, and creeping bentgrass. PCNB, chloroneb, and chlorothalonil all give effective management [125].

Snow mold caused by *Sclerotinia borealis* has been reported in Canada, Alaska, Sweden, Norway, Finland, and the USSR. It has been found on Kentucky bluegrass, red fescue, perennial ryegrass, tall fescue [18], and bentgrass [125]. The disease is similar to other gray snow molds, with grayish mycelium present near the advancing snow margins. Dull black sclerotia can be found on the surface of infected leaves. The disease is most severe in the northern part of Canada [85]. PCNB is an effective fungicide in the management of *Sclerotinia borealis*.

Diseases: Flag smut and stripe smut

Pathogens: Flag smut—*Urocystis agropyi* (Preuss) Schrot
Stripe smut—*Ustilago striiformis* (Westend.) Niessl

Hosts: Kentucky bluegrass, creeping bentgrass, colonial bentgrass

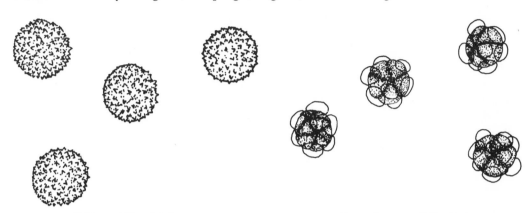

Ustilago striiformis teliospores   *Urocystis agropyi* teliospores

The smuts, along with *Fusarium* blight, are the most destructive diseases of *Helminthosporium*-resistant Kentucky bluegrass cultivars. They are systemic and perennial, which means that once a plant becomes infected it will remain so for life. Furthermore, all plants arising from an infected mother plant will be infected also. A smut-infected plant is always in a weakened condition and any additional stress will kill it. The most common form of stress is drought, and it is not unusual to see entire lawns that are heavily infected with stripe or flag smut die when people go on vacation in the summer and neglect to have someone water the grass. The smuts can be distinguished easily under a microscope. The teliospores of stripe smut occur singly, while those of flag smut occur together in groups of three to five, known as "spore balls," which are surrounded by sterile cells.

The following discussion is mainly about stripe smut on Kentucky bluegrass because little work has been done on flag smut, although flag smut may be the more important disease of the two. Plants infected with flag smut are killed more readily than are plants infected with stripe smut. Consequently, a year after infection has occurred it is difficult to find plants that have flag smut, but plants affected by the less severe stripe smut remain (C. F. Hodges, personal communication).

Stripe Smut on Bentgrass. Although most of the attention has been given to stripe smut on Kentucky bluegrass, stripe smut can be a serious problem on creeping bentgrass as well. It is often difficult to see on bentgrass cut at putting-green height, because there is so little leaf surface. Stripe smut has been reported on the cultivars Evansville, Pennlu, Seaside, Toronto (C-15), Washington (C-50), Arlington (C-1), Congressional (C-19), Old Orchard (C-52), and Penncross [58]. I have observed stripe smut to be a problem mainly on Toronto creeping bentgrass in the Midwest. If it occurs on Penncross, that is the exception rather than the rule. The disease usually starts thinning the turf in high areas or heavily trafficked areas (e.g., where the cup is cut). Recovery of the turf around the cup following a day with heavy play will be slow. *Poa annua* rather quickly invades such weakened areas on Toronto creeping bentgrass greens. Stripe smut is a slow-moving disease which is difficult to detect in Toronto creeping bentgrass greens because of the height at which they are mowed, and except for the thinning, slow growth, and invasion of annual bluegrass, it may go unnoticed.

Symptoms

From a distance infected turf looks clumpy because the stripe smut fungus causes the infected bluegrass plants to grow more upright than the healthy plants [61]. Stripe smut tends to kill individual plants, leaving bare spots that contribute to the clumpy appearance. Smut-infected plants do not tiller as profusely as healthy plants, and so weed grass and broadleaf weeds, rather than Kentucky bluegrass, fill the bare spots.

Light yellow blades of grass are the first symptoms of stripe smut. As the disease advances, the leaf blades begin to curl and show parallel black stripes running the length of the blade (see fig. 4-5). If you touch these stripes, a black, sootlike dust—the spores of the stripe or flag smut fungus—will rub off. Older infected blades will be twisted, curled, and shredded from the tips down.

Occurrence

The stripe smut fungus overwinters as mycelium in the crown and other vegetative parts of an infected plant. It can also survive as teliospores in the soil for many seasons. Infection of seedlings can occur through the coleoptiles or through axillary crown buds or rhizome nodes [62].

Symptoms of stripe smut are most commonly seen in the spring and fall during periods of wet cool weather when the daytime temperature is below 70 °F. They gradually dis-

Figure 4–5.   Close-up of a stripe-smut-infected Marion Kentucky bluegrass plant

appear as the weather becomes warmer. Although the symptoms are most evident during cool weather, very little turf is lost then. Most turf loss occurs during hot dry summer weather (when the grass is under heat and drought stress) or in open winters that subject plants to desiccation and cold-temperature stress.

Stripe smut is a systemic disease that is perennial in the grass plant. *Systemic* means that the fungus is internal and can spread throughout the plant's vascular system. (The striping on the grass blades is due to the fungus growing only in the veins.) *Perennial* means that once a plant is infected it will remain so for life, although symptoms may not always be visible. Under certain environmental conditions foliar symptoms may be absent even though the fungus is still present in the crown of the infected plant. Protected in the crown, the fungus can survive adverse conditions for months and then become active when conditions are right.

The stripe smut fungus cannot attack through the foliage; it can attack only through the lateral buds on the rhizomes. (But leaves, tillers, and rhizomes arising from infected crowns are infected also.) This limited ability to infect probably explains why the disease is usually serious only on turf that is at least 3 years old. And it is also the reason that stripe smut becomes a problem only in sod fields that have been in cultivation for many years, allowing spores to accumulate in the soil. The spores are thick-walled and can remain alive in the soil for many years.

Stripe smut produces specific races that attack specific cultivars of Kentucky bluegrass. Gaskin [48] was the first to demonstrate the existence of these races. All races of stripe smut belong to the species *Ustilago striiformis*, but each race has unique characteristics resulting from its own particular genetic makeup. Each race of stripe smut will attack only specific Kentucky bluegrass cultivars.

The spores of *U. striiformis* are often referred to as chlamydospores because they are thick-walled and can survive in the soil for many years, but they are more correctly called teliospores. The binucleate teliospores undergo karyogamy followed by meiosis, which gives rise to haploid nuclei. The teliospores then germinate to form a promycelium, which in turn produces uninucleate (haploid) sporidia. Sporidia of opposite mating types fuse to form a dikaryon (n + n). It is only the dikaryon which can infect. The possibility is great that new forms of virulence will develop during mating and the formation of the dikaryon. Therefore, the fact that a cultivar is resistant today doesn't mean it will be resistant forever. A "resistant" cultivar is simply one that is resistant to the stripe smut races prevalent today, most of which are specific for Merion and Windsor.

Management

Cultural Practices

Keep nitrogen applications to a minimum during the summer months—no more than ½ pound of nitrogen per 1000 square feet per month. Turf infected with stripe smut should not be allowed to dry out. A healthy Kentucky bluegrass turf will become dormant when dry and will recover when it is irrigated, but a lawn with stripe smut will die when it becomes dry.

Resistant Cultivars

There are several Kentucky bluegrass cultivars that are resistant to stripe smut, but their resistance is likely to be temporary. The stripe smut fungus has the potential to produce new races, and once a Kentucky bluegrass becomes widely grown, a race of

U. striiformis which can attack it will probably develop. Cultivars that are currently resistant are certainly preferable to cultivars that are already susceptible, but you should be on the lookout for problems in the future. What is needed is identification of Kentucky bluegrass cultivars that have horizontal resistance to stripe smut (see chapter 8). In the meantime, it is a good idea to blend three or four of the better Kentucky bluegrasses. Then if a new race of stripe smut that is specific to one of the cultivars in the blend develops, the other cultivars will remain healthy and the turf will not be ruined.

Chemical Management

Stripe smut is an internal disease and can be managed chemically only by the use of systemic fungicides. For the systemic fungicides to be effective they must be drenched into the root system immediately after application. The best results are obtained in the fall when the temperatures become cool or in early spring when the grass plants are dormant. Benomyl, thiophanate-methyl, and thiophanate-ethyl are systemic fungicides which have been used to manage stripe smut. This is not a permanent solution, however, and repeated application will have to be made in subsequent years; moreover, it is only a matter of time before *U. striiformis* develops resistance to the benzimidazole systemic fungicides.

In addition to the destruction wrought by the stripe smut fungus itself, Kentucky bluegrass varieties infected with stripe smut lose their resistance to *Helminthosporium* melting-out. The systemic fungicides also cause Kentucky bluegrass cultivars resistant to *Helminthosporium* melting-out to become susceptible. Because of this, it is recommended that turf infected with stripe smut receive an application of a good *Helminthosporium* fungicide as well as a systemic fungicide to control the stripe smut [70]. Overseeding the infected turf with a blend of resistant Kentucky bluegrass or creeping bentgrass cultivars is the best solution.

Disease: Yellow tuft (downy mildew)

Pathogen: *Sclerophthora   macrospora* (Sacc.) Thirum, Shaw, and Naras

Hosts: Kentucky bluegrass, creeping bentgrass, annual bluegrass, fine-leaf fescues, tall fescue, perennial ryegrass, *Poa trivialis*, colonial bentgrass, velvet bentgrass

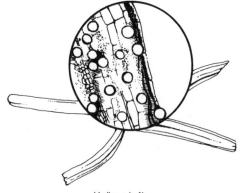

Yellow tuft

In the 1950s Tarjan and others associated yellow tuft with parasitic nematodes [134, 135] but this was never verified. Mueller et al. [95] found the downy mildew fungus *Sclerophthora macrospora* associated with yellow tuft, and Jackson and Deroeden [71] later demonstrated that *S. macrospora* is the causal agent.

Symptoms

The symptoms are small yellow spots in the turf, from ¼ inch to 3 inches in diameter. Infected turf may appear spotted, as though droplets of herbicide had been misapplied to the area. Examination of the tufts reveals a dense cluster of yellow shoots, which can be seen arising out of a single axillary bud at the node or terminals of a stem [71].

Occurrence

Yellow tuft most commonly occurs in the cool weather of the spring and fall. *S. macrospora* can overwinter and oversummer as mycelium in the infected plant or as oospores in the grass plants and in the debris. With the advent of cool moist weather, mycelium in infected plants produces sporangia, which germinate and release motile zoospores that can infect healthy plants. The disease is unsightly, but usually causes little serious damage. However, I have observed severe damage to two-year-old and younger Penncross creeping bentgrass during warm weather. The damage is greatest in areas where surface drainage occurs and on greens where excessive amounts of nitrogen fertilizers have been applied before the advent of warm weather.

Management

Cultural Practices

The addition of iron ($Fe_2 SO_4$) will help to mask the symptoms. No more than ½ pound of nitrogen per 1000 square feet per month should be applied in June, July, and August, and it may be even better to make no applications at all.

Resistant Cultivars

Little is known about resistance to yellow tuft, but some of the more susceptible Kentucky bluegrasses are A-20, Adelphi, Bonnie Blue, Baron, and Merion. Toronto and Penncross creeping bentgrass are very susceptible also.

Chemical Management

There are no commercially available chemicals that can be used to manage yellow tuft. A Ciba-Geigy experimental fungicide, to be sold under the trade names Subdue and Ridomil, has been shown to manage the disease (N. Jackson, personal communication).

chapter five

VIRAL, MYCOPLASMAL, AND NEMATODE DISEASES OF TURFGRASSES

VIRAL AND MYCOPLASMAL DISEASES

There are eight viral diseases and one mycoplasmalike disease known to affect turfgrass [18]. Of these, St. Augustine decline seems to be the only one of economic importance. This may be the true situation; or it could be that there are viral problems in many of the important turfgrass species but the plants are symptomless carriers; or viruses could be expressing themselves as part of a complex of problems that might include edaphic factors, fungi, nematodes, and various environmental stresses. Control of one or more aspects of such a complex might lessen the effect of a virus and cause it to go unnoticed. The greatest potential for harm from viruses is probably in seed-production fields. Many viral diseases of other grasses (wheat, barley, oats, etc.) tend not to destroy the host but merely to reduce yields.

The eight viral diseases are St. Augustine decline (SAS), barley yellow dwarf, ryegrass mosaic, oat necrotic mottle, western ryegrass mosaic, bromegrass mosaic, sugarcane mosaic (maize dwarf mosaic), and *Poa* semilatent virus. The one suspected mycoplasmal disease is aster yellows. St. Augustine decline will be discussed in detail, since it is the only viral disease of turfgrass that is economically important. For information on the other viral diseases and the mycoplasmalike disease, consult the book by Couch [18].

The pathogen responsible for SAD is the *Panicum* mosaic virus, or St. Augustine decline virus. The host, St. Augustinegrass, is one of the major turfgrass species in the South. In Texas and Florida, SAD damages or destroys more St. Augustinegrass than any other disease. An estimated 3 million dollars in turf replacement value was lost in Corpus Christi, Texas, in 1966.

The first symptom of SAD is mild chlorotic mottling of the leaf blades (fig. 1-5). The mottling becomes worse the second year, and in the third year the grass plants will die, leaving dead areas which are filled in by weedy grass and broadleaf weeds. The disease is most severe when St. Augustinegrass is grown under conditions of low nitrogen or drought, or where nematodes or insects are a problem [88].

SAD is mechanically transmitted. Since all the St. Augustinegrass turfs are sodded, sprigged, or stolonized (sprigging being the most common method of establishment), once the disease becomes established in a St. Augustinegrass nursery it can be spread throughout the nursery by mowing and over a large area when the sprigs are sold. Likewise, once SAD gets into a neighborhood where the mowing is done by contractors, it can spread quickly from lawn to lawn.

Figure 5–1. Foliar symptoms of St. Augustine decline (SAD); 1 = no disease, 5 = severe disease (Photograph courtesy of Dr. Don Blasingame)

Management

Cultural Practices

Good turf maintenance will slow the progress of the disease, but the decline and eventual loss of the St. Augustinegrass turf is inevitable. Nitrogen applications can temporarily mask the presence of SAD, but in time the symptoms will reappear.

Resistant Cultivars

Texas A & M University, in cooperation with the University of Florida, has developed a cultivar of St. Augustinegrass called Floratam, which is resistant to SAD. This, of course, sounds like the obvious solution to the SAD problem, both for new lawns and for reestablishing St. Augustinegrass in turfs destroyed by SAD. In addition to its resistance to SAD, Floratam is reported to be resistant to the chinch bug, which also is devastating to St. Augustinegrass. Unfortunately, the agronomic characteristics of Floratam are not sufficiently good to make it a desirable turfgrass species, especially in the northern part of the St. Augustinegrass growing area.

Chemical Management

There are no chemicals that will manage SAD.

NEMATODES

Nematodes are small nonsegmented worms, usually eel shaped, which live in soil and water or on hosts (plants or animals). They are colorless and range from $\frac{1}{10}$ to $\frac{1}{75}$ of an inch in length (see fig. 5-2). All nematodes that are plant parasites are obligate parasites. They feed by means of a stylet, a hollow, spearlike structure located in the anterior (head) end (fig. 5-3). With its stylet the nematode punctures living cells to

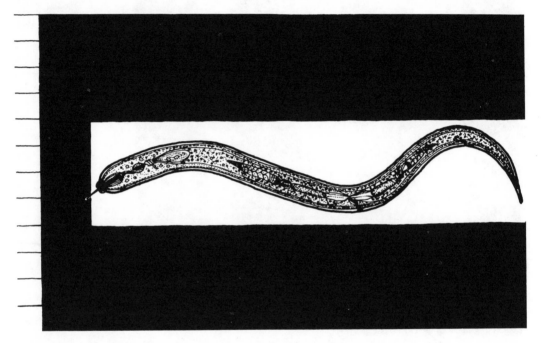

Figure 5–2. Ectoparasitic nematode and No. 50 thread, both at a magnification of 270 ×. The common button thread, whose diameter is approximately 12 times that of the worm, is visible to the naked eye; the nematode is microscopic and invisible.

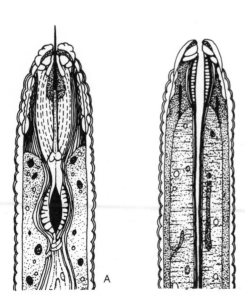

Figure 5–3. *A*, plant-parasitic nematode with stylet; *B*, free-living nematode without stylet

obtain food. The stylet is like a syringe through which the nematode draws a cell's contents into its own body. Before withdrawing the cell's contents the nematode injects digestive secretions that start decomposing the cell's protoplasm. Some of the injected substances cause physiological changes that make grass plants more susceptible to other problems, such as diseases caused by fungi. In other words, the wounds that some types of nematodes make while feeding may allow other parasites or saprophytes to enter.

The two main classifications of nematodes are based on their feeding habits. *Ectoparasitic* nematodes (fig.5-4) feed with their bodies outside the plant root, and *endoparasitic* nematodes (fig. 5-5) enter the plant root and feed from within the root. Ectoparasitic nematodes are more common on turfgrass, which is fortunate because they are easier to manage.

Figure 5-4. Ectoparasitic nematodes feeding on a turfgrass root

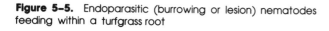

Figure 5-5. Endoparasitic (burrowing or lesion) nematodes feeding within a turfgrass root

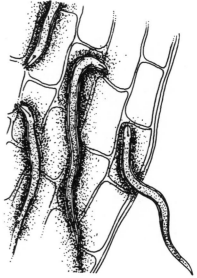

Pathogenicity

Nematodes that are plant parasites and that live in a weed-free stand of turf must feed on the roots of the turfgrass. The question that has been baffling turfgrass scientists is, How much damage are they doing? A single nematode has a negligible potential for doing damage, but it doesn't take long for nematode populations to reach a level where they can do great harm. The life cycle (i.e., egg to egg) of nematodes pathogenic to plants may be as short as 10 days, but 30 to 45 days is normal. Depending on the species, one female can lay up to 2000 eggs. Nematode populations vary throughout the season. If you suspect that nematodes are present, take samples every month throughout the growing season to see how the population fluctuates. This information will help you work out strategies to control the problem with nematicides.

How many nematodes constitute a problem? The answer depends on the species of nematode. As few as 10 sting nematodes (*Belonolaimus longecaudatus*) per 100 cubic centimeters are a real problem, whereas 300 stunt nematodes (*Tylenchorhynchus* spp.) per 100 cubic centimeters are a potential problem. The data to support these numbers come from laboratory and greenhouse experiments carried out in controlled environments with pasteurized soil to eliminate other biological factors such as microorganisms, insects, and even other nematode species. It is understood that the direct application of the results of laboratory and greenhouse experiments to field conditions is not always possible, but these data can help you decide how to approach field situations.

How many nematodes are necessary to cause damage when soil is water-soaked following heavy rains? How many are necessary to weaken a plant or alter its physiology so that weak pathogens like *Fusarium roseum* or *Pythium graminicola* can become serious? How many nematodes constitute a problem when more than one species is found in association with a plant? Do 300 nematodes per 100 cubic centimeters of soil have the same effect on a grass plant growing at 70 °F as they do on a grass plant growing at 90 °F or more? The point is that the pathogenic potential of a nematode population is influenced by a complex of biotic and abiotic factors. Laboratory experiments elucidate individual components of the complex, but all aspects of the situation must be taken into consideration when you make decisions about a particular field situation.

Sampling

Your sampling technique is important if laboratory estimates of the nematode populations are to be accurate. Collect a pint of soil randomly from an area suspected of harboring nematodes. Put it in a container, preferably a plastic bag, label it properly, and take it to a test laboratory immediately. If this is not possible, place the sample in a refrigerator (*not* a freezer) until it can be taken to a laboratory. Many nematodes will die if subjected to high temperatures or drying (for example, being left on a desk or in a truck for a day or two) and the information you receive from the laboratory may not reflect the true population.

Inaccurate and misleading information can also result from sampling too late, that is, sampling an area so badly deteriorated that there are only a few live plants left. Nematodes are obligate parasites and once their food source, the plant roots, is destroyed, the population declines. This could lead to an erroneous conclusion that nematodes aren't the problem. If much turf has already been killed, it is advisable to collect soil samples from adjacent healthy areas. If tests show high nematode populations in the areas where turf looks healthy, you must keep a close watch for further signs of deterioration.

Locality

It is easier to recognize nematode problems in the warm-season grasses of the South than in the cool-season grasses of the North. This is primarily due to the longer periods of warm weather in the South. Nematodes are a problem on turfgrass when they cause severe thinning and shortening of the root system (see fig. 5-6). A turfgrass plant with such a root system may survive when it is growing at a cool or moderate temperature, but it will not survive long periods of high temperature. Even when adequate water is available, the damaged root system cannot take up water fast enough to replace the water being lost through transpiration. Heald and Perry [57] point out that nematode problems are most serious in the sandy coastal soils of Florida, which are more subject to drought than are heavier soils. This supports the hypothesis that symptoms are caused by the interaction of nematodes, drought, and high temperature.

In the North, symptoms of nematode problems are more subtle. Because of the more moderate climate, turfgrass plants attacked by nematodes can endure severe damage to the root system and still survive, especially if they get adequate water. Because of its damaged roots, turf with a high nematode population wilts faster than healthy turf, but in the North, irrigation can rectify this. Sometimes the only noticeable difference between a golf course putting green with a high nematode population and one with few nematodes or none at all is how much quicker the green with the high nematode population wilts. Another reason that symptoms in the North are different from those in the South is that the turfgrass and nematode species involved in the host-parasite relationship are different.

Biological interactions usually are not simple, and this is true of nematode problems in turf. In northern turfgrasses, nematodes often interact with other plant pathogens.

Figure 5–6. Kentucky bluegrass root shortened by stump nematode *Tylenchorhynchus dubius* (left), and a healthy nematode-free root (right)

The more moderate the climate, the more these interactions will affect the symptoms. There are many examples of crops being affected by nematode-fungus interactions, but only a few such interactions have been noted on turf. This may be because the leading turf researchers of the 1950s and early 1960s were mainly concerned with comparing turf treated with nematicides to untreated turf and did not pay much attention to environmental stress, fungal interactions, or microsymptoms. Many laboratories have used nematode extraction techniques that do not adequately assess the total nematode population, and frequently nematodes have been identified only at the generic level, even though species identification is necessary for proper analysis.

Vargas and Laughlin [152] demonstrated an interaction between the stunt nematode *Tylenchorhynchus dubius* and *Fusarium roseum* in the development of *Fusarium* blight symptoms. But this is not to say that *Fusarium* blight is always an interaction between *T. dubius* and *F. roseum*. Nematodes do not appear to be associated with *Fusarium* blight in climates of high temperature and high humidity, and sod laid on compacted subsoil can also develop macrosymptoms without a nematode-*Fusarium* interaction. The nematode-*Fusarium* interaction can, however, play an important role in the development of *Fusarium* blight symptoms in moderate climates (see fig. 5-7). (The north-central region appears to have more species and higher population densities of stunt nematodes than most other regions of the country.) Similar interactions have been observed with stripe smut in Kentucky bluegrass and *Helminthosporium* leaf spot in fine-leaf fescue. Plots with reduced nematode populations following a nematicide application exhibited less severe damage from stripe smut and leaf spot.

Figure 5-7. *Fusarium* blight-cyst nematode damage on a Kentucky bluegrass turf

Specific Nematodes

Nematodes that affect turfgrass are listed in table 5-1. Their common and scientific names are given, along with the names of grass species or cultivars on which they are known to be a problem. The sting nematode and the spiral nematode deserve special mention because they are such important parasites of turfgrass.

Sting Nematode (*Belonolaimus* spp.)

The sting nematode is a large ectoparasitic nematode that feeds on the tips of roots. It can cause severe damage in relatively low numbers (less than 10 per 100 cubic centimeters of soil), with its long stylet and the vigorous manner in which it feeds. It is the most important turfgrass pest in Florida. It is known to be a problem on St. Augustinegrass, centipedegrass, and zoysiagrass [57]. Christie et al. [15] described the symptoms produced by the sting nematode as "stubby root" because of the knoblike appearance of the root tips on the few remaining rootlets (fig. 5-8). The short root systems may be accompanied by stunted top growth and yellowing.

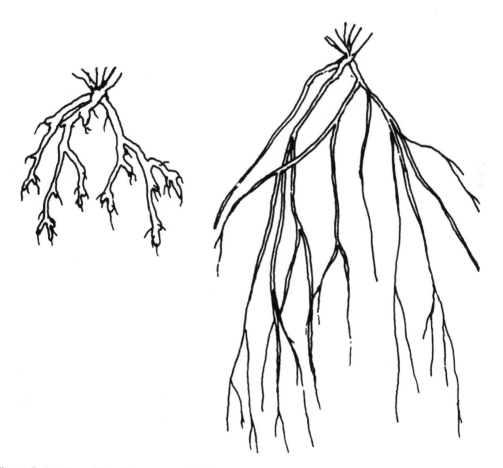

Figure 5–8. Normal, healthy grass root (left), and short, swollen roots of a turfgrass plant attacked by stubby-root nematodes (right)

Table 5-1. Pathogenic Turfgrass Nematodes, Symptoms, and Turfgrass Species with Which They Have Been Associated

Common Name	Scientific Name	Associated Turfgrass Species	Symptoms
Endoparasitic Nematodes			
Burrowing nematode [14, 39, 74]	*Radopholus similus*	Bermudagrass St. Augustinegrass	Yellowing and stunting of top growth; stunting of root system; brown sunken lesions, often quite large.
Cyst nematode [28, 29]	*Heterodera major*	Tall fescue Fine-leaf fescues Perennial ryegrass Rough bluegrass Annual ryegrass	Yellowing of top growth. Tiny knobs (cysts) on the root system, which are white when first formed and later turn light brown.
	H. punctata	Creeping bentgrass Colonial bentgrass St. Augustinegrass Kentucky bluegrass	
	H. leuceilyma	St. Augustinegrass	
Lesion nematode [136, 139]	*Pratylenchus brachyurus*	Bermudagrass Kentucky bluegrass	Yellowing of the top growth. Large brown lesions form on the root system. Severe pruning of root system often takes place.
	P. penetrans [30, 91, 100]	Tall fescue Kentucky bluegrass	
	P. pratensis	Kentucky bluegrass	
	P. zeae	Zoysiagrass	
	Pratylenchus spp.	Bermudagrass Centipedegrass St. Augustinegrass Zoysiagrass	
Root-knot nematode [8, 55, 64, 65, 93, 101, 107, 108, 115, 133]	*Meloidogyne arenaria*	Bermudagrass	Yellowing and stunting of top growth; swelling of the roots; knots or galls present.
	M. hapla	Bermudagrass Kentucky bluegrass St. Augustinegrass	
	M. incognita	Creeping bentgrass Bermudagrass Kentucky bluegrass Rough bluegrass	
	M. naasi	Creeping bentgrass Colonial bentgrass Tall fescue Perennial ryegrass Annual bluegrass Kentucky bluegrass Rough bluegrass	
	M. graminis	Bermudagrass Kentucky bluegrass St. Augustinegrass Zoysiagrass	Top growth stunted and yellow; wilting evident; roots brown and stunted; root enlargement and galls small and often difficult to see.
Grass root-gall nematode [126]	*Ditylenchus radicoloa*	Annual bluegrass	Large galls evident on roots.

Table 5-1 — *Continued*

Common Name	Scientific Name	Associated Turfgrass Species	Symptoms
Ectoparasitic Nematodes			
Awl nematode [98]	*Dolichodorus* spp.	Bermudagrass	Stunted roots and yellow foliage.
Dagger nematode	*Xiphinema americanum*	Bermudagrass Zoysiagrass Kentucky bluegrass Centipedegrass St. Augustinegrass	Yellowing and stunting of top growth; stunted root systems with reddish brown to black lesions.
Lance nematode [28, 109]	*Hoplolaimus* spp.	Bermudagrass Annual bluegrass Centipedegrass St. Augustinegrass Zoysiagrass	Stunting of top growth. Swelling of roots at feeding areas.
Pin nematode [21, 22, 23, 91]	*Paratylenchus hamatus*	Kentucky bluegrass Tall fescue	Stunting of top growth, with shortened inter-nodes; root systems increase in size but have fewer lateral roots. Tillering increases. Lesions on infected roots.
	P. projectus	Tall fescue Fine-leaf fescues Kentucky bluegrass	
Ring nematode [15, 49, 74, 127, 133]	*Criconemoides cylindricum*	Kentucky bluegrass Zoysiagrass Bermudagrass Centipedegrass	Stunting and thinning of turf. Stunted roots with brown lesions.
	Criconemoides spp.	St. Augustinegrass Fine-leaf fescues Annual bluegrass Creeping bentgrass	
Sheath nematode [4]	*Hemicycliophora* spp.		Yellowing of top growth.
Spiral nematode [28, 29]	*Helicotylenchus digonicus*	Kentucky bluegrass	Yellowing and thinning of turf stand. Stunted discolored root systems.
	H. erythrinae [30, 91, 100]	Bermudagrass Creeping bentgrass Kentucky bluegrass St. Augustinegrass Zoysiagrass	
	H. melancholicus	Bermudagrass	
	H. microlobus	Kentucky bluegrass	
	H. nannus	Bermudagrass Zoysiagrass	
	H. platyurus	Kentucky bluegrass	
	H. pumilus	Kentucky bluegrass	
Sting nematode [91, 93]	*Belonolaimus gracilis*	St. Augustinegrass	Yellowing of turf foilage may be evident; stunt-ing of root system with lesions evident.
	B. longicaudatus	Bermudagrass St. Augustinegrass Zoysiagrass	

Table 5-1 — *Continued*

Common Name	Scientific Name	Associated Turfgrass Species	Symptoms
Stubby root nematode [104, 105, 106]	*Trichodorus christiei*	Bermudagrass Tall fescue Kentucky bluegrass St. Augustinegrass	Stunting and yellowing of top growth; large brown lesions on roots; root tips swollen due to feeding of nematode.
	T. primitivus	Bermudagrass	
	T. proximus	St. Augustinegrass	
	Trichodorus spp.	Centipedegrass Zoysiagrass	
Stunt nematode (stylet nematode) [80, 81, 82, 127, 136]	*Tylenchorhynchus actus*	Bermudagrass	Stunting and thinning of top growth; short stunted root system; brown discoloration of roots; lesion usually lacking; wilting often evident.
	T. claytoni	Annual bluegrass Kentucky bluegrass Creeping bentgrass Zoysiagrass	
	T. dubius	Creeping bentgrass Kentucky bluegrass Fine-leaf fescues Annual bluegrass	
	T. maximus	Kentucky bluegrass	
	T. nudus	Kentucky bluegrass	
	Tylenchorhynchus spp.	Centipedegrass St. Augustinegrass Zoysiagrass	

Spiral Nematode (*Helicotylenchus* spp.)

Perry et al. [100] found *Helicotylenchus digonicus* to be responsible for "summer dormancy," a disease associated with unthrifty Kentucky bluegrass in Wisconsin turf. *H. digonicus* greatly reduced the number and size of the Kentucky bluegrass roots during the spring and early summer, and the symptoms of summer dormancy developed with the arrival of high temperatures and drought stress. The reduction of nematode populations with nematicides improved the quality of the turf and prevented summer dormancy.

The characteristic symptoms of summer dormancy are a thin stand which is difficult to maintain, curtailment of growth of new turfgrass plants from rhizomes or stolons, and pale or chlorotic narrow leaf blades and brown roots. Generally the turfgrass plants grow well in the spring, then decline and exhibit the disease symptoms in the summer, and resume good growth in the fall. This complex of environmental stress and disease supports the idea that nematodes have an important role in symptom development.

Management

Sanitation

Sanitation is important with most diseases, but it is especially important in preventing nematode problems. Clean seed or sod is of little use in preventing foliar fungal diseases because most are airborne. It is different with nematodes. They have to be in the soil before it is seeded or sodded, brought in on the seed or sod, or brought in later with topdressing soil or cultivating equipment. Starting with nematode-free soil is a good way to prevent or delay severe nematode problems. If you are buying vegetative plant parts, such as sod, stolons, or sprigs for establishment, and the plant parts come from a nursery infested with nematodes pathogenic to turfgrass, chances are that you will acquire a nematode problem. The same is true of topdressing material. Having a nematode analysis run before you purchase vegetative parts or topdressing may be well worth the minimal cost.

Fumigation prior to planting or replanting is advisable for soil already infested with nematodes. Fumigation of a golf course from tee to green is expensive, but it is within most budgets, at least for the greens. Even if the surrounding areas are infested, at least the young turf will have a chance to establish itself without the added stress of nematodes. It may be several years before the nematodes reinvade the fumigated area and become sufficiently numerous to create a problem. But do not go to the trouble of fumigating and then bring in nematode-infested plants or soil.

Cultural Practices

Watering. The development of nematode symptoms can often be prevented by adequate and properly timed watering. Frequent light watering is better than a few deep waterings. Although deep watering is usually recommended to develop a good root system, this works only on healthy turf. A nematode-infected turf is not healthy. It has a shortened, devitalized root system, with most of the roots in the top inch of soil or, even worse, in the top inch of thatch. When the top inch dries out (the thatch will dry out faster than the soil), the plants begin to wilt and die. Any water below the top inch is useless. The old theory that the plant roots will follow the water down does not apply, because the nematodes will prevent this from happening. During periods of hot weather, light syringing around noon may be necessary to prevent wilting.

Fertilization. Proper fertilizing, like proper watering, can alleviate a nematode problem enough so a satisfactory turf can be maintained. It is usually wise to keep phosphorus and potassium at adequate levels based on soil tests (see chapter 7). Nitrogen should be applied lightly (less than ½ pound of actual nitrogen per 1000 square feet). High levels of nitrogen increase top growth, which is perhaps already too great for the nematode-damaged root system and produce succulent plants, which are more susceptible to heat and drought stress. Moreover, a devitalized root system cannot use large amounts of nitrogen efficiently, and the excess is lost through leaching or volatilization.

Heald and Burton [56] found that plots fertilized with organic nitrogen (activated sewage sludge, or Milorganite) had a smaller population of *Belonolaimus longicaudatus* than plots receiving inorganic nitrogen (ammonium nitrate). Fertilization with organic nitrogen also resulted in increased root and top-growth weights.

Chemical Management

There are two types of nematicide, fumigant and nonfumigant. Fumigant nematicides usually give broad nematode control [9], but they must be applied to the soil prior to planting. Nonfumigant nematicides tend to be effective against some species of nematodes but not against others, so that although the dominant nematode species may be reduced, other species that previously were not a problem may increase to the point that they become one [80, 83, 150]. Both fumigant and nonfumigant nematicides have a drawback common to all soil pesticides—their effectiveness depends somewhat on the type and texture of the soil. They are most effective on light sandy soils low in organic matter and least effective in heavy clay, silt, silt-type soil, and soil high in organic matter, such as muck and peat soils. Higher rates of application may therefore be required in soils that are heavy or that contain a lot of organic matter.

It seems that the timing of nematicide treatments is important. If it is true that nematodes weaken a grass plant by shortening its root system or that they open the way to fungus attacks by altering the plant's physiology, then nematicides should be applied early, to allow recovery of weakened roots and to prevent fungus infection. On the other hand, if nematodes simply put additional stress on plants already weakened by disease, then nematicides should be applied later in the season (fig. 5-9). There is probably no single correct answer.

Fumigant Nematicides. Fumigants include methyl bromide, chloropicrin, ethylene dibromide, and 1,3-dichloropropene alone or in combination with 1,2-dichloropropane. As mentioned earlier, they must be applied prior to planting. They should be applied at a depth of 6 to 8 inches (the depth of a normal turfgrass root zone) and allowed to volatilize and move up and out of the soil, killing the nematodes in the process. It is ideal if you can use specialized fumigation equipment that delivers fumigant at 6 to 8 inches below the surface, but this often is not possible.

The labels on most fumigants specify an average number of days that must elapse between treatment and planting or replanting. However, if the soil temperature remains cool or if rainy weather keeps the soil excessively wet, it may take longer for the fumigant to volatilize, and you must postpone planting. The soil temperature must be at least 50 °F for fumigant nematicides to work. Lower temperatures may result in poor control or delayed planting or both.

Nonfumigant Nematicides. Nonfumigant nematicides are organophosphate or carbamate derivatives which are highly toxic to humans (see the LD_{50} chart in chapter 6). They are usually sold as granular formulations, but this practice may be changing because birds pick up the granules.

The key to effective application of nonfumigant nematicides is getting the active ingredient into the root zone. Heavy watering following a nematicide application is recommended and aerification before application will help to get the nematicide down to the root zone.

Figure 5-9. Wilting of turfgrass caused by high populations of ring and stunt nematodes (left). No symptoms of wilt are evident in the nematicide-treated plot (right).

People often associate nematicides with fungicides rather than with insecticides, a habit of thought which may have dire consequences. All pesticides should be handled with extreme caution. Most people, however, tend to get a little careless when handling fungicides, especially when previous carelessness has caused no noticeable harmful effects. But careless handling of nematicides can be fatal. (See chapter 6 for information on the safe use of pesticides.)

Resistant Cultivars

Little research has been done on the resistance of turfgrass cultivars to nematodes. Sledge [115] has reported that *Meloidogyne graminis*, a root-knot nematode (fig. 5-10), did not complete its life cycle on Ormond bermudagrass, Emerald zoysiagrass, or Floratine St. Augustinegrass, but much more work needs to be done. Although it is important to study turfgrass resistance to all nematodes, priorities need to be established. Turfgrass scientists should not hope for a supercultivar resistant to all nematodes any more than they should expect to find one cultivar that is resistant to all diseases or to all insects. The one or two most severe nematode problems on a given species should be determined, and then a program should be established to breed for resistance to those nematodes. Minor nematode problems can, it is hoped, be solved culturally, the theory being that, like minor fungus problems, they should be easier to manage culturally and, if need be, chemically. Of course, a major assumption is that the new cultivar will not be susceptible to new and highly pathogenic nematodes. Significant research will need to be done over the next 10 to 20 years if we are to understand nematode problems in turf. Important topics for research include nematode-fungal interactions, resistant cultivars, chemical management, and biological management.

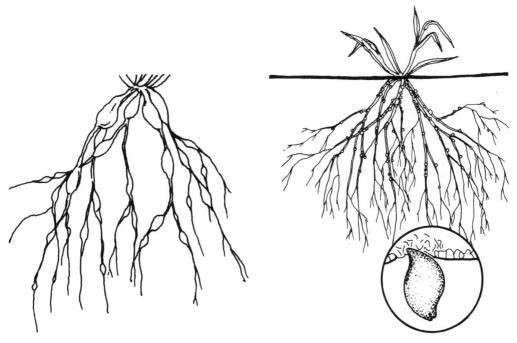

Figure 5-10. Root-knot nematode galls on a turfgrass root system

Figure 5-11. Turfgrass roots infected with cyst nematodes

chapter six

FUNGICIDES

Fungicides belong to a group of chemicals called pesticides, which are used to protect plants from pests. Other pesticides include insecticides, which control insects; nematicides, which control nematodes; and herbicides, which control weeds. Too often the term pesticide is used incorrectly to mean only insecticides. Actually, it refers to the entire group of chemicals used to control pests of plants and animals.

The term fungicide is applied to all chemical plant protectants that manage fungal diseases. Many fungicides, however, do not kill the fungus, but merely inhibit its growth by preventing germination of spores or stopping growth of the hyphae or mycelium after germination. Such chemicals are really fungistats (growth inhibitors) rather than fungicides. The benzimidazole systemic fungicides (benomyl, thiophanate-methyl, thiophanate-ethyl) are examples of fungistats. Even though they are fungistats, when applied as eradicants (i.e., after the disease is present), they will stop the spread of a fungus by preventing it from entering new plant tissue.

GENERIC NAMES, CHEMICAL FORMULAS, AND TRADE NAMES

Most turfgrass managers know the fungicides they use by their trade names. Trade names are given to fungicides by manufacturers or distributors; the names are registered with the U.S. patent office to prevent others from using them for their products. This practice is intended to protect the company selling the fungicide, but it also protects the user. It is confusing enough to try to remember the trade names of the many fungicides; it would be even harder to memorize the chemical compositions of different fungicides with the same trade name. The fungicides are listed by generic name, chemical formula, and trade name in table 6-1 (the listing is alphabetical by generic name).

Some fungicides are sold as combination products containing two or more fungicides. Some of these are listed in table 6-2. To find the chemical formula of a listed ingredient, look under its generic name in table 6-1.

Is a fungicide sold by one company better than the same fungicide sold by another company? The answer is no. As a matter of fact, most of the time a fungicide is manufactured by one company and sold to another for distribution or packaging under a different label or trade name. The only possible substantive difference between the two products is a difference in the concentration of the active ingredient.

Table 6-1. Common Names, Chemical Compositions, and Trade Names of Some Widely Used Fungicides

Common Name	Chemical Name or Mixture	Trade Names
Anilazine	2,4-Dichloro-6-(O-chloroanilino)-s-triazine	Dyrene, Proturf Fungicide III, Dymec 50
Benomyl	Methyl-1-(butylcarbamoyl)-2-benzimidazolecarbamate	Tersan 1991, Proturf Fertilizer + DSB fungicide
Cadmium compounds	Cadmium chloride	Caddy
	Cadmium chloride (8.3%) plus thiram (75%)	Cad-trete
	Cadmium sebacate 5%, potassium chromate 5%, malachite green 1%, auramine 0.5%, thiram 16%	Kromad
	Cadmium succinate 60% (29% cadmium)	Cadminate
Captan	N-(Trichloromethylthio)-4-cyclohexene-1,2-dicarboximide	Captan 50W, Captan 75W, Orthocide
Chloroneb	1,4-Dichloro-2,5-dimethoxybenzene	Tersan SP, Proturf Fungicide II
Cycloheximide	3-(2-(3,5-Dimethyl-2-oxocyclohexyl)-2-hydroxyethyl)glutarimide	Acti-dione TGF
Chlorothalonil	(2,4,5,6-Tetrachloroisophthalonitrile)	Daconil 2787, Proturf 10IV
Dinocap	2,4-Dinitro-6-(2-octyl)phenyl crotonate	Karathane, Mildex
Etridiazol (ethazol)	5-Ethoxy-3-trichloromethyl-1,2,4-thiadiazole	Koban, Terrazole
Iprodione	3-(3,5-Dichlorophenyl)-N-(1-methylethyl)-2,4-dioxo-1-imidazolidinecarboxamide	Chipco 26019, Rovral
Maneb	Manganese ethylene bisdithiocarbamate	Manzate
Mancozeb	Coordination product of zinc ion and manganese ethylene bisdithiocarbamate	Fore, Formec 80
Maneb plus zinc sulfate	Manganese ethylene bisdithiocarbamate plus zinc sulfate	Tersan LSR
Mercury compounds — Inorganic	Mercuric & mecurous chloride	Calo Clor, Calo Gran
PCNB	Pentachloronitrobenzene	Terraclor 75, Scotts F + F II, Turfcide
PMA (PMAS)	Phenylmercury acetate	PMA, PMAS, Puraturf No. 10
Thiophanate-ethyl	Diethyl[(1,2-phenylene)bis(iminocarbonothioyl)]bis[carbamate]	Cleary's 3336
Thiophanate-methyl	Dimethyl[(1,2-phenylene)bis(iminocarbonothioyl)]bis[carbamate]	Fungo 50, Spot Kleen, Proturf Systemic Fungicide, Topmec 70
Thiram	Tetramethylthiuram disulfide	Tersan 75, Spotrete, Thirmad
Thiabendazole	2-(4-Thiazoyl)benzimidazole	Mertect 160, Tobaz
Zineb	Zinc ethylene bisdithiocarbamate	Dithane Z-78, Acme Zineb 75W

Table 6-2. Composition of Some Fungicide Mixtures

Generic Makeup of Mixture	Trade Name
Cycloheximide + thiram	Acti-dione Thiram
Cycloheximide + PCNB	Acti-dione RZ
PMA + thiram	Proturf Broad Spectrum Fungicide
Thiophanate-ethyl + thiram	Bromosan
Thiophanate-methyl + maneb	Duosan

The benzimidazole systemic fungicides merit special mention here because they are all basically the same in that they break down into chemically similar active ingredients. Benomyl and thiophanate-methyl break down into benzimidazole O-methylcarbamate (MBC), and thiophanate-ethyl breaks down into benzimidazole O-ethylcarbamate (EBC) (see fig. 6-1). Both MBC and EBC prevent cell division by inhibiting chromatid migration during mitosis [25, 78].

In this case, "chemically different" fungicides that are sold under different labels break down into similar active ingredients after application. However, even though their modes of action are essentially identical, different benzimidazole systemic fungicides can differ in their effectiveness in managing turfgrass diseases because of external factors such as pH that may affect the conversion of the parent compounds into MBC or EBC. The benzimidazole systemic fungicide that works best in your area should be used, because no benefit will be derived from alternating them in attempts to manage different diseases or to prevent fungicide resistance.

Thiobendazole is another benzimidazole-type systemic fungicide; its structural formula is given in figure 6-1. It does not convert to either MBC or EBC, but it does have a similar mode of action most of the time [25]. (There are indications that it also has a different mode of action which appears to be pH related, but this has not been demonstrated in the field.) Thiobendazole is a marginal turfgrass fungicide at best, useful only in the management of dollar spot. It is too phytotoxic to be used in high concentrations, and even at low concentrations (for managing dollar spot) it may injure turf during warm weather.

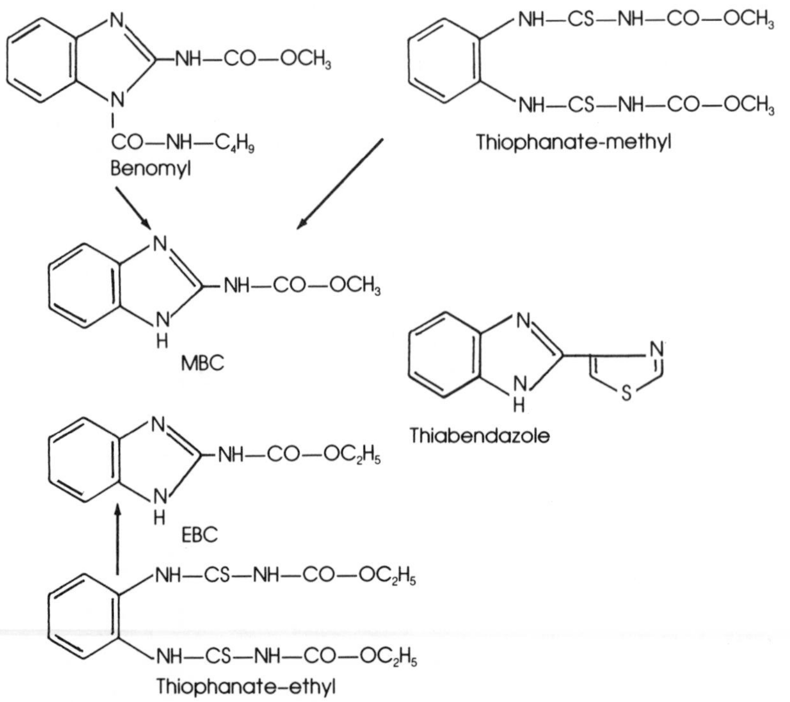

Figure 6-1. Chemical structures of some benzimidazole fungicides and their breakdown products (see text for nomenclature)

SYSTEMIC AND NONSYSTEMIC (CONTACT OR SURFACE) FUNGICIDES

The major difference between systemic and nonsystemic (contact) fungicides is the means by which they control turfgrass diseases. A contact fungicide is applied to the foliage, where it prevents or halts infection. It forms a protective shield around the outside of the plant. The contact fungicides have the general disadvantage of being exposed to weathering and photodecomposition, and on turf they are exposed to an additional hazard: mowing. Turfgrass is constantly being mowed, and as the old foliage is mowed off the new foliage that replaces it is unprotected. This is especially a problem on greens that are mowed daily. Also, turf is watered nightly during most of the summer, and so the fungicide that isn't mowed away may be washed away.

The benzimidazoles are the most commonly used systemic fungicides. They differ from contact fungicides in that they are taken up by the plant: they are absorbed by the roots and foliage and then translocated upward. The only other registered systemic fungicide is chloroneb, which acts as both a contact and a systemic fungicide [154].

Since the benzimidazole systemic fungicides can be root-absorbed, they can persist after the treated foliage is mowed off; new foliage will obtain some systemic fungicide from redistribution and from the fungicide that the roots continue to pick up from the soil. The systemic fungicide will eventually be tied up, broken down (degraded), or leached from the soil, and will then no longer be available. At such a time an additional application will be needed. A benzimidazole systemic fungicide will give protection for 3 to 6 weeks, depending upon the soil type and disease pressure. Turfgrass that is growing in sandy soil usually requires more frequent fungicide application than does turfgrass growing in loam, silt, or clay.

Systemic fungicides have controlled diseases, such as *Fusarium* blight and stripe smut that once were considered uncontrollable. *Fusarium* blight is primarily a root and crown disease, and its control requires a systemic fungicide that can be taken up by the roots and redistributed within the plant. It would be impossible to completely surround the root and crowns of an established turfgrass plant with a contact fungicide without removing the plant and dipping it into a fungicide solution. Stripe smut is a systemic disease which is internal to the turfgrass plant, and external fungicides will have no effect on it. An internal fungicide like the benzimidazole systemic fungicides must be used to treat such a disease. Since they are fungistats, they must be applied before new tissue growth occurs in order to prevent the fungus from moving into it. Thus in managing stripe smut it is recommended that the benzimidazole systemic fungicides be applied after the grass goes dormant in the fall or before it breaks dormancy in the spring [69]. The systemic fungicides can also be applied for stripe smut management in the late summer or early fall, just as the cool weather begins and the plants start to initiate new stolons and rhizomes [145]. An application made at that time avoids the *Helminthosporium* problem brought on by applications of the benzimidazole systemic fungicides to dormant turfgrass [70]. (See the section on stripe smut in chapter 4.)

The benzimidazole systemic fungicides are not the panacea they were once thought to be. Their greatest assets have been their low-concentration residual management of dollar spot and the fact that they are the only fungicides that manage *Fusarium* blight and stripe smut. However, turfgrass pathogens like *Sclerotinia homoeocarpa* (dollar spot) have quickly developed resistance to them. For the management of dollar spot, they must be used in conjunction with contact fungicides to delay the development of resistance. For *Fusarium* blight and stripe smut management there is currently little choice but to use them until resistance develops. The benzimidazole systemic fungicides will not control

Helminthosporium melting-out, and there is evidence that they actually increase the severity of the disease [70]. Severe *Helminthosporium* leaf spot outbreaks also have occurred where the benzimidazole systemic fungicides were used for the management of *Fusarium* patch exclusively.

As noted above, the benzimidazole systemic fungicides are the only fungicides available for the management of *Fusarium* blight and stripe smut, which means there is little choice but to use them on an exclusive basis. Will the organism causing these diseases develop resistance to the benzimidazole systemic fungicide? Yes, it has already been reported with *Fusarium roseum* [117]. Resistance probably will be reported soon for *Ustilago striiformus* (stripe smut) also. Since there is no other alternative, systemics must be applied on an exclusive basis where chemical management of disease is desired.

The other course of action is to recognize that chemical management is only a temporary solution, at least until other fungicides are found, and instead begin a renovation program and reestablish the infected turf area with a blend of resistant bluegrass cultivars. For information on resistant cultivars, see chapter 8.

RESISTANCE TO FUNGICIDES

Resistance occurs when a fungus which was sensitive to a fungicide becomes resistant to it. This can occur in three ways: a spontaneous mutation of the fungus, the fungicide causing a mutation of the fungus, or the fungicide selecting out and eliminating sensitive individuals in the fungus population so that only the resistant ones remain. The last of these three modes of action is the most likely one [78].

Resistance to fungicides is not new; its occurrence has been known for years [78]. It is also no stranger to the turf area, as cadmium- and Dyrene-resistant strains of *Sclerotinia homoeocarpa* have been reported by Cole, Taylor, and Duich [17]. However, it has never been as widespread and developed as quickly as it has to the benzimidazole systemic fungicides. Resistance usually occurs during the second or third season that the benzimidazole systemic fungicides are used. The speed with which resistance has developed to the benzimidazole systemic fungicides appears to be related to their specific mode of action. They inhibit cell division by preventing the sister chromatids from migrating to the poles during the metaphase of mitosis [25]. This means that fungi which can prevent the fungicide from doing this will not be controlled by it, while the sensitive fungi will. It would be more difficult for a fungus strain to block the mode of action of a contact fungicide, since such fungicides are believed to have many modes of action that affect different processes of the fungal cell.

AVOIDING RESISTANCE PROBLEMS

The use of a fungicide year after year for the management of a particular disease leads to the development of resistance. This has occurred for cadmium, Dyrene, and the benzimidazole systemic fungicide (benomyl) used in *Sclerotinia* dollar spot management programs. Resistance has developed also to the benzimidazoles used for managing powdery mildew and *Fusarium* blight. Indeed, resistance to the benzimidazole fungicides has occurred on most crops where they have been used. (They often have been the only fungicides used in a disease management program, which has led to even quicker development of resistance.) One reason that the benzimidazole systemic fungicides have been used on an exclusive basis is economic. Management of dollar spot can be obtained for 3 to 6 weeks with one application of ½ to 1 ounce of a benzimidazole systemic fungicide per 1000 square feet. A contact fungicide would have to be applied every 10 to 14 days, in concentrations of 2 to 6 ounces per 1000 square feet, to achieve the same degree of control. However, an effective *Sclerotinia* dollar spot contact fungicide must be used sometime during the dollar spot season to delay resistance if the economic benefits of the benzimidazole systemic fungicides are to continue to be realized.

PROPER USE OF SYSTEMIC FUNGICIDES

The benzimidazole systemic fungicides (e.g., benomyl, thiophanate-methyl, thiophanate-ethyl) are the best fungicides ever marketed for the control of *Sclerotinia* dollar spot. They manage *Sclerotinia* dollar spot in lower concentrations and for a longer period of time than do any other fungicides. Therefore, the benzimidazole systemics should be used during the heaviest part of the dollar spot season for maximum benefit. The 3 to 6 weeks' control with 1 ounce per 1000 square feet means a savings of material and labor, but somewhere before the end of the first dollar spot season and before the beginning of the brown patch season a contact fungicide must be applied to delay the development of resistance. A second application of benzimidazole should be made at the end of the *Rhizoctonia* brown patch season and the beginning of the second *Sclerotinia* dollar spot season. (*Sclerotinia* dollar spot usually has two seasons—an early one in late spring and early summer, and a second one in later summer and early fall. Between these are sandwiched a *Rhizoctonia* brown patch season and sometimes a *Pythium* blight season.) Another contact fungicide should be used at least once in the early fall, and the first fungicide application the next spring should be a contact fungicide also to try to eliminate any resistant strains of *S. homoeocarpa*. Not just any contact fungicide will do. It must be a contact fungicide which manages *Sclerotinia* dollar spot and *Rhizoctonia* brown patch. This means that one must use such fungicides as anilizine, chlorothalonil, and cycloheximide, because such fungicides as maneb or mancozeb, which are not effective against *Sclerotinia* dollar spot, will not delay the development of resistance.

Alternating the benzimidazole systemic with the contact fungicides will probably delay the development of resistance, not prevent it. This should not be surprising, in light of the fact that alternating insecticides does little to prevent the development of resistance to them. In fact, entomologists now recommend using one class of insecticide (e.g., organophosphates) until resistance develops (approximately 5 years), and then switching to another class (e.g., carbamates) for the next 5 years. There is evidence that where they are alternated, resistance to both insecticides will occur in that 5 years.

This does not mean that fungicides should not be alternated, because only the benzimidazoles have only one mode of. action. Resistance to the contact fungicides would take years to develop, even if they were used all alone in a fungicide program. What it does mean is that alternating contact fungicides and benzimidazole systemic fungicides may only delay the development of resistance to the benzimidazole. When resistance occurs, the systemic fungicides will have to be deleted from the fungicide program.

The reason that resistance to the benzimidazoles develops may be twofold: they have only one mode of action, and they are very effective at eliminating sensitive strains. For example, three 1-ounce applications per 1000 square feet on the Michigan State University plots in 1973 prevented any development of dollar spot in those plots for all of 1974. In one test plot area at MSU the resistant strain of *S. homoeocarpa* developed after the benzimidazole fungicides were used on an exclusive basis for 2 years. Five years later, during which time the plots had not received any benzimidazole fungicide treatments, only benzimidazole-resistant strains of *S. homoeocarpa* could be isolated. The benzimidazole systemic fungicides may thus be their own worst enemy. If the fungicides had only suppressed sensitive strains of *S. homoeocarpa* instead of apparently completely eliminating them, the benzimidazole-sensitive strains might have been able to keep the resistant strains at low levels, as they apparently had done for years before the application of the benzimidazole systemics.

End of Myth

The myth that alternating benzimidazole systemic fungicides that have different trade names will prevent the development of resistance has almost been laid to rest. They all have a similar mode of action, and resistance to one benzimidazole systemic fungicide means resistance to all of them regardless of the trade name or color of the container in which they are sold. (See table 6-1 for more details.)

Conclusions

It is obvious that the best fungicide disease-management program includes both contact and systemic fungicides. For a specific program in your area and on your type of turf, see chapters 11 and 12.

SAFE HANDLING OF FUNGICIDES

Chemical Storage

Fungicides are among the safest pesticides, but they are nonetheless pesticides and should be treated accordingly (see table 6-3 and fig. 6-2 for toxicity data). They should be stored in a room that is well ventilated and away from areas where people are apt to congregate. The preferable storage location would be a separate building, or at least a building that is used only to store equipment. For exact requirements, consult OSHA and FEPCA regulations. Remember—it is your life, and inhaling those pesticide fumes daily cannot do anything but shorten it.

Proper Clothing

When handling pesticides you may need to wear rubber gloves, boots, goggles, and an aspirator (face mask). It is advisable also to wear a rubber rain suit when applying pesticides. After application of the pesticides, the clothing should be thoroughly washed. People still insist on wearing leather boots and cloth or leather gloves; however, leather absorbs pesticides and retains them. Every time your boots or gloves become wet, whether from water or sweat, the pesticides in the leather can come in contact with your skin and be absorbed by your body.

CRITERIA FOR SELECTING A FUNGICIDE

The first criterion should be how well the fungicide works (table 6-4); that is, which is the best fungicide for the disease problem? The second criterion should be the safety of the product vis-à-vis the turfgrass. Most fungicides, properly applied, will

Table 6-3.   Oral and Dermal Toxicity Ratings for Turfgrass Fungicides and Nematicides

	LD$_{50}$(mg/kg)	
	Oral	Dermal
Class 1. Highly toxic	1–50	1–200
Class 2. Moderately toxic	50–500	200–2,000
Class 3. Low order of toxicity	500–5,000	2,000–20,000
Class 4. Very low order of toxicity	over 5,000	over 20,000

Warning Statement on Label	Probable Oral Lethal Dose for 150-lb Person
Class 1. Poison	Few drops to 1 tsp
Class 2. Danger	1 tsp to 1 oz
Class 3. Warning	1 oz to 1 pt (1 lb)
Class 4. Caution	1 pt to 1 qt (2 lb)

Generic Name	Oral LD$_{50}$[a]	Dermal LD$_{50}$[a, b]	Type[c]
Anilazine	2710	M	F
Benomyl	9590	L	F
Captan	9000–15,000	L	F
Chloroneb	>11,000	>5,000	F
Cycloheximide	1.8–2.5	S	F
Chlorothalonil	>3750	>10,000	F
Dasanit	2–10	3–30	N
Maneb	6750–7500	<1000	F
Mancozeb	8000	8000	F
PCNB	1650–2000	M	F
Thiram	780	S	F
Zineb	>5200	>1000	F
Dinocap	980–1190	9400	F
Terrazole	2000		F
Thiabendazole	3100		F
Dibromochloropropane	172	1,420	N
Phenamephos	8–9	72–84	N
Vapam	1,260	4,640	F,N
Vorlex	305	M	F,N
Oxymal	5.4–37	2,960	N

[a] LD$_{50}$ = Dosage that would be fatal to one-half of those exposed.

[b] S = severe reaction, M = mild reaction, L = little reaction.

[c] F = fungicide, N = nematicide.

not harm the grass, but some fungicides have greater safety factors than others. For example, PCNB is an excellent fungicide for the control of brown patch, but application of PCNB when the temperature is in the 80s may cause yellowing and death of the treated turf. If another fungicide that has a greater safety factor will do the job, then it should be used. The third criterion should be the applicator's safety in handling the product. The fourth criterion is the cost per unit area of applying the fungicide.

Ease of Handling

The fungicide should go into suspension or solution readily at all temperatures and should not settle out in the spray tank.

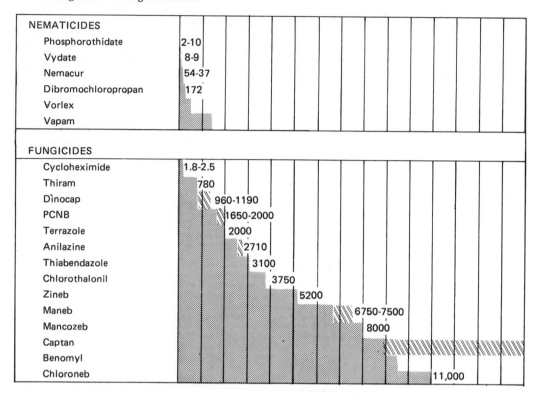

Figure 6–2. LD$_{50}$ oral toxicity ratings (mg/kg of body weight) for some turfgrass fungicides and nematicides

Cost

Cost should be a consideration only when two or more products do the same job equally well. Otherwise, always buy a product on the basis of effectiveness, safety, and ease of handling. The cost of a fungicide can be deceiving. The only cost that really matters is the cost per unit area (usually per 1000 square feet). For example, a pound of systemic fungicide will cost about $8 to $10 per pound, while a contact fungicide will usually cost either $2 to $4 or $4 to $5 per pound, but most contacts must be applied at a concentration of 4 to 6 ounces per 1000 square feet ($2-to-$4-per-pound contacts) or 2 to 4 ounces per 1000 square feet ($4-to-$5-per-pound contacts) while the systemics require only 1 ounce per 1000 square feet. The important thing to remember is *not to buy* any fungicide by how much it costs per pound; buy it only on the basis of how much it will cost per unit area. If you can't figure it out using the formulas given in the next section, have your chemical salesman do it for you—if he can't, then you need a new salesman!

SPRAYER CALIBRATION

Sprayer calibration is really quite simple, and yet it is one of the most difficult subjects to teach. The difficulty in teaching or learning it can only be related to the fact that mathematical calculations are involved, and the very thought of math sends instant fear

Table 6-4. Fungicide Efficacy on Various Turfgrass Diseases

	Dollar Spot	Brown Patch	Pythium Blight	Anthracnose	Red Thread	Helminthosporium	Fusarium Blight	Stripe Smut	Powdery Mildew	Rusts	Fusarium Patch	Typhula Blight	Gray Leaf Spot	Copper Spot	Spring Dead Spot
Acti-dione TGF	G	G	NC	F	—	F	NC	NC	G	E	NC	F	—	NC	—
Acti-dione Thiram	E	E	NC	F	E	G	NC	NC	G	E	NC	F	—	NC	G?
Acti-dione RZ	E	E	NC	NC	—	G	NC	NC	NC	E	NC	F	E	NC	—
Bromosan	E	G	NC	E	E	G	—	—	—	—	F	NC	—	E	—
Caddy	E	NC	NC	—	—	F	NC	NC	NC	NC	F	F	—	E	—
Cadminate	E	NC	NC	—	—	F	NC	NC	NC	NC	F	F	—	E	—
Cadtrete	E	NC	NC	—	—	F	NC	NC	NC	NC	F	F	—	E	—
Calo Clor	—	—	—	—	—	—	—	—	—	—	E	E	—	—	—
Calo Gran	—	—	—	—	—	—	—	—	—	—	E	E	—	—	—
Chipco 26019	E	E	NC	F	—	E	F	NC	NC	NC	E	NC	—	—	—
Cleary's 3336	E	G	NC	E	F	NC	E	E	E	NC	G	NC	—	E	G?
Daconil 2787	E	E	NC	E	E	E	NC	NC	NC	E	NC	G	E	E	G?
Duosan	E	E	NC	E	E	G	—	—	—	E	E	NC	—	E	—
Dyrene	E	G	NC	NC	E	E	NC	NC	NC	NC	NC	F	E	—	—
Fore	NC	E	NC	E	E	G	NC	NC	NC	E	E	NC	E	—	—
Fungo 50	E	G	NC	E	F	NC	E	E	E	NC	G	NC	—	—	G?
Karathane	NC	NC	NC	NC	NC	NC	NC	NC	E	NC	NC	NC	NC	NC	—
Koban	NC	NC	E	NC	NC	NC	NC	NC	NC	NC	NC	NC	NC	NC	NC
Kromad	E	G	NC	NC	E	F	NC	NC	NC	NC	G	F	G	E	—
PMAS	—	—	—	—	—	—	—	—	—	—	E	G	—	—	—
Proturf Fertilizer + DSB Fungicide	E	G	NC	E	G	NC	G	G	G	NC	G	NC	—	—	—
Proturf 10IV Fungicide	G	G	NC	—	—	G	NC	NC	NC	—	NC	F	—	—	—
Proturf F, F II	G	E	NC	—	—	E	NC	NC	NC	NC	NC	E	—	—	—
Proturf Fungicide II	NC	NC	G	—	—	NC	NC	NC	NC	NC	NC	F	—	—	—
Proturf Fungicide III	G	G	NC	—	—	G	NC	NC	NC	NC	NC	NC	—	—	—
Proturf Broad Spectrum Fungicide	—	—	—	—	—	—	—	—	—	—	E	G	—	—	—
Proturf Fertilizer + Fungicide	—	—	—	—	—	—	—	—	—	—	E	G	—	—	—
Proturf Systemic Fungicide	G	F	NC	—	—	NC	F	—	—	NC	—	NC	NC	—	—
Spotrete	G	F	NC	F	F	F	NC	NC	NC	NC	NC	F	—	—	—
Terraclor 75 (Turfcide)	G	E	NC	NC	—	G	NC	NC	NC	—	NC	G	—	—	G?
Tersan 75	G	F	NC	F	F	F	NC	NC	NC	NC	NC	F	—	—	—
Tersan 1991	E	G	NC	E	F	NC	E	E	E	NC	G	NC	—	—	G?
Tersan LSR	NC	E	NC	E	—	G	NC	NC	NC	E	F	NC	—	E	—
Tersan SP	NC	NC	E	NC	NC	NC	NC	NC	NC	NC	NC	G	—	—	—
Dithane Z-78	NC	G	NC	F	G	F	NC	NC	NC	E	NC	NC	E	—	—

Key: E = excellent control, G = good control, F = fair control, NC = no control, — = not applicable or not known.

Note: All agricultural chemicals recommended in this chart should be applied in accordance with the directions on the manufacturer's label as registered under the Federal Insecticide, Fungicide, and Rodenticide Act. Mention of a trademark or proprietary product does not constitute a guarantee or warranty of the product by the author or the publisher and does not imply approval to the exclusion of other products that may also be suitable. Some products recommended in this chart may not be registered on the particular disease for which a rating is given. These ratings are based on experimental fungicide trials. Such products should not be used until they are fully labeled for the specific disease. The efficacy of these products is primarily based on the author's experience and efficacy of a product may be different in other areas of the world.

through many people. The calculations are quite simple, and no one should have any trouble using the formulas in this section to calibrate a sprayer.

Calibrating a sprayer isn't just something that is nice to do, it is a *necessity!* I know of no other way to apply accurately the proper amount of fungicide to a given area, and that is the principle behind fungicide application. It reminds me of the time that I was called to look at a disease problem that "no" fungicide was controlling. By the time I arrived, very little turf was left on the four affected greens—mainly because the superintendent had applied to the affected greens four potent fungicides each at a concentration of 8 ounces per 1000 square feet in a little over a week. As nearly as I could tell, the disease in question was *Rhizoctonia* brown patch. I asked to see the record of the spray schedule, and sure enough the fungicides that the superintendent used should have controlled brown patch. Besides, he said, "It only occurred on four greens." I suggested that something could be wrong with his sprayer calibration, even though it didn't seem likely at the time since only four greens were affected. At this I noticed a strange look on his face, and I said, "You do calibrate your sprayer don't you?" To which he replied, "Of course not, nobody does. You know, it's the old case for the front nine and the old case for the back nine." I said, "No, I don't know the old case for the front nine and the old case for the back nine. How can you possibly know how much you are getting on each green, or even if what you are getting on any of them is correct?" He was sure that couldn't be the problem, because two of the affected greens were on the front nine and two of the affected greens were on the back nine. So I asked him what order they sprayed them in. He told me that he sent his men out to the far end of the course on the front nine, and sprayed the back nine in the same way. The last two greens on both nines were the ones with the problems, and I suggested that this might be because the sprayer wasn't calibrated and the people spraying had to hurry over the last two greens on each nine when they discovered that they were running out of liquid in the spray tank.

Needless to say, my suggestion fell on deaf ears. Next year he doubled his fungicide budget, but didn't calibrate his sprayer. His system didn't work any better than it had before, and fortunately for the sake of the profession he is no longer in it.

The superintendent who followed him believed in calibration, and for the first time in 5 years grass was maintained on those four greens. The membership believed that the new superintendent could walk on water, because he kept grass on those greens all season long. It really wasn't a matter of his walking on it, just calculating how much was coming out of his sprayer.

Application Rate

There are four factors that affect application rate: ground speed, pressure, type or size of nozzles, and density of liquid. You need to develop a system wherein the first three remain constant and only the last one varies.

Ground Speed

Select a speed that can be used for all areas. If you are walking while treating a green, learn to walk at a comfortable, constant speed. For most people, this is their normal walking speed.

Pressure

Spray with the lowest possible pressure that gives a full pattern to ensure proper overlap between nozzles (see fig. 6-3). The trouble with people who own high-pressure

Figure 6-3. Misapplication of a granular snow-mold fungicide—spreader was not properly overlapped

sprayers is the same as the problem with people who own high-powered cars—since they have all that power they feel a need to use it. Save the higher pressures for spraying tall trees. The higher the pressure, the smaller the droplet, and the smaller the droplet, the greater the drift problem. If you aren't concerned about your neighbor (and you should be), look at it from a practical viewpoint—what drifts away isn't giving protection where it is needed.

Types of Nozzles

Flat fan nozzles are still the most widely used. You should select one that you can use for all types of spraying. The nozzles should be changed yearly, because wettable powder formulations are abrasive and will enlarge the opening.

Density of Liquid

There is obviously very little that can be done to control liquid density. It will vary from one material to another and with concentration of fungicide. The more dense the liquid in the spray tank is, the slower it will flow through the nozzles. For precise application each chemical and rate should be checked individually.

Calibration

The purpose of calibration is to determine how much liquid your sprayer is putting out per 1000 square feet. The initial calibration usually is done with water. It is assumed that you have already selected the ground speed, the pressure, and the type of nozzles you want. Fill the tank with water, mark off 1000 square feet, and determine how much water it takes to cover the area. (This can be determined by refilling the tank with a known quantity of water.) Another method of determining sprayer output is to collect the liquid from one nozzle while covering the 1000 square feet and then multiply that volume of liquid by the number of nozzles. For either method, the process should be repeated three or four times, or until consistent output is obtained. If the rate is not satisfactory, the pressure can be raised or lowered, the ground speed changed, or the nozzles replaced with ones that have a larger or smaller opening.

The basic output per unit area of the sprayer is the key to calibration. For the sake of discussion, let's say that the output of the sprayer is 2 gallons per 1000 square feet. The amount of fungicide that must be added to the tank can then be determined by plugging figures into a simple formula.

$$\frac{\text{ounces per 1000 sq ft recommended on label}}{\text{output of sprayer (gal) per 1000 sq ft}}$$

$$= \frac{\text{total ounces required in tank}}{\text{tank size or amount of water in tank}}$$

Example 1. How much fungicide must be added to a 200-gallon tank to give an application rate of 4 ounces per 1000 square feet if the sprayer output is 2 gallons per 1000 square feet?

We know:
   Sprayer output = 2 gal/1000 sq ft
   Rate required = 4 oz/1000 sq ft
   Tank size = 200 gal

We want to find out how many ounces of fungicide to add to the 200-gallon tank.

$$\frac{\text{ounces required per 1000 sq ft}}{\text{sprayer output}} = \frac{\text{fungicide needed}}{\text{tank volume}}$$

$$\frac{4 \text{ oz}}{2 \text{ gal}} = \frac{x}{200 \text{ gal}}$$

Cross multiply:
$$(2 \text{ gal}) \, x = (4 \text{ oz}) \, (200 \text{ gal})$$
$$2x = 800 \text{ oz}$$
$$x = 400 \text{ oz}$$

Thus we need 400 ounces (25 pounds) of fungicide. As long as the same ground speed, pressure, and nozzles are used, the sprayer will be applying 4 ounces of fungicide per 1000 square feet. Note that we needn't know how large each green or fairway is.

Example 2. Assume that only one green of 5000 square feet needs to be treated. The sprayer output is 0.5 gallons per 1000 square feet, and the recommended rate of application for the fungicide is 2 ounces per 1000 square feet. How much water and chemical must be added to the tank?

We know:
   Fungicide needed per 1000 sq ft = 2 oz
   Sprayer output = 0.5 gal/1000 sq ft
   Area to be sprayed = 5000 sq ft

We need to determine the amount of water to be added to the spray tank fir

$$\frac{\text{sprayer output}}{\text{unit area}} = \frac{\text{water needed}}{\text{area to be treated}}$$

$$\frac{0.5 \text{ gal}}{1000 \text{ sq ft}} = \frac{x}{5000 \text{ sq ft}}$$

$$1000x = 2500 \text{ gal}$$

$$x = 2.5 \text{ gal}$$

Thus 2.5 gallons of water must be added to the tank to spray 5000 square feet. How much fungicide must be added to 2.5 gallons of water?

$$\frac{\text{ounces required}}{\text{sprayer output}} = \frac{\text{fungicide needed}}{\text{tank volume}}$$

$$\frac{2 \text{ oz}}{0.5 \text{ gal}} = \frac{x}{2.5 \text{ gal}}$$

$$0.5x = 5 \text{ oz}$$

$$x = 10 \text{ oz}$$

So we need 10 ounces of fungicide in 2.5 gallons of water to treat 5000 square feet, provided the same pressure and ground speed are used. (For practical purposes, 3 or 3.5 gallons of water and 12 or 14 ounces of fungicide would be added to the spray tank, because when the level in the tank becomes too low the pump often loses its prime. Also, many sprayers cannot spray out the last gallon or so accurately.

There is one other type of problem that may be encountered, especially with herbicide mixtures in which different amounts of the same active ingredients (ai) are present in products sold by different companies. 2,4-D is a good example. Although this book deals only with fungicides, this information may come in handy. Since commercial 2,4-D contains various amounts of active ingredient, university recommendations are often given in terms of percent ai.

Example 3. A university recommendation calls for the application of 3 ounces of active ingredient per 1000 square feet for any product containing benomyl. The product you have is a 75% wettable powder (WP). If it were a 100% WP, 1 ounce would be equivalent to 1 ounce of ai; since it contains only 75% ai, you must determine the amount required to obtain 1 ounce of ai.

How much of the 75% formulation of benomyl is needed to get 3 ounces of ai? This is determined by dividing 100 by 75.

$$\frac{100}{75} =: 1.3$$

To obtain 1 ounce of ai, 1.3 ounces of a 75% WP must be used. Since 3 ounces of ai are required, you need 3.9 ounces of the benomyl, 75% WP (1.3 × 3 = 3.9).

If the university recommendation calls for 3 ounces of ai per 1000 square feet, the sprayer is calibrated to put out 1 gallon per 1000 square feet, and it is a 200-gallon sprayer, the amount of benomyl 75% WP that must be added to the sprayer can be determined by plugging the data into the proportions.

$$\frac{\text{ounces required}}{\text{sprayer output}} = \frac{\text{benomyl 75\% WP needed}}{\text{tank volume}}$$

$$\frac{3.9 \text{ oz}}{1 \text{ gal}} = \frac{x}{200 \text{ gal}}$$

$$x = 780 \text{ oz}$$

To apply 3 ounces of *ai* per 1000 square feet with a 200-gallon tank filled to capacity, you need 780 ounces of benomyl 75% WP.

The area that can be covered by one tankful of the mixture can be determined as follows:

$$\frac{\text{sprayer output}}{\text{unit area}} = \frac{\text{sprayer volume}}{\text{total area}}$$

$$\frac{1 \text{ gal}}{1000 \text{ sq ft}} = \frac{200 \text{ gal}}{x}$$

$$x = 200,000 \text{ sq ft (a little more than 4 acres)}$$

CALCULATIONS TO SAVE YOU MONEY

It is difficult to teach people to buy a chemical or a fertilizer on the basis of its cost per unit area rather than its cost per pound. I still have former students tell me what a great deal they got on a case of fungicide or a ton of fertilizer because it cost only so much a pound or a ton. When I ask them how many square feet or how many acres it will treat, too often the answer is What difference does it make? Well, it makes a lot of difference. Let me illustrate with some examples.

Example 4. Fungicide A costs $2.00 per pound, fungicide B costs $10.00 per pound, and both will manage dollar spot. Fungicide A, at $2.00 per pound, appears to be the better buy. But is it?

The cost that counts is the cost per 1000 square feet, not the cost per pound. Assume fungicide A is applied at a rate of 8 ounces per 1000 square feet and fungicide B at a rate of 1 ounce per 1000 square feet. Since there are 16 ounces in a pound, the cost per ounce of fungicide A is $2.00/16, or 12.5¢, and the cost per ounce of fungicide B is $10.00/16, or 62.5¢. At a rate of 8 ounces per 1000 square feet, fungicide A would cost 12.5¢ × 8 or $1.00 per 1000 square feet. Fungicide B, applied at a rate of 1 ounce per 1000 square feet, would cost 62.5¢ per 1000 square feet. Thus fungicide B turns out to be the better buy.

Remember, it is the cost per unit area that you consider when buying fertilizer and chemicals, not the cost per pound! By following the steps in example 4, you can figure out cost per 1000 square feet. If you don't want to do the figuring yourself, ask your salesman to do it for you. (As I said before, if he can't, you need a new salesman.)

Consider one more example, this time with fertilizer. It is with fertilizers and herbicides that people most often make the mistake of buying on the basis of cost per pound instead of cost per 1000 square feet.

Example 5. Fertilizer A is a 15-0-0 mixture that costs $150.00 per ton, and fertilizer B is a 35-0-0 mixture that costs $300.00 per ton. You want to apply 1 pound of actual nitrogen per 1000 square feet. Which fertilizer is the better buy?

The numbers 15 and 35 on the labels give the percentage of nitrogen per pound. To get 100% (1 pound) actual nitrogen you must apply 100/15 or 6.67 pounds of fertilizer A. With fertilizer B you will need 100/35 or 2.86 pounds.

Since there are 2000 pounds in a ton, the cost per pound of fertilizer A is $150.00/2000 or 7.5¢, and the cost per pound of fertilizer B is $300.00/2000 or 15¢ . The cost per 1000 square feet of fertilizer A is 6.67 × 7.5¢, or 50¢; the cost per 1000 square feet of fertilizer B is 2.86 × 15¢, or 43¢. Thus fertilizer B is cheaper to use, even though it costs more per ton.

When buying fertilizer you must be aware that there are different forms of nitrogen and take that into account. The point I'm making here, however, is that you should buy fertilizer according to the cost of actual nitrogen per unit area, not the cost per ton.

chapter seven

CULTURAL ASPECTS OF TURFGRASS DISEASE MANAGEMENT

Cultural management is, of course, only one aspect of a comprehensive program for managing turfgrass disease. The other major components of a disease management program, resistant cultivars and chemical management, will be discussed in chapters 11 and 12, which describe disease management programs. This chapter deals with the effects of soil fertility, soil pH, watering, and mowing on turfgrass diseases.

SOIL FERTILITY

Nitrogen

Adding nitrogen to the soil makes some turfgrass diseases worse but reduces the severity of others (see, for example, fig. 7-1.) Some diseases in each category are listed below.

Severity Increased by Nitrogen	Severity Decreased by Nitrogen
Pythium blight	Rust
Rhizoctonia brown patch	*Corticium* red thread
Fusarium blight	*Sclerotinia* dollar spot
Stripe smut	Anthracnose
Fusarium patch	
Typhula blight	
Helminthosporium diseases	
Gray leaf spot	

Once you know the effect of nitrogen on disease development, timing the nitrogen applications becomes the next important consideration. Nitrogen applied in the spring is not going to solve a stem rust problem in the fall. Likewise, the addition of 2 or 3 pounds of nitrogen in the late summer and fall will not aggravate *Fusarium* blight, but 2 or 3 pounds applied in the spring can make *Fusarium* blight worse.

Timing nitrogen applications to make a particular disease less severe is not as simple as it may seem. In the course of one growing season a single turfgrass species may be subject to a variety of diseases, all of which must be taken into account. It would be ideal if each turfgrass species were susceptible to only one disease, for then it would be easy to plan nitrogen applications. Unfortunately, as things are, a program of nitrogen

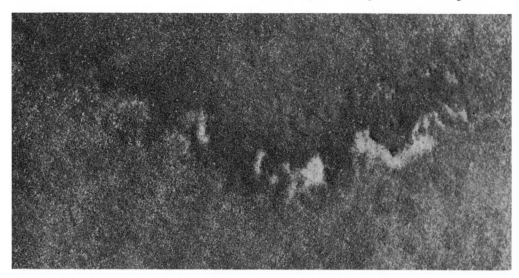

Figure 7-1. *Fusarium* patch on annual bluegrass in the fairy-ring zone of stimulation where the susceptibility of the grass has been increased by excess nitrogen

fertilization that alleviates one disease may worsen another. Luckily, tables that show the times of the year when fertilizing with nitrogen will make a particular disease worse are available. (See the tables in chapters 11 and 12.) The following list shows the times of year when certain common diseases are encouraged by fertilization with nitrogen.

Spring	Summer	Fall
Fusarium blight	Stripe smut	*Helminthosporium*
Helminthosporium	*Pythium* blight	diseases
diseases	*Rhizoctonia* brown patch*	*Typhula* blight
	Gray leaf spot	*Fusarium* blight
		Spring dead spot

In scheduling nitrogen applications you must balance disease management with the nutrient needs of the turfgrass plant. Grass plants need nitrogen, and so you cannot simply eliminate all nitrogen applications in the interests of disease management. You should apply nitrogen at the time of year when it will assist disease management the most.

Phosphorus and Potassium

After nitrogen, the two elements most important for growing plants are phosphorus and potassium. The role of these elements in controlling diseases has not been determined, although Couch [18] and Madison [90] both explain how the interaction of nitrogen, phosphorus, and potassium affects specific diseases. If most turfgrasses were subject to only one serious disease it might be worthwhile to maintain relative concentrations of nitrogen, phosphorus, and potassium designed to mitigate that disease. But, unfortunately, most turfgrass species have many diseases during a single growing season, and while it is fairly easy to regulate the nitrogen level, it is difficult to alter the amounts of phosphorus and potassium available to the plant. Phosphorus and potassium

*_Rhizoctonia_ brown patch is also a problem in the St. Augustine growing area in late spring and early fall.

Table 7-1. Recommended Annual Phosphate (P$_2$O$_5$) Applications (Bray P$_1$-Extractable)

Soil Test (lb P/acre)	General Turf (lb/1000 sq ft)	(lb/acre)	High-Maintenance Turf[a] (lb/1000 sq ft)
Less than 15 (very low)	3	130	4
16–25 (low)	2	85	3
26–40 (medium)	1	45	2
41–70 (high)	0	0	1
More than 70 (very high)	0	0	0

[a]Includes greens and tees.

Table 7-2. Recommended Annual Potash (K$_2$O) Applications (Neutral 1 N Ammonium Acetate-Extractable)

Soil Test (lb K/acre)	General Turf (lb/1000 sq ft)	(lb/acre)	High-Maintenance Turf[a] (lb/1000 sq ft)
Less than 50 (very low)	4	170	5
51–101 (low)	3	130	4
101–175 (medium)	2	85	3
175–250 (high)	1	45	2
More than 250 (very high)	0	0	1

[a]Greens, tees, and other high-maintenance turfs on sandy soils with high irrigation rates.

tend to be insoluble and thus are not readily leached. It is easy to raise the level of these nutrients in the soil but hard to bring it back down quickly. It would be very difficult to implement any program that required raising and lowering the levels of phosphorus and potassium throughout the season. The simplest solution is to maintain adequate levels of phosphorus and potassium and vary the amount of nitrogen.

What are adequate levels of phosphorus and potassium? Guidelines are given in tables 7-1 and 7-2, which are based on recommendations from the Michigan State University Soil Testing Lab. Other labs may use different methods of testing soil.

Sulfur

Sulfur is known to be a fungicide. It may act directly as a fungicide or indirectly as a plant nutrient. Davidson and Goss [26] were able to eliminate *Ophiobolus* patch by applying sulfur, and Goss and Gould [51] demonstrated control of *Fusarium* patch with sulfur. Most of this work was done in the Pacific Northwest, and the researchers believe their results are good enough that they can make recommendations for the use of sulfur under conditions similar to those that obtained in the experiments. Outside of the Pacific Northwest, however, little research has been done on how sulfur affects turfgrass diseases. In other parts of the country, therefore, sulfur should be applied initially on small plots to determine its effect under local conditions. If large quantities of sulfur are used, the soil pH should be checked annually.

Iron

Iron is a minor element that is applied when turf becomes chlorotic because of a lack of available iron in the soil or because of poor rooting. When soluble iron is applied to foliage it is a matter of only half an hour or so before the turf looks darker and greener. Iron sulfate is generally used, although other forms of soluble iron are available. If you desire a darker green turf, adding iron is a much safer way to get it than applying nitrogen. Adding excessive amounts of nitrogen will only encourage disease development, and you may be left with brown turf or bare ground instead of the lovely dark green grass you envisioned.

Iron sulfate can be used to mask the symptoms of yellow tufts disease. While this won't control the problem, it will make turf infected with yellow tufts look better.

SOIL pH

The soil pH should be maintained at the optimum level for turfgrass growth (between 6 and 7). Although some diseases do respond to changes in soil pH, it is not practical to combat turfgrass diseases by adjusting pH. For example, you cannot easily change the soil pH from 5 to 7 to fight one disease and then change it back again when a different disease comes along. (If only one disease is a problem, then changing the pH to manage that disease might be practical.) Since the effect of pH on turfgrass diseases is usually related to the levels of nitrogen, phosphorus, and potassium, it is much simpler to maintain proper pH and adequate levels of phosphorus and potassium and adjust the amount of nitrogen.

Most of the recommendations for adjusting the phosphorus and potassium levels and the pH have been inspired by laboratory and greenhouse experiments. But it is one thing to make these changes for grass grown in a pot and inoculated with a single disease, and another to make them under field conditions where you must contend with tons of soil and many diseases. Laboratory and greenhouse experiments should be tried under field conditions before the results are used as a basis for recommendations.

Sulfur will lower the soil pH. As mentioned above, you should apply sulfur only to small plots until you have determined its effect in your locality. Lime will raise the pH. Consult the turfgrass experts in your area before using sulfur, lime, or gypsum.

WATERING

Proper watering can help minimize turfgrass diseases. Too often watering schedules are based solely on the physiological requirements of the grass plant or the convenience of the superintendent, while the pathological effects of water are ignored. Most turf managers water in the late afternoon or early evening. This wets the turfgrass plant and debris (mat, top thatch) and allows fungi to germinate, grow, and infect all night, since normally very little drying takes place before sunrise. Watering early in the evening also promotes the formation of guttation water.

The best time to water is just before sunrise. The water dilutes the nutrient-rich dew and, by breaking up the droplets, allows quicker drying after the sun rises. An exception is turf infected with *Fusarium* blight, which needs light periods of frequent daily waterings at about midday during dry weather. (Midday watering prevents only the symptoms of *Fusarium* blight; it does not eliminate the disease.)

Turf should be watered to prevent wilting. Watering healthy turf deeply once a week is usually sufficient during cool weather. More frequent waterings are wasteful, can be expensive, and in general will encourage the development of short root systems. Daily watering is sometimes necessary to prevent wilt on golf course greens and on annual bluegrass fairways during hot weather. Turf infected with *Fusarium* blight should also be watered daily to prevent severe turf loss during warm weather. The condition of the grass determines how much water you should apply. Healthy turf should be watered deeply and infrequently in the spring of the year to encourage deep root growth. As the soil on top begins to dry out, the roots travel deeper in search of water. A deep root system established in the spring will help the turf through the summer, when the roots naturally become shorter. The same is true for fall irrigation and survival of grass plants through the winter. However, if a plant has a short root system due to nematodes, *Fusarium* blight, or stripe smut, deep watering will not be effective, because the diseased and shortened roots cannot draw water from below the root zone. Turf with this problem requires light, frequent waterings even during the cool weather of spring and fall. What you must keep in mind is that diseased turf has to be watered differently from healthy turf.

DRAINAGE

Good drainage is just as important as proper watering. In the transition zone and the warm-season grass areas, *Pythium* blight requires chemical management. But in the northern region of the cool-season grassbelt *Pythium* blight indicates a drainage problem, and if you correct the drainage problem you will also clear up most of the *Pythium* blight. Other diseases that are made worse by poor drainage are *Rhizoctonia* brown patch, *Fusarium* patch, and *Typhula* blight.

Air drainage is important, too. Diseases like *Fusarium* patch, *Pythium* blight, *Rhizoctonia* brown patch, and gray leaf spot are more severe where air drainage is poor. Removing or pruning some trees, especially the lower limbs, will increase the air circulation and make these diseases less severe.

MOWING

Height of Cut

Grass should not be mowed shorter than its minimum competitive mowing height (see table 7-3). For some species, like creeping bentgrass, this can be as short as ⅛ inch, although ¼ inch is more practical and ½ inch would be preferable (but is not possible on greens). Other species—Kentucky bluegrass, for example—have a minimum competitive height of ¾ inch, and certain cultivars must be even higher. It has been suggested that the "new" Kentucky bluegrasses could be cut shorter and still compete with other grasses such as annual bluegrass. Maybe they could, if they didn't have to sustain traffic. But traffic can't be eliminated from a golf course fairway, and a fairway is the only place requiring a lower cutting height; there is no reason to mow home lawns so short. Turfgrass plants mowed shorter than their optimal height of cut are, in general, more susceptible to diseases.

Table 7-3. Mowing Heights of some Turfgrass Species

Species	Minimum Height (in.)	Preferred Height (in.)
Creeping bentgrass	⅛	¼–1
Kentucky bluegrass	¾	2–3
Fine-leaf fescue	½	2–3
Bermudagrass	¼	½–2
St. Augustinegrass	¾	2–3
Zoysiagrass	¾	2–3
Annual bluegrass	⅛	¼–1

Seasonal variation in mowing heights can be beneficial. A lower cutting height during cool weather retards thatch development, whereas higher mowing heights during warm weather may lower the temperature around the crowns and help the grass to survive the stress period.

Frequency

How often you mow depends on how much the turf is used. In any case, you must make sure that no more than one-third of the top growth is removed during a single mowing. A golf green needs daily mowing (6 days a week), and fairways and tees require mowing daily to once a week (three times a week is common). For areas of general use, such as parks, home lawns, and athletic fields, mowing once a week is usually sufficient.

Mowing makes wounds through which pathogenic fungi can enter the plant and infect it. The more you mow, the more fresh wounds the grass will have. A dull mower inflicts more and bigger wounds than a sharp mower. Wounds made by a sharp mower are cleaner and heal faster than the tearing and shredding caused by a dull mower.

Clippings

It is not clear what effect clippings have on disease development. There is little evidence to support the theory that clippings left on the ground increase inoculum levels and thereby encourage disease. In fact, clippings seem to have little direct effect on disease development, and they do not contribute to thatch. With some diseases, like those caused by helminthosporiums, large amounts of inoculum may be present in the crown area and root zone; however, there is little evidence that the disease is worse where clippings are left than where they are removed. Even when clippings are removed, there appears to be plenty of inoculum for an epidemic. If you want to prevent the *Helminthosporium* diseases, plant a resistant grass variety and leave the clippings debate to the plant pathologists!

Golf course greens have more diseases than other turfs, although the clippings are removed. For diseases with airborne inoculum, like the rusts, smuts, powdery mildews, and *Helminthosporium*, removal of clippings is useless as a preventive measure. In the case of root diseases, removing the clippings obviously won't affect the inoculum level.

Leaving the clippings does, however, affect the total nitrogen and potassium available to the plant. Turfs from which the clippings are removed require more nitrogen than turfs on which clippings are left. Leaving the clippings could aggravate diseases like stripe smut, *Pythium* blight, *Rhizoctonia* brown patch, and *Fusarium* patch by increasing the amount of nitrogen and by the shading or mist-chamber effect, especially if there are a lot of clippings. But you can adjust your fertilizing schedule to compensate for the extra nitrogen from the clippings, and you will save money because you won't need to buy as much nitrogen.

Disease Management by Mowing

Rust and red thread can be managed by mowing. Recommendations for managing these diseases call for increasing the nitrogen level. However, if you add nitrogen and do not mow, you will actually make the disease worse, not better. This has been demonstrated many times in the laboratory. On the control plot infected foliage is mowed off before the rust has a chance to sporulate, or produce a fruiting body. Since rust has a 10-to-14 day cycle from infection to sporulation, mowing once a week will keep it from becoming a serious problem.

chapter eight

USING DISEASE RESISTANCE IN TURFGRASS MANAGEMENT

Diversity is the rule of nature. Rarely, whether in grassland or forest, is an extensive monostand found. Most of the single-species plant communities that exist today have been purposely developed to satisfy agricultural or aesthetic needs. Monocropping has been successful with annual crop plants, especially since the development of selective herbicides, but it has proved more difficult to establish and maintain single stands of perennial turfgrasses. Mixtures of turfgrass species and blends of turfgrass cultivars are now being used in efforts to imitate the patterns of nature. In this chapter the reasons for blending and mixing will be examined, and the two forms of resistance—horizontal and vertical—explained.

MIXTURES AND BLENDS

A *mixture* consists of two or more turfgrass species planted together; a *blend* is two or more cultivars of the same species planted together. The purpose of using a mixture or a blend is to create a diversified plant community which will have greater resistance to stress and disease, and thus greater longevity, than a stand composed of a single species or cultivar. Simply mixing any two species or cultivars, however, will not necessarily improve quality or increase longevity; appropriate species or cultivars must be selected. Mixing a fine-leaf fescue with a common Kentucky bluegrass (*Poa pratensis*) in a home lawn, for example, results in a plant population capable of producing acceptable turf under a range of environmental stresses. Thus, Kentucky bluegrass will usually predominate in areas that receive full sun, and the fine-leaf fescue will thrive in shaded or droughty areas. Although theoretically sound, this mixture does not always produce a uniform turf. Sometimes the fine-leaf fescue tends to persist in the areas of full sunlight, often as individual clumps or patches which detract from the lawn's appearance.

The principle of blending cultivars to achieve disease-resistant turf is applicable to all turfgrasses. In the cool-season regions, Kentucky bluegrass blends are the most common, and therefore most of the following information deals with that species, but the principles of blending apply to other grasses as well.

Blends vs. Single Cultivars

Until the mid-1960s, most universities and commercial seed companies recommended planting single cultivars, particularly if high quality was desired. Then, in the mid-1960s, researchers began to blend Kentucky bluegrass cultivars, with an apparent improvement in turfgrass quality. Reevaluation suggests, however, that the quality of blended turf may not be better after all. (Data are available in turfgrass conference reports and turfgrass field reports from several universities.) The sort of misinterpretation that has occurred is shown by the following hypothetical example evaluating resistance to *Helminthosporium* melting-out in Kentucky bluegrass. Experimental results like those in table 8-1 have been reported as demonstrating that a blend of Merion and common Kentucky bluegrass is superior to common Kentucky bluegrass. The quality rating was increased from 8 for common Kentucky bluegrass alone to 4 for the blend, and the percentage of infection was reduced from 70 percent for common Kentucky bluegrass alone to 40 percent for the blend. Overlooked, however, was the fact that Merion alone had a quality rating of 2, with only 10 percent infection. The blend is indeed an improvement over common Kentucky bluegrass, but it is inferior to Merion alone. (For more information on the averaging effect of blending, see Vargas and Turgeon [155].)

Table 8-1.   Hypothetical Melting-out Ratings

	Percentage of Turf Infected	Quality Rating (1 = best, 9 = poorest)
Merion	10	2
Common	70	8
Merion–common blend	40	4

Blending will not cure all turfgrass ills. A blend of two improperly selected cultivars may produce a less desirable turf than a single superior cultivar would (see, for example, fig. 8-1).

"Super" Blends

The theory that a blend can be made that will suit all situations is untenable. Blends must be developed for specific uses, such as high-maintenance turf, low-maintenance turf, or shaded turf. Attempting to develop a blend that meets all those needs will result in fair-to-poor turf for all areas, because the cultivars that are not adapted to the environment and cultural regime of an area will deteriorate, lowering the turf quality. The preferred practice is to seed or sod with a blend developed for a particular environment and cultural regime. Small exceptions, such as shaded portions of a home lawn, can be seeded or sodded with appropriate single cultivars instead of with the blend.

Should Blends Include a Common Type?

There is a theory that blends of Kentucky bluegrass should include a common type along with improved types.* Two reasons for including a common type are (1) it keeps the cost of seed down, and (2) if the seed or sod receives low maintenance, the common type will predominate. Common Kentucky bluegrasses, however, are susceptible to *Helminthosporium* melting-out; the improved types are resistant. (The terms "common" and "improved" are open to question.) There is thus an obvious danger in adding the susceptible grasses to a blend.

---

*The term "common" applied to Kentucky bluegrass denotes susceptibility to *Helminthosporium* melting-out; the term "improved" denotes resistance to the disease.

Figure 8–1.   *Left,* Merion, a Kentucky bluegrass cultivar that is resistant to *Helminthosporium* melting-out; *right,* a blend of Kentucky bluegrass cultivars (Prato, Delta, and Park) that all are susceptible to melting-out.

Vargas and Turgeon [155] found that blending common types like Kenblue and Park with the resistant cultivars Merion, Nugget, and Pennstar produced turf of lower quality than stands of single resistant cultivars. After 4 years, the blends Pennstar-Kenblue, Pennstar-Park, Nugget-Kenblue, Nugget-Park, and Merion-Park were still of intermediate quality during the time of year when *Helminthosporium* melting-out was active, indicating that the common types had not been eliminated from the blends. (This probably happened because the large amounts of inoculum produced on the susceptible cultivars broke down the resistance of the improved cultivars, preventing them from gaining a competitive advantage.) The hypothesis that *Helminthosporium* melting-out would quickly eliminate the common type from such blends was thus disproved. Only in the Merion-Kenblue blend was there an indication that the common type, in this case Kenblue, was being eliminated from the blend. This was observed in the fourth season. Some might conclude that in this case the combination was justified. Yet for 4 years the turf has been of lower quality than Merion itself, and this condition undoubtedly will continue for at least another 2 years until all of the Kenblue has been eliminated. The result of the Merion-Kenblue blend is a lawn of intermediate quality for 6 years. The normal life span of a first-class turf given no renovation (to remove perennial weedy grasses) is 5 to 10 years. Thus 6 years have been wasted. Moreover, the weakened condition of the common component during the spring, when *Helminthosporium* melting-out occurs, allows perennial weedy grasses to invade. When the Kenblue is finally eliminated from the blend, what will be the result? A monostand of Merion! If that was the goal, what was the purpose of the blend? Even in a blend of two resistant cultivars and one susceptible cultivar, if the susceptible cultivar is eliminated after a period of time the genetic diversity is reduced by one-third, and poorer quality has been tolerated while this was occurring. A blend of three disease-resistant cultivars would have given a lawn of superior quality, and the genetic diversity contributed by all three cultivars would have been present for the life of the turf.

HORIZONTAL AND VERTICAL RESISTANCE

Plants have two types of resistance to disease, specific and generalized [144]. Specific resistance (also called vertical resistance) occurs when plant x is bred or selected for resistance to a specific race of a pathogen, for example, race 1 of pathogen a. Generalized, or horizontal, resistance occurs when plant x is bred or selected for resistance to all existing races of a particular pathogen or without regard to whether races of the pathogen exist. Specific resistance in its highest form is immunity, or complete freedom from infection. Generalized resistance is usually less than immunity, but results in fewer infections, smaller lesions, longer intervals between infection and sporulation, and fewer spores. These results are brought about by a reduction in the amount of inoculum.

Specific resistance is most effective against pathogens lacking a sexual stage and having only one life cycle a year. A pathogen that has a sexual cycle, or that has repeating asexual cycles throughout the growing season, is more likely to develop a race able to overcome specific resistance. Generalized resistance, on the other hand, is effective against pathogens whether or not they have a sexual cycle or a repeating asexual cycle. The possible development of new races is not important, since generalized resistance is resistance to all races of a pathogen.

The following discussion treats resistance in the context of three important diseases of Kentucky bluegrass—*Helminthosporium* melting-out, stripe smut, and *Fusarium* blight.

Helminthosporium Melting-out

The successful development, through hybridization and selection, of cultivars of Kentucky bluegrass resistant to *Helminthosporium* melting-out is a classic example of generalized resistance. Merion Kentucky bluegrass was the first melting-out-resistant cultivar to be discovered and developed. The fact that its resistance has been sustained for over 30 years shows how effective horizontal resistance is. A number of Kentucky bluegrass cultivars developed since then also have excellent resistance to *Helminthosporium* melting-out.

If two cultivars, one susceptible and one resistant to *Helminthosporium* melting-out, are blended, you might expect that the susceptible cultivar would become infected and the resistant one would not. But remember that horizontal resistance means a lowered inoculum level (see fig. 8-2). A resistant cultivar such as Merion tends to keep the inoculum level low during the 4 or 5 weeks that melting-out is active, but the presence in the blend of a susceptible common type like Park nullifies this effect by bombarding the Merion with inoculum. The horizontal resistance of Merion may be partly broken down, causing it to express a higher incidence of the disease than if it had been growing as a monostand. Merion may therefore fail to gain the expected competitive advantage over the susceptible cultivar. Evidence for this was found by Vargas and Turgeon [155].

Does combining horizontally resistant cultivars improve horizontal resistance to a specific disease? So far, the answer is no. Vargas and Turgeon [155] reported that blending horizontally resistant cultivars did not lessen the incidence of disease or improve turf quality.

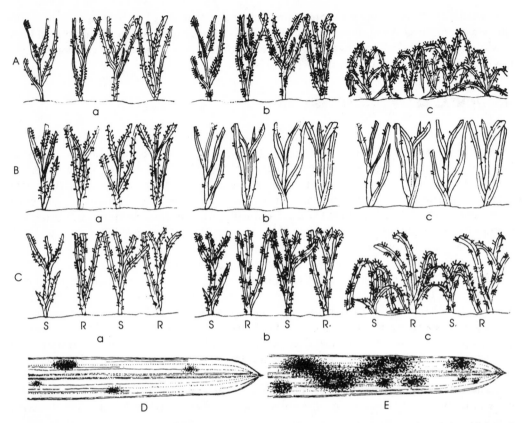

Figure 8–2.   Misuse of a blend for disease resistance when good horizontal resistance already is available. *A*, susceptible cultivar: *a*, initial inoculum arrives from susceptible cultivar; *b*, rapid buildup of inoculum in subsequent generations; *c*, susceptible plants dying. *B*, resistant cultivar: *a*, inoculum arrives; *b*, little inoculum is produced in susequent generations; *c*, resistance by inoculum reduction prevents epidemic. *C*, blend of susceptible *(S)* and resistant *(R)* cultivars: *a*, inoculum arrives on blend; *b*, large buildup of inoculum on susceptible cultivar partially breaks down resistance of resistant cultivar; *c*, combination of susceptible and resistant cultivars yields a turf of intermediate quality. *D*, lesions on resistant cultivar. *E*, lesions on susceptible cultivar.

Stripe Smut

Blending vertically resistant species can prevent multirace host-specific pathogens from destroying a turfgrass stand. Some diseases to which Kentucky bluegrasses have vertical resistance are stripe smut, caused by *Ustilago striiformis*; powdery mildew, caused by *Erysiphe graminis*; and rusts caused by several species of *Puccinia*. Powdery mildew is a problem mainly in the shade, and the easiest way to deal with it is to plant a mildew-resistant grass in shady places. Rusts, with the exception of stripe rust, are a minor problem on slow-growing turf and can usually be managed with adequate moisture and nitrogen. Stripe smut is thus the only major disease of Kentucky bluegrass that requires blending for its management. A combination of three or four Kentucky bluegrass cultivars resistant to current races of stripe smut should provide the broad genetic base required to prevent a race of stripe smut from extensively damaging a stand of turf.

Most of the current stripe smut races are specific for Merion and Windsor. The race that attacks Merion can be designated race 1, and the race that attacks Windsor, race 2. A suitable blend of Kentucky bluegrasses might contain Touchdown, Parade, Majestic, and Adelphi, all resistant to races 1 and 2. Suppose that races 1 and 2 hybridize and produce race 3, which turns out to be specific for Parade. The vertical resistance of the other three cultivars to race 3 ensures that stripe smut will not ruin the turf. The amount of inoculum produced is not a factor in vertical resistance. Race 3 cannot attack the other cultivars, and the disease affects only the Parade plants. However, since resistance to stripe smut is specific, cultivars that are resistant today may be as susceptible as Merion and Windsor tomorrow, as new races of stripe smut develop and become dominant in the population.

Horizontal resistance to stripe smut probably does exist in Kentucky bluegrass, but has been overlooked because the breeding and selecting programs have focused on achieving immunity to stripe smut. What we need to find are cultivars with sufficient general resistance so that no more than 10 or 20 percent of the plants in a population ever become infected with stripe smut. The same is true for other turfgrass species and other diseases, such as rusts and powdery mildew. Breeding for generalized resistance is much more difficult and usually more time consuming than is breeding for specific resistance, but the rewards can be much greater. Loegering et al [86] have proposed a system for evaluating horizontal resistance on a single-plant basis. Their system merits careful examination by turfgrass breeders who are trying to find cultivars resistant to multirace pathogens like rusts, smuts, and powdery mildew.

Fusarium Blight

Fusarium blight is a major disease of Kentucky bluegrass. Whether resistance to this disease is generalized or specific has not yet been determined. The apparent resistance of some cultivars for several years after their release suggests vertical resistance to the current races of *F. roseum* and *F. tricinctum*. On the other hand, blends of susceptible cultivars with cultivars thought to be resistant become infected as though resistance were horizontal.

HIGH–MAINTENANCE TURF

High-maintenance Kentucky bluegrass turfs should consist of cultivars resistant to *Helminthosporium* melting-out, stripe smut, and *Fusarium* blight—the three major diseases of Kentucky bluegrass. Resistance to melting-out is horizontal, and resistance to *Fusarium* blight appears to be horizontal too, so blending will do little to improve resistance to those two diseases. Resistance to stripe smut, however, is vertical (at present, anyway), and therefore a blend of three or four cultivars resistant to both melting-out and *Fusarium* blight is needed to ensure genetic diversity sufficient to prevent a single race of stripe smut from destroying the turf.

Resistance to disease is not the only criterion for cultivar selection; environmental and cultural adaptation are very important too. A successful cultivar must withstand environmental stress. For example, a cultivar that lacks cold-temperature hardiness cannot survive in the North; resistance to disease will not save it. Cultivars also must be suited to the management regimen under which they will be grown. Kentucky bluegrasses should not repeatedly be mowed to ½ inch, and most cultivars do not grow well in the shade. Fine-leaf fescues will not thrive if irrigation is excessive or drainage is poor. Resistance to disease is no solution to these problems.

Ideally, all cultivars in a blend should meet all three criteria—disease resistance, environmental adaptation, cultural adaptation. An exception may be made if there is no cultivar known to be horizontally resistant to a multirace pathogen. A single cultivar that meets all three criteria will be superior to a blend containing cultivars that do not meet all three criteria.

chapter nine

THE COOL-SEASON GRASSES—
A PLANT PATHOLOGIST'S POINT OF VIEW

Seven principal turfgrasses are grown in the northern turfgrass growing area: creeping bentgrasses, colonial bentgrasses, Kentucky bluegrasses, annual bluegrasses, fine-leaf fescues, tall fescues, and perennial ryegrasses. In this chapter, I will discuss the strong and weak points of each. I will also include information about where each turfgrass is culturally and environmentally adapted and how it should be maintained.

Although as a plant pathologist, I believe the most important characteristic of a grass is its resistance to disease, I am not blind to all other facts, and I realize that a turfgrass must have good agronomic qualities too. The most disease-resistant turfgrass in the world is not practical, desirable or salable if it looks like pasture grass when it is mowed. On the other hand, a turfgrass with the best agronomic characteristics is just as impractical and undesirable if it is susceptible to a serious disease. Unfortunately, such a turfgrass *is* salable, as evidenced by the large number of commercially available turfgrasses that are susceptible to serious diseases. This state of affairs is often the fault of university people who list all the agronomic attributes of a turfgrass variety, but fail to mention the diseases to which it is susceptible, mention only the diseases to which it is resistant, or fail to mention anything at all about its disease resistance or susceptibility.

The three turfgrasses for which this problem is most evident are Kentucky bluegrasses, fine-leaf fescues, and perennial ryegrasses. That is not to say that other grasses don't also have problems. Creeping bentgrass, which is grown on golf course greens, is probably the most disease-susceptible turfgrass species of all, but golf course greens are considered high-maintenance turf and receive the fungicide treatments necessary to manage or prevent diseases. Kentucky bluegrasses, fine-leaf fescues, and perennial ryegrasses are grown on areas generally considered to require moderate to low maintenance, such as golf course fairways, home lawns, and park and recreation areas. No one wants to treat these areas weekly for turfgrass diseases.

To cite a specific example, Prato Kentucky bluegrass is a turfgrass that has very high root density, low growth habit, medium green color, and resistance to powdery mildew. It sounds like a pretty good grass until someone tells you it is very susceptible to *Helminthosporium* melting-out, stripe smut, and stem rust. (You can usually forget about the stripe smut and rust because Prato is so susceptible to *Helminthosporium* melting-out that it probably won't be around long enough to catch the other diseases.) Another example of a Kentucky bluegrass is South Dakota certified. The word certified has the connotation today of being something special. The only thing it is certified for is the fact that it was grown in South Dakota, and again it is futile to expand on its agronomic characteristics since it is so susceptible to *Helminthosporium* melting-out that a stand of it will be severely thinned and badly invaded by weeds a few years after establishment. A third Kentucky bluegrass cultivar that is susceptible to *Helminthosporium* melting-out is Palouse (fig. 9-1).

In this chapter an attempt will be made to distinguish the desirable turfgrass species and cultivars from the undesirable on the basis of their susceptibility or resistance to the major turfgrass diseases affecting each species. The minor diseases can usually be managed easily by cultural or chemical means. Even though turfgrass diseases are the most important considerations in selecting a turfgrass species or cultivar, a cultivar must also be environmentally and culturally adaptable. Bermudagrass won't do well in Maine, and the best Kentucky bluegrass cultivar won't do well in Florida. Nor can you mow Kentucky bluegrass at ¼ inch and expect it to compete with *Poa annua*. It is just as foolish to recommend a grass on the basis of its agronomic characteristics while knowing that a major disease like stripe smut, *Fusarium* blight, or spring dead spot is going to destroy it.

CULTIVAR RECOMMENDATIONS

There is nothing sacred about cultivar recommendations, and a cultivar that is resistant today may not necessarily be so tomorrow. That is not a "cop-out"—the cultivars recommended in this chapter have the greatest known resistance to the important diseases today. But fungi, like plants, have the ability to change their genetic makeup, and may overcome certain types of resistance. Also, there is the possibility of a new or previously unimportant disease developing or becoming important on a new cultivar. Manhattan

Figure 9-1. Palouse Kentucky bluegrass severely thinned by *Helminthosporium* melting-out *(Helminthosporium vagans)* during cool spring weather

perennial ryegrass and *Corticium* red thread provide a good example of this. Before Manhattan was introduced, red thread was not considered an important problem on perennial reygrass, but now Manhattan is no longer recommended in many areas because of its susceptibility to this disease. Another example is provided by Merion Kentucky bluegrass. It was widely grown because of its excellent resistance to *Helminthosporium* melting-out. After a period of years, stripe smut, which was considered a minor problem on common Kentucky bluegrass, became a major problem on the cultivar Merion. Then *Fusarium* blight, a disease that was completely unknown before the introduction of Merion, became a major problem.

Many turfgrass experts today believe that Merion Kentucky bluegrass has too many disease problems to warrant its recommendation as a desirable turfgrass. A question often asked by the public is "Why, when it is such a poor grass, was Merion so widely used?" The reason that Merion Kentucky bluegrass was so widely grown is its excellent resistance to *Helminthosporium* melting-out. It was the first, and for years the only, Kentucky bluegrass cultivar with such resistance. Perhaps the reason we never saw *Fusarium* blight as a serious problem in the common-type Kentucky bluegrasses was that *Helminthosporium* melting-out caused the severe thinning of the turf and subsequent invasion by weeds that make the symptoms of *Fusarium* blight difficult to discern. The same fate faces every new cultivar released today.

Cultivar recommendations can be made only on the basis of present-day knowledge and must be changed whenever new information becomes available. (The practice of changing cultivars periodically is a hard one for sod growers, landscapers, and others to understand, yet it often is employed by growers of agronomic and horticultural crops.) Even though it is known that the resistance of a cultivar may change and that it may become susceptible, one should use the cultivars that have the best resistance known today in preference to those that are known to be susceptible to major diseases. It makes no sense to start with susceptible cultivars for which there is no hope of success. (For a further discussion of this subject, see chapter 8.)

THE BENTGRASSES

Creeping Bentgrass (*Agrostis palustris* Huds.)

The creeping bentgrasses are some of the most disease-susceptible turfgrasses. The species can be considered a desirable one only because of its aggressive nature (which allows quick recovery from disease or injury), the fact that it can be maintained as low as ⅛ inch and still be competitive, and because it is used primarily on golf course greens where expensive fungicide spray programs are affordable. (I know that someone is going to point out that he knows of a golf course that has bentgrass fairways. Don't bother—I have seen them, and many golf course superintendents would like to have for their total budget what the superintendents of those courses spend on fungicides alone in trying to maintain those creeping bentgrass fairways.)

Diseases

The three bentgrass species (creeping, colonial, and velvet) are all susceptible to *Sclerotinia* dollar spot, *Rhizoctonia* brown patch, *Helminthosporium* diseases, *Pythium* blight, *Typhula* blight, and *Fusarium* patch. The degree of susceptibility varies among bentgrass species and cultivars, but the variance is slight. The literature is full of discussions of differential susceptibilities of bentgrasses, especially creeping bentgrass, to the various diseases. However, recommendations based on these putative differences aren't worth very much. For example, Penncross creeping bentgrass is listed as moderately resistant to dollar spot [4]. Yet whenever Penncross is grown in an area where dollar spot is a problem, the grass requires fungicide treatments for management of the disease.

Uses

Penncross, Cohansey, and Seaside are three creeping cultivars that can be recommended for turfgrass use. (One must bear in mind, of course, that a heavy fungicide program will be required for disease prevention.) The jury is still out on two others, Emerald and Penneagle. Penncross, Penneagle, Seaside and Emerald are available as seed; Cohansey is a vegetatively propagated cultivar. Seaside is a blend of several selections and will readily segregate into its individual components. Penncross is made up of three selections. It is also reported to separate out into its individual components, although I have not personally observed this. If it does separate, it certainly doesn't do so to the same degree as does Seaside. Based on my observations, Penncross and Cohansey are the preferred cultivars.

A brief mention of Toronto creeping bentgrass (C-15) is in order. This vegetatively propagated cultivar used to be the elite bentgrass in the Midwest. It was represented to be genetically homogeneous, but there is now good evidence that at least two distinct strains exist. One strain is susceptible to a disease that has been called "C-15 problem." The other strain is not affected by this disease, but it is susceptible to stripe smut. Stripe smut weakens the turf so that it doesn't recover well from traffic, injury, or other diseases.

Until its disease problems are resolved, purchasing Toronto is like buying a horse that once was the greatest in the world even though you know that it now is afflicted with a terminal illness. Believe it or not though, some people are still buying Toronto. I submit that any golf course superintendent who puts in Toronto greens is doing so at great risk to his or her career.

Cultivars

Recommended

Cohansey (C-7)
Penncross
Seaside

Not Recommended

Arlington— Not competitive enough
Congressional— Not competitive enough
Pennlu— Stripe smut
Toronto (C-15)— Stripe smut + C-15 problem
Washington— Not competitive enough

No Opinion

Emerald
Penneagle

Colonial Bentgrass (*Agrostis tenuis* Sibth.)

The colonial bentgrasses are susceptible to a wide range of diseases, from dollar spot to the snow molds. Because of their susceptibility to disease and lack of a vigorous creeping habit they are not desirable as turfs for putting greens. They are also not desirable in high-quality turf areas because costly fungicide programs can be avoided by using species that have better disease resistance.

Uses

Do the colonial bentgrasses have a place in modern turfgrass culture? Yes, as a component of mixtures for fairway and general turfgrass areas where, if they die, something else can fill in for them. They survive best in mixtures in the coastal areas of northern Europe and the Pacific Northwest.

Cultivars

The following cultivars are listed, without recommendation, so that you will know what to ask for.

Astoria
Boral
Exeter
Highland
Holfior

Velvet Bentgrass (*Agrostis canina* L.)

Velvet bentgrass lacks the disease resistance and competitive ability necessary to make it a desirable turfgrass species for high-maintenance turf areas like golf course greens. Velvet bentgrass is even more susceptible to disease than is creeping bentgrass. In addition, it doesn't wear well, is not very tolerant of high temperatures, and has a tendency to lie flat in the summertime, thus making an undesirable putting surface. In short, because of disease problems and lack of competitive ability, it simply will not compete with annual bluegrass, which eventually will take over. In order to maintain existing velvet bentgrass greens for as long as possible, minimal amounts of nitrogen should be used and the turf should be watered infrequently. A good fungicide program is also necessary.

Cultivars

The following velvet bentgrass cultivars are listed for your information, but no recommendation is given.

Acme
Kernwood
Kingstown
Piper
Raritan

THE BLUEGRASSES

Kentucky Bluegrass (*Poa pratensis* L.)

The greatest advances in turfgrass breeding and selection have been made with the Kentucky bluegrasses. There are already almost too many Kentucky bluegrasses to name, with new ones arriving on the scene every day. The reason for the explosion in the development of Kentucky bluegrass is simple economics. Most general turf areas in the cool-season turfgrass belt are seeded or sodded to Kentucky bluegrass. For a comparison of the relative amounts of creeping bentgrass and Kentucky bluegrass that commonly are planted, just think of how small an area a golf course green occupies compared to the fairways and roughs. Because of the large acreages involved, not only universities but also many private seed companies have been involved in developing Kentucky bluegrass.

While the burgeoning number of new Kentucky bluegrasses has provided a great variety of colors and textures to choose from, it has also caused great confusion. The buyer wonders which variety is the best. The advertisements in the trade journals suggest that they all are super grasses, but this isn't so. The limiting factors in their use, after all is said and done about color, texture, and lower growth habit, are their environmental adaptability, cultural adaptation, and resistance. For no matter how many other good qualities a variety has, if it is not resistant to the major turfgrass diseases and environmentally and culturally adaptable, it won't be around long enough for you to enjoy it.

You can, of course, apply fungicides to manage some turfgrass diseases, but there is an easier way. It is called selecting the right cultivars to start with. The diseases of Kentucky bluegrasses and their avoidance by the proper selection of varieties are discussed below.

Diseases

The easiest way to manage diseases of Kentucky bluegrass is through sound cultural practices and the use of cultivars which offer the best resistance to the major diseases. These major diseases are *Helminthosporium* melting-out, which is caused by *Helminthosporium vagans; Fusarium* blight, caused by *Fusarium roseum* and *Fusarium tricinctum;* and stripe smut, caused by *Ustilago striiformis* (fig. 9-2). The minor diseases of Kentucky bluegrasses are powdery mildew caused by *Erysiphe graminis,* the rusts caused

Figure 9-2. A stripe-smut-infected Merion Kentucky bluegrass turf. The infection has caused the grass plants to become clumpy and upright in their growth.

by *Puccinia* spp., and fairy ring caused by various fungi, mostly in the class Basidiomycetes.

First, let's dispose of the minor diseases. Powdery mildew is a problem on some Kentucky bluegrass varieties (e.g., Merion, Cheri, Baron, and Fylking) when they are grown in the shade. It can be avoided by the simple expedient of not planting susceptible varieties in the shade. The rusts are a problem on slow-growing turfs, usually because of a lack of nitrogen. The problem can be eliminated by increasing the amount of nitrogen applied or the frequency of its application so that the turf is mowed at least once a week. The third minor disease, fairy ring, is really not a disease in the sense of a pathogen attacking a grass host; it is a fungus growing in the thatch or organic matter. The fungus breaks down the organic matter as it grows, releasing nitrogen which produces the zone of stimulation (the dark green turf associated with the ring). The body (mycelium) of the fungus is hydrophobic and forms a layer that is impervious to water. Consequently, the turf in the area of the main body of the fungus dies from lack of water. The only successful management practices are removal of the fairy ring along with the contaminated soil and fumigation. Fairy rings are most often found in turf areas where tree branches, roots, or trunks have not been removed, or where they have been used as fill. Avoidance of such practices will help to prevent the development of fairy rings.

Most turfgrass managers do not consider *Helminthosporium* melting-out a major disease problem in Kentucky bluegrass. This is because of the many resistant cultivars that are available. The main reason Merion has been so popular and so widely grown is that for many years it was the only cultivar available which had resistance to *Helminthosporium* melting-out. Today, *Fusarium* blight and stripe smut receive all the notoriety as the major diseases of Kentucky bluegrass. However, if it were not for the many melting-out-resistant cultivars available, *Fusarium* blight and stripe smut would not be as important as they are today—*Helminthosporium* melting-out would have eliminated the desirable Kentucky bluegrasses long before *Fusarium* blight and stripe smut could become a problem.

There are many cultivars with excellent resistance to *Helminthosporium* melting-out, but *Fusarium* blight and stripe smut must also be taken into consideration. Merion has excellent resistance to *Helminthosporium* melting-out, but it is very susceptible to stripe smut and *Fusarium* blight. Fylking, Nugget, and Pennstar also have excellent resistance to *Helminthosporium* melting-out, but all are highly susceptible to *Fusarium* blight. The use of any of these cultivars may result in an unsatisfactory turf.

A list of Kentucky bluegrass cultivars and their resistance and susceptibility to the various diseases is given in table 9-1. The cultivars available today that have the best resistance to all three diseases are Adelphi, Baron, Cheri, Victa, Edmundi, Majestic, Parade, Brunswick, and Touchdown. Since blends give added strength to a turf, especially with respect to such diseases as stripe smut, a blend of three or four of these Kentucky bluegrass cultivars would be ideal. This is not to say that these cultivars will remain resistant, or that some new disease won't come along and destroy them. However, based on our present knowledge, these are the best varieties available. At least there is a chance of having a disease-free turf if one uses these disease-resistant cultivars; no such chance exists when you use such disease-susceptible cultivars as Merion, Fylking, Pennstar, Nugget, and Windsor.

Uses—Low-Maintenance Turf Areas

There are some areas in which the planting of the elite cultivars is not recommended. These are low-maintenance areas such as roadsides, parks, and general-use areas where

Table 9-1. Disease Resistance and Susceptibility of 38 Kentucky Bluegrass Cultivars

Cultivar[a]	Melting-out	*Fusarium* Blight	Stripe Smut	Dollar Spot
A-20	R	MR–S	R	R
Adelphi	R	R	MR	R
Aquilla	MR	MR	R	MR
Baron[b]	MR	MR–S	MR	R
Bensun (A-34)	MR	S	R	R
Birka	MR	MR–S	R	R
Bonnieblue	R	S	R	R
Bristol	R	MR–S	R	R
Brunswick	R	MR	R	R
Campina	S	R	R	MR
Cheri[b]	MR	MR–S	MR	MR
Cougar[b]	S	—	—	—
Delft[b]	S	S	R	R
Edmundi	R	R	R	R
Enita	S	S	R	R
Entoper	S	S	R	R
Fylking	R	S	MR	MR
Galaxy	R	S	S	R
Geronimo	R	S	S	MR
Glade	S	MR	R	MR
Kenblue[b]	S	S	MR	MR
Majestic	R	MR	MR	R
Merion	R	S	S	S
Monopoly	R	MR	R	R
Newport	S	S	S	S
Nugget	R	S	R	S
Parade	R	MR	MR	MR
Park[b]	S	MR	MR–S	R
Pennstar	R	S	R	R
Plush	R	S	R	R
Prato	S	—	—	—
Ram #1	S	MR	R	S
Ram #2	MR	S	R	MR
Rugby[b]	R	R	S	R
Sydsport	R	S	R	S
Touchdown	R	MR	R	S
Vantage	S	R	R	R
Windsor	MR	R	S	R

Key: R = resistant, MR = moderately resistant, S = susceptible.

[a] Common was not included because what is sold today is the cultivar Newport.

[b] These varieties may be used in a blend or in a mixture with the fine-leaf fescues for general-use turf areas which receive less than 2 pounds of nitrogen per season and no supplemental irrigation.

less than 2 pounds of nitrogen per 1000 square feet per season and no supplemental irrigation are to be applied. In these areas, the common Kentucky bluegrass types should be used. They will survive better under conditions of low maintenance than will the improved Kentucky bluegrass cultivars, which have high nitrogen and irrigation requirements. The turf should be maintained at a minimum 3-inch height of cut for best results. Of course, this turf will not have the appearance of a first-class turf composed of properly fertilized and irrigated elite cultivars. It will, however, look and survive better than elite cultivars grown under conditions of low maintenance.

Annual Bluegrass (*Poa annua* L.)

You may have a tough time buying annual bluegrass seed at your local seed store, but don't let that bother you, because annual bluegrass has a way of seeding itself at no expense. I realize that treating annual bluegrass as a desirable turfgrass species is going to be met with amazement in some quarters, because some people still consider it to be strictly a weed. But treating annual bluegrass strictly as a weed is the equivalent of living in the Dark Ages and thinking that the world is flat. Annual bluegrass, or "poa" as it is affectionately known, is a fact of life in the northern areas of the cool-season turfgrass region. It makes up over 80 percent of the golf course fairways and tees over 10 years old, and at least half the greens. Most chemical-control programs intended to eradicate or prevent the growth of annual bluegrass have failed; many because good annual bluegrass cultural-control programs weren't conducted in conjunction with them. It is about time we faced up to the fact that annual bluegrass can be a good turfgrass species. It is widely grown and, until a satisfactory means of eradication is found, it should be treated as desirable. For a more detailed discussion of all aspects of annual bluegrass, see reference 6.

Diseases

Annual bluegrass is susceptible to *Sclerotinia* dollar spot, *Rhizoctonia* brown patch, *Pythium* blight, *Helminthosporium* leaf spot, anthracnose, *Corticium* red thread, *Typhula* blight, and *Fusarium* patch. All of these diseases are important and, if not controlled, will destroy annual bluegrass turfs. One other disease, HAS decline (whose major component probably is anthracnose), deserves special mention because it generally has been overlooked as a disease of annual bluegrass (fig. 9-3), and perhaps of the fine-leaf fescues, perennial ryegrass, and some Kentucky bluegrass cultivars as well [146, 149]. It has been my experience that what has been called *Pythium* blight and high-temperature killing of annual bluegrass is in reality HAS decline. It thus seems that controlling this disease complex, along with the more obvious diseases such as *Sclerotinia* dollar spot, *Rhizoctonia* brown patch, and *Pythium* blight, would allow the growing of fine annual bluegrass turfs during the summer in the northern parts of the cool-season turfgrass region.

Annual bluegrass is resistant to the *Helminthosporium* melting-out diseases, *Fusarium* blight, stripe smut, powdery mildew, and stem rust.

Uses

Annual bluegrass can be used on golf course fairways and putting greens, although it certainly is less desirable on the latter because it forms many seedheads in the spring. An adequate irrigation system is necessary to maintain annual bluegrass in hot weather.

Its resistance to disease gives annual bluegrass a competitive advantage over the Kentucky bluegrasses. When a Kentucky bluegrass turf is thinned by one or more of the diseases to which annual bluegrass is resistant (*Helminthosporium* melting-out, stripe smut, *Fusarium* blight), the annual bluegrass seeds that are always present in the soil begin to germinate in the voids (see fig. 9-4).

Annual bluegrass is more competitive than Kentucky bluegrass when a turf is maintained at mowing heights of less than 1 inch, when nitrogen levels are high, and when irrigation is frequent. When such management regimens are employed, as they often are on golf course fairways, annual bluegrass will become the dominant species.

Annual bluegrass will also replace creeping bentgrass turf that is damaged by disease. With the exception of anthracnose, creeping bentgrass is susceptible to all the dis-

Figure 9–3. *Top,* annual bluegrass fairway infected with HAS decline, 10 days after treatment of the left side with fungicide. *Bottom,* treated (left) and untreated (right) portions of same fairway 2 months later.

Figure 9–4. *Helminthosporium* melting-out thinning Kentucky bluegrass during cool spring weather. The annual bluegrass (with seedheads) is not affected by the disease and will probably invade the thinned out areas.

eases that annual bluegrass is. If disease causes an open spot in a turf, annual bluegrass usually will germinate before creeping bentgrass can recover and fill the void. If, on the other hand, annual bluegrass is destroyed by disease, there is enough of its seed in the soil to germinate and replace the destroyed turfgrass when conditions become favorable for doing so.

One final word about annual bluegrass. Before you decide to replace annual bluegrass with something else (and heaven alone knows how you are going to do it without losing your job), ask yourself what you are going to replace it with. You say Kentucky bluegrass. Fine, but you had better get the membership to allow you to mow it to a height of no less than 1 to 1½ inches, because it won't compete with annual bluegrass if it is cut shorter than that. The fairways should receive as little irrigation as possible, and should be watered only when there is evidence of wilting. (This, of course, means that the members will be playing on hard fairways in the summer.) Lastly, applications of nitrogen should be kept to a minimum because excessive amounts encourage the invasion of your Kentucky bluegrass turf by annual bluegrass.

No, you say creeping bentgrass. Fine again, but now you have at least tripled your fairway fungicide budget. If you don't control *Helminthosporium* leaf spot, *Sclerotinia* dollar spot, *Rhizoctonia* brown patch, *Pythium* blight, *Fusarium* patch, and *Typhula* blight, the diseased spots in your creeping bentgrass turf will be filled by—you guessed it—annual bluegrass.

Creeping bentgrass fairways must be dethatched mechanically in the spring or they become puffy and scalped in the summer. The cost of mechanical dethatching must therefore be added to your maintenance budget, because annual bluegrass will fill the voids left by scalping. Golfers don't care whether it was scalping or disease that caused the turf to turn brown. To them, brown is brown and they don't like it. Most golfers couldn't tell annual bluegrass from crabgrass, let along from Kentucky bluegrass or creeping bentgrass, but they can tell green grass from brown, and they usually aren't very fond of brown.

How about the perennial ryegrasses? They are vigorous enough to establish themselves in an existing annual bluegrass turf and are the only alternative available where established annual bluegrass fairways exist. Problem solved? Not quite. Like the other turfgrass species, perennial ryegrasses have their share of disease problems. They are susceptible to *Helminthosporium* brown blight, *Corticium* red thread, crown rust, *Rhizoctonia* brown patch, and *Pythium* blight. Furthermore, although the new cultivars mow better than the old common perennial ryegrass, they still don't mow like Kentucky bluegrass, and they have a shabby appearance during the warm summer months. Lastly, and perhaps most importantly, it is not easy to determine which perennial ryegrass cultivars are best for use on golf course fairways, which ones compete best with annual bluegrass, and what the cultivars' maintenance requirements are. The perennial ryegrasses may someday offer a viable alternative to annual bluegrass, but a lot of research still is necessary before solid recommendations can be made.

TALL FESCUE (*FESTUCA ARUNDENACEA* SCHREB.)

In many areas tall fescue is considered to be a weed, especially when it occurs as single plants, or small groups thereof, in a monostand of a species like Kentucky bluegrass, bermudagrass, or red fescue. However, it can be a desirable turfgrass species for home lawns in the Kentucky bluegrass-bermudagrass transition zone, and for general-purpose use in roadsides and parks in much of the cool- and warm-season turfgrass regions.

Diseases

Because of tall fescue's limited use, and the fact that it is treated as a perennial weedy grass, little research has been done on its susceptibility to disease. In general, tall fescue is susceptible to *Helminthosporium* net blotch and leaf spot, crown rust, *Fusarium* patch, *Fusarium* blight, *Ophiobolus* patch, and *Rhizoctonia* brown patch (fig. 9-5). There are undoubtedly differences in the susceptibilities of different cultivars to these and other diseases; the differences will be discovered as tall fescue is grown more widely as a turf type and as more research is done.

Uses

Tall fescue is used in such areas of low maintenance as roadsides, general park areas, and industrial lawns, and in high-maintenance areas such as home lawns. Because of its wear tolerance, it is also especially well adapted for use on sports turfs and playgrounds in the cool-season grass region; it is used in polystands with bermudagrass and bahiagrass in the warm-season grassbelt [4]. It also can be grown in monostands on home lawns, as it often is in the Kentucky bluegrass-bermudagrass transition zone and in the southwestern United States.

Tall fescue tolerates conditions of low maintenance, especially drought, and it will thrive if nitrogen and supplemental irrigation are applied. It will winter-kill, and it is not really adapted for the extreme northern parts of the cool-season grass region. When

Figure 9-5. *Rhizoctonia* brown patch on a tall fescue turf (Photograph courtesy of Dr. Robert E. Partyka)

it is seeded in polystand with Kentucky bluegrass, the tall fescue should constitute at least 70 percent of the mixture by weight. The turf will then not exhibit the clumpy appearance associated with tall fescue when it is not the dominant species in a polystand. Tall fescue should *not* be used on golf course fairways because of its inability to withstand environmental stresses and disease pressure at a low cutting height.

Cultivars

The following tall fescue cultivars are listed so that you will know what to ask for if you are ordering one. There is not enough information available on their resistance or susceptibility to disease to make a recommendation possible.

Alta
Goar
Fawn
Kenmont
Kentucky 31
Kenwell

THE FINE-LEAF FESCUES

Chewings fescue (*Festuca rubra* L. subspecies *commutata* Gaud.)
Creeping fescue (creeping red fescue) (*F. rubra* L. subspecies *trichophylla* Gaud.)
Spreading fescue (creeping red fescue) (*F. rubra* L. subspecies *rubra*)
Hard fescue (*F. longifolia* Thuill.)
Sheep fescue (*F. ovina* L.)

Disease remains the limiting factor in the widespread use of the fine-leaf fescues as turfgrass. It used to be thought that *Helminthosporium* leaf spot was the only important disease of the fine-leaf fescues, but some new cultivars have problems with such other diseases as *Sclerotinia* dollar spot, anthracnose, *Corticium* red thread, *Fusarium* patch, and rust. The fine-leaf fescues could well be the grass of the future if it proves possible to incorporate disease resistance into a desirable turf type. They have low water and nitrogen requirements, and as our natural resources become scarcer and more expensive, such species will replace those that require more water and nitrogen if disease resistance adequate for survival without fungicide treatments can be incorporated into them. When fungicide treatment is required to maintain a fine-leaf fescue turf, one natural resource, and its attendant cost, is simply being substituted for another.

Uses

Do the fine leaf fescues have any uses today? Yes, in areas where low-maintenance turf is used—the same areas, generally speaking, where you would use common Kentucky bluegrass. These are areas where no supplemental irrigation is supplied and where nitrogen fertility is at a minimum. The fine-leaf fescues' nitrogen requirements are between 1 and 3 pounds of actual nitrogen per 1000 square feet per season; 1½ pounds per 1000 square feet is probably the ideal amount. The quickest way to get rid of a fine-leaf fescue is to overwater it and overfertilize it with nitrogen. In other words, nothing gets rid of a fine-leaf fescue turf faster than does the installation of automatic irrigation systems. This often happened when the members of a golf course decided that they wanted green fairways in the summer, and that the only way to do that was to install an irrigation system. Once an irrigation system is installed, enough water is usually supplied (overwatering in many cases) to keep the fairways soft and green through the summer. The fine-leaf fescues then begin to disappear and annual bluegrass begins to take over.

The fine-leaf fescue turfs may go dormant or off-color (brown) in the summer. It is to be hoped that the incorporation of disease resistance into the fine-leaf fescues will make them better able to tolerate water, at least as it relates to disease development, so that green fescue turfs can be maintained through the summer.

The fine-leaf fescues have been placed in such low-maintenance turf areas as roadsides, parks, and golf course roughs. The species also is used in Europe in polystands with colonial or creeping bentgrass for putting and bowling greens. The fine-leaf fescues are especially well adapted to well-drained, sandy soil and to conditions of low pH (5.5 – 6.5) with little or no added fertility and no supplemental irrigation.

Spreading fescue (*Fescuta rubra* subspecies *rubra*) may have the greatest potential for widespread use if a cultivar that has a true creeping habit (spreads laterally by producing rhizomes) can be found. Even though the species is commonly called creeping fescue, 30 percent or fewer of the plants in any given turf actually have a true creeping habit. At least 70 percent of the plants must have a true creeping habit if the turf is to be acceptable for general use on golf course fairways. (It is reported that 100 percent of the plants of the cultivar Fortress are of the spreading type.)

Cultivars

The recommendations given in table 9-2 are made with the understanding that the cultivars listed do have disease problems, especially *Helminthosporium* leaf spot, and are not suitable for high-maintenance turf areas.

Table 9-2. Disease Resistance and Susceptibility of the Fine-Leaf Fescues

Fine-Leaf Fescue	Leaf Spot	Dollar Spot	Red Thread
Chewings Fescue			
Banner	S	R	—
Cascade	S	—	—
Highlight	S	R	—
Jamestown	S	R	—
Koket	S	R	—
Oregon Chewings	S	—	—
Wintergreen	S	R	R
Creeping Fescue			
Dawson	S	S	—
Golfrood	S	S	R
Oasis	S	S	—
Jade	S	R	—
Spreading Fescue			
Boreal	S	—	—
Fortress	S	R	—
Illahee	S	—	—
Pennlawn	S	R	S
Ruby	S	R	S
Hard Fescue			
Biljart (Scott's C-26)	MR	R	MR
Scaldis	—	—	R
Sheep Fescue			
Seed availability is limited			

Key: S = susceptible, R = resistant, MR = moderately resistant.

MEADOW FESCUE (*FESTUCA ELATIOR* L.)

Meadow fescue is a tufted species that produces a few short rhizomes. In spite of this, it is not as clumpy as tall fescue when grown in a polystand. In many ways it appears like tall fescue when mowed, although its blades are not as coarse. It tends to blend-in better than does tall fescue in a polystand with Kentucky bluegrass. Although it does not have the wear- or heat-tolerance of tall fescue, one cultivar, Beaumont, does have superior cold-temperature hardiness.

Diseases

Meadow fescue is especially susceptible to *Helminthosporium* net blotch, *Rhizoctonia* brown patch, and crown rust. It is reported to be susceptible also to *Pythium* blight, *Fusarium* patch, and stripe smut. As is the case with tall fescue, cultivars of meadow fescue probably exhibit differing susceptibilities to disease. Information about such differential susceptibilities will become available as meadow fescue becomes more widely grown.

Uses

Meadow fescue is recommended for use in polystands with Kentucky bluegrass in such general-maintenance areas as parks, roadsides, and industrial lawns. It may be useful in polystands with Kentucky bluegrass in sports turfs, especially in northern areas where tall fescue is winter-killed.

Cultivars

There is not enough information available on susceptibility and resistance to disease to warrant recommendations. The following cultivars are listed for purposes of knowing what to ask for, but again, they are not recommended.

Beaumont
Ensign
Minor
Trader

THE RYEGRASSES

Perennial ryegrass (*Lolium perenne* L.)
Italian ryegrass (annual ryegrass) (*Lolium multiflorum* Lam)

The perennial ryegrasses have become the new kid on the block. They are competing with the Kentucky bluegrasses for use on golf course fairways, home lawns, and in general turf areas. In 1977, an estimated 30 million pounds of perennial ryegrass seed were sold. A great deal of effort, by both universities and private companies, has gone into breeding and selecting new cultivars. It is unfortunate, however, that the major emphasis has been on improving mowability of the perennial ryegrasses and that little attention has been given to disease resistance. Now that a fairly high level of improved mowability exists, perhaps attention can be turned toward developing cultivars with improved disease resistance.

The improved perennial ryegrasses do mow better than common perennial ryegrasses, but they still are not as mowable as Kentucky bluegrass, fine-leaf fescue, or creeping bentgrass. This is especially true during warm weather. Mowing equipment must be kept sharp to prevent shredding, which will result in the turf's having an undesirable white cast. It may be difficult to prevent this from happening when rotary mowers are used.

Diseases

The ryegrasses are susceptible to *Helminthosporium* brown blight, crown rust, *Fusarium* patch, *Rhizoctonia* brown patch, *Corticium* red thread, stripe smut, *Typhula* blight, and *Pythium* blight, although variation in susceptibility exists among cultivars. *Helminthosporium* brown blight is an almost universal problem on the ryegrasses; it occurs in the cool weather of spring and fall. In the northern parts of the cool-season turfgrass region, the perennial ryegrasses that aren't winter-killed are severely injured by *Fusarium* patch and *Typhula* blight. In the coastal areas of North America and Europe, where cool weather in the spring and fall slows the growth rate of turfgrass, crown rust and *Corticium* red thread are serious problems. *Pythium* blight is a problem in the warm-season turfgrass areas, where perennial ryegrass is used to overseed dormant bermudagrass, and in the transition and cool-season zones, where the new improved perennial ryegrasses are being used as fairway grasses (see fig. 9-6).

The perennial ryegrasses are the most susceptible of all the desirable turfgrasses to *Pythium* blight, *Rhizoctonia* brown patch, *Corticium* red thread, and crown rust. There are

Figure 9-6. *Pythium* blight on a perennial ryegrass lawn (Photograph courtesy of Dr. Bobby G. Joyner)

differences among cultivars in their susceptibilities to some of these diseases, and cultivars with resistance should be used in preference to those without. But other factors, such as heat tolerance, cold tolerance, and competitive ability, must also be considered when one is selecting a perennial ryegrass cultivar. There has not been enough research conducted on the cultural requirements of ryegrass under different maintenance regimens to make specific cultivar recommendations possible. The selection of cultivars listed in table 9-3 has been made simply on the basis of resistance to disease.

Uses

Italian ryegrass is used primarily as a nurse grass where quick establishment is needed prior to the germination and establishment of the permanent grasses. This is especially the case where slow-germinating Kentucky bluegrasses are used on erosion-prone areas.

One of the major uses of perennial ryegrass is the overseeding of bermudagrass greens when they go dormant in the fall. The perennial ryegrasses supply a desirable green color and, probably more importantly in the long run, protect the bermudagrass from excessive wear while it is dormant. The seeding rate used is around 30 pounds per 1000 square feet! Dormant bermudagrass fairways on some golf courses also are overseeded to improve their color, but a much lighter rate of seeding is used.

Many golf course superintendents who have given up trying to grow bermudagrass and Kentucky bluegrass in the transition zone between the warm- and cool-season grassbelts have turned to perennial ryegrass. They may be sitting on powder kegs. *Pythium* blight is difficult to control on perennial ryegrass fairways during hot, humid weather. Both Kentucky bluegrass and bermudagrass are susceptible to *Pythium* blight,

Table 9-3.   Disease Resistance and Susceptibility of the Perennial Ryegrasses

Cultivar	Brown Blight[a]	Brown Patch[b]	*Pythium* Blight	Red Thread	Crown Rust
Yorktown II	R	R	S	S	R
Diplomat	R	R	S	—	S
Omega	R	R	S	MR	S
Birdie	S	R	S	MR	S
Citation	S	R	S	MR	S
Derby	S	R	S	—	S
Manhattan	R	S	S	S	S
NK-200	S	S	S	S	S
Pennfine	S	MR	S	MR	S
Yorktown	R	S	S	S	S
Campus	S	S	S	—	S
Eton	S	S	S	—	S
Game	S	S	S	—	S
Linn	S	S	S	—	S
NK-100	S	S	S	S	S
Paramount	S	S	S	—	S

Key: R = resistant, MR = moderately resistant, S = susceptible.

[a] *Helminthosporium siccans.*

[b] *Rhizoctonia solani.*

but neither is as susceptible as the perennial ryegrasses. Fungicidal control of *Pythium* blight on the perennial ryegrasses during periods of extreme high temperature and humidity may be difficult.

The ryegrasses are also used in seed mixtures on sports turfs and for overseeding worn areas. Mowing quality may be poor, and diseases such as *Helminthosporium* brown blight, crown rust, and *Corticium* red thread can be a problem, especially in the fall when sports fields are used for football. These factors must be taken into consideration when making a decision to use perennial ryegrass.

chapter ten

THE WARM–SEASON GRASSES—
A PLANT PATHOLOGIST'S POINT OF VIEW

THE ZOYSIAGRASSES (*ZOYSIA* WILLD.)

The jury is still out on zoysiagrass as far as disease susceptibility is concerned. Either more definitive research needs to be done or, if it has been done, its results need to be distributed more widely. Zoysiagrass is slow to establish itself, but it eventually forms a dense turf that is practically weed-free. Zoysiagrass is also slow to recover from injury, which may be an undesirable characteristic for golf course fairways and tees. Zoysiagrass does have great potential for general turfgrass areas as well as for golf course fairways in the warm climatic zone and in the bermudagrass-Kentucky bluegrass transition zone. Its cultural requirements and disease resistance and susceptibility still require further study.

While zoysiagrass has great potential for the warm climatic zone, it is not well adapted to cool temperatures. It does have winter hardiness that allows it to survive, but it discolors (brown) with the first cool weather of the fall and does not green-up until late spring or early summer. This means that anyone who plants zoysiagrass in the cool-season grass region can expect a green turf for 2 or 3 months per year and a brown turf for 9 to 10 months. In spite of this difficulty, large advertising campaigns that describe the slow-growing, less-mowing, weed-free, dense-turf virtues of zoysiagrass appear every year in large metropolitan areas. The advertisements don't mention the fact that zoysiagrass is slow to green-up and becomes off-color early in the fall.

Diseases

Zoysiagrass is reported to be susceptible to *Sclerotinia* dollar spot, *Rhizoctonia* brown patch, rust (*Puccinia zoysia*), and *Helminthosporium* disease. The degree to which zoysiagrass is susceptible to each of these diseases, and whether they will be limiting factors in its use, must be determined on a cultural basis.

Uses

Zoysiagrass can be used on home lawns, parks, golf course tees and fairways, and as a border grass on approaches to prevent the bermudagrass on the fairway from invading the bentgrass green.

Cultivars

There are several improved zoysiagrass cultivars. They are listed below for informational purposes, but no recommendation is made.

Meyer—*Z. japonica*
Midwest—*Z. japonica*
Emerald—*Z. japonica* × *Z. tenuifolia*
FC1352—*Z. matrella*

CENTIPEDEGRASS (*EREMOCHLOA OPHUIROIDES* (MUNRO.) HACK.)

Diseases

Rhizoctonia brown patch, *Sclerotinia* dollar spot, centipedegrass decline, and nematodes can cause severe injury.

Uses

Centipedegrass is grown mostly on low-maintenance turf areas. It will not persist where soil pH is high or where high concentrations of nitrogen and excess water are applied. Centipedegrass is used on home lawns or other areas where minimal care is given and where there is little traffic. Like the fine-leaf fescues and certain Kentucky bluegrasses, it does quite well under such low-maintenance conditions. Disease problems, as well as the direct effects of high maintenance, may be responsible for the loss of centipedegrass under intense culture. Oklawn is one improved cultivar of centipedegrass that is available, although seed supply is limited. It was released by the Oklahoma Agricultural Extension Service, and is apparently well adapted for that area. No disease information is available.

BUFFALOGRASS (*BUCHLOË DACTYLOIDES* (NUTT.) ENGELM.)

Buffalograss grows naturally in many mowed, unirrigated areas of the warm arid climatic zone. It persists in unirrigated fairways and roughs on golf courses. Very little selecting or breeding has been done with this species, but as natural resources become scarcer it could become an important species, especially in arid and semiarid areas of the warm arid climatic zone.

Diseases

There is no information available on the susceptibility of buffalograss to disease.

Uses

Buffalograss is the fine-leaf fescue of the arid and semiarid warm climatic zone. It survives well in areas where no supplemental irrigation and little or no supplemental nitrogen are applied. Irrigation and the application of nitrogen will cause buffalograss to decline.

ST. AUGUSTINEGRASS (*STENOTAPHRUM SECUNDATUM* (WALT.) KUNTZE)

St. Augustinegrass, like most of the warm-season grasses, is currently propagated only vegetatively. It has been widely used on home lawns, industrial grounds, and parks. It is not cold-tolerant and is restricted mainly to the southern part of the warm humid climatic zone.

Diseases

St. Augustinegrass is susceptible to *Rhizoctonia* brown patch, especially in the shade (fig. 10-1), gray leaf spot, downy mildew, *Sclerotinia* dollar spot, and St. Augustine decline virus (SADV). A resistant cultivar of St. Augustinegrass was found by some fine cooperative efforts between the University of Florida and Texas A & M University. This resistant cultivar is called Floratam. Unfortunately, while Floratam has good resistance to SAD, it lacks good turfgrass quality in terms of leaf texture. It also lacks shade adaptation and, in comparison to Texas common, it lacks low-temperature hardiness.

Cultivars

There are two other cultivars that can be grown where SAD virus is not a problem: Bitter Blue and Floratine. However, if SAD virus is a problem, Floratam should be grown in areas where it forms a suitable turf. Floratam has excellent resistance also to the chinch bug, which can be a devastating problem on St. Augustinegrass. Breeding programs currently under way should produce St. Augustinegrass cultivars that are resistant to SAD and also have good turfgrass quality.

BERMUDAGRASS (*CYNODON* SPP., L. C. RICH)

Bermudagrass is one of the most important warm-season turfgrasses. It has a wide range of uses, from golf course greens, tees, and fairways to home lawns, athletic fields, institutional grounds, cemeteries, roadsides, and general park areas. A few of the improved cultivars can be mowed as low as ¼ inch, although heights of ¾ to 1 inch are preferred for general-purpose use. One of the things that makes bermudagrass so

Figure 10–1. *Rhizoctonia* brown patch on St. Augustinegrass (Photograph courtesy of Dr. Don Blasingame)

popular is its recuperative capability after it has been thinned by traffic, disease, or insects. Bermudagrass does have poor low-temperature tolerance. Also, it loses color in the cool weather of the fall and doesn't green-up until soil temperatures rise to 50 °F in the spring.

Diseases

Bermudagrass is susceptible to spring dead spot (fig. 10-2), *Helminthosporium* diseases, *Rhizoctonia* brown patch, *Sclerotinia* dollar spot, *Pythium* blight, rust, and *Fusarium* patch. Spring dead spot (SDS) is the limiting factor in the successful growth of bermudagrass as a turfgrass species in many areas of the warm climatic zone. The colder the winter, the more severe is spring dead spot. The disease is an especially severe threat to bermudagrass in the transition zone and in cooler areas of the warm climatic zone.

Bermudagrass golf greens that are on a heavy fungicide spray program very seldom have a problem with spring dead spot. Wilcoxen [159] showed that repeated fungicide application on fairways during the growing season reduced the amount of SDS. While more research needs to be conducted on chemical management of SDS, it may be worth trying such a program where quality bermudagrass with a reduced incidence of spring dead spot is desired.

Bermudagrass is a high-maintenance turfgrass that responds well to nitrogen. It does best when adequately irrigated.

Bermudagrass has more diseases listed for it than do the other warm-season grasses. This is due in part to the fact that it has been studied more, and also because it has been used on golf courses more than has any other warm-season species. It also has been subjected more than has any other warm-season grass to high-intensity cultural practices, and this has led to the discovery of its disease problems.

Figure 10–2. Spring dead spot on a bermudagrass golf course fairway (Photograph courtesy of Dr. Bill Daniels)

Cultivars

The cultivar Midiron is currently being represented as resistant to spring dead spot. If it has resistance, or if this resistance holds up, it will be a major breakthrough and will greatly expand the area in which bermudagrass can successfully be grown. It should also supply the genetic material to start a breeding program to develop other cultivars with resistance to SDS.

Four species of bermudagrass are grown as turfgrasses: *Cynodon dactylon* (L) Pers., *Cynodon transaalensis* Burtt-Davy, *Cynodon magennisii* Hurcombe, and *Cynodon incompetus* var. *hirsutus* (Stent) de Wet et Harlan. Several of the improved cultivars are listed below. They may be used in areas where spring dead spot is not a problem or where fungicide programs are used.

C. dactylon
    Ormond
    U-3
C. dactylon × *C. transvaalensis*
    Midiron
    Midway
    Santa Ava
    Tex Turf 10
    Tifdwarf
    Tiffine
    Tifgreen
    Tifway
C. Magennisii
    Sunturf

OTHER PROBLEMS OF WARM–SEASON TURFGRASSES

Insect and nematode problems (fig. 10-3) are more severe in warm climates than they are in cool ones. This is not to say that the cool-season grasses don't have nematode or insect problems, but these problems are more numerous and occur more frequently on the warm-season grasses.

Figure 10–3. Lawn severely thinned by nematodes (Photograph courtesy of Dr. Don Blasingame)

chapter eleven

DISEASE MANAGEMENT STRATEGIES FOR GOLF COURSES

COOL-SEASON GRASSES—GREENS

The Bentgrasses

Recommended Species

Let us start with the easy one, turfgrasses for golf course greens. You are talking about creeping bentgrass. Yes, some people still plant velvet bentgrass, and if you want a grass that is extremely susceptible to common bentgrass diseases, won't compete well with annual bluegrass, becomes unmanageably puffy in hot weather, and provides one of the poorest-quality putting surfaces ever, please don't let me discourage you from planting velvet bentgrass.

Creeping bentgrasses can be assigned to one of two classes on the basis of the way in which they are established; there are those that can be established only vegetatively and those that can be established either vegetatively or from seed. Toronto (C-15) and Cohansey (C-7) are the two most popular vegetatively established cultivars. Unfortunately, Toronto has developed too many disease problems, which leaves Cohansey as the only widely grown, vegetatively established creeping bentgrass cultivar that can be recommended. Cohansey does have a light green color that some people find objectionable, but aside from its color it is a fine creeping bentgrass for golf course greens.

The elite of the seeded cultivars is Penncross creeping bentgrass. It has good wear tolerance [5] and is vigorous enough to compete fairly well with annual bluegrass if diseases are controlled and proper cultural practices are followed. Seaside creeping bentgrass is another widely used seeded cultivar. It is a blend of many strains of creeping bentgrass, and unfortunately they are not uniform in color and tend to segregate themselves into many different patches of various shades of green. (Penncross also is a blend of three strains of creeping bentgrass, but segregation is not a serious problem.) The overall susceptibilities to disease of Seaside and Penncross are about the same, but Seaside is not as vigorous a cultivar as Penncross, and it will have a harder time competing with annual bluegrass. Two new seeded types of creeping bentgrass that have been introduced are Emerald and Penneagle, but neither has been grown widely enough to make possible a recommendation one way or the other.

Diseases

Creeping bentgrasses are susceptible to *Sclerotinia* dollar spot, *Rhizoctonia* brown patch, *Pythium* blight, *Typhula* blight, *Fusarium* patch, *Helminthosporium* leaf spot, and red leaf spot. A fungicide and nitrogen fertility schedule for your area can be found in tables 11-1 through 11-3 and 11-7 through 11-8.

Maintenance Programs

Irrigation. The greens are obviously the most important single part of a golf course. A few bare spots on tees and fairways may go unnoticed, but they never will be unnoticed on a green. In order to keep the greens free of bare spots, an adequate watering system and good surface and subsurface drainage are essential. Standing water in hot weather can be as damaging as too little water. When purchasing an irrigation system, get a good one. It will be cheaper in the long run to spend a little extra money to do it correctly rather than nickle-and-diming yourself to death trying to correct problems later with stop-gap measures that only make a bad situation temporarily acceptable.

Golf course greens should be watered as needed to prevent wilting. The amount of water used will depend on such things as soil type, time of year, and species of grass. Remember that creeping bentgrass greens should be kept on the dry side to prevent the invasion of annual bluegrass.

Mowing Height. Creeping bentgrass greens can be mowed to between ⅛ and ⁵⁄₁₆ inch. Most golf course superintendents mow to between ³⁄₁₆ and ¼ inch. The closer the greens are mowed, the more difficult they will be to maintain during stress periods, but the faster and truer they will putt, provided that other cultural practices are followed.

Fertility. Excessive use of nitrogen is one way to lose your grass in a hurry. To most people, a healthy turf is one that is dark green. A healthy turf is one that has good density; it may or may not be dark green. As more nitrogen is supplied, more top growth is produced, but this is usually at the expense of the root system. Nitrogen causes the foliar tissue to become more succulent, and the more succulent it becomes, the more susceptible it becomes to many serious diseases such as *Pythium* blight, *Rhizoctonia* brown patch, and *Helminthosporium* leaf spot. Too much nitrogen also will make golf course greens more susceptible to wilting, desiccation, and wear.

There is no pat formula for determining the amount of nitrogen that should be applied, and that is why growing grass is an art as well as a science. The amount of nitrogen that is optimum varies with the length of the growing season, soil type, amount of watering, and other factors. However, there is a general rule of thumb: No more than 3 pounds of nitrogen per 1000 square feet should be applied in the northern regions of the cool-season turfgrass belt, and no more than 4 pounds per 1000 square feet should be applied in the southern regions. These are maximum permissible concentrations, and less nitrogen should be used where possible.

If a dark green color is desired use iron, because trying to obtain a dark green color with nitrogen will only lead to a lot of grief. Adequate levels of phosphorus and potassium should be maintained; their concentrations can be determined by a soil test. The phosphorus (P_2O_5) level should be between 40 and 70 pounds per acre, and the potassium (K_2O) level should be between 175 and 250 pounds per acre [114]. Phosphorus and potassium need be applied only once a year, preferably in the fall. A fertility program similar to the above should be followed with annual bluegrass greens and tees, although excess nitrogen will certainly favor the annual bluegrass over the creeping bentgrass. See tables 11-1, 11-3, and 11-8 for a typical nitrogen fertility schedule for your area.

Cultural Practices. Cultural practices that must be carried out on a golf course green if a quality putting surface is to be maintained include vertical mowing, brushing, and combing, or, to remove graininess, all three. Topdressing should be done to reduce thatch and provide a firm putting surface. Spiking, usually weekly, will help break up surface compaction, and coring one to three times a season during cool weather will relieve compaction in the 1- to 3-inch depth where it is a problem.

Annual Bluegrass

I know that this sounds blasphemous, but the simple fact is that annual bluegrass exists on the majority of the golf course greens in the cool-season grassbelt and, since there is no effective, safe means of eliminating it, replacing it with something else, and preventing it from coming back, it must at least be classified as a functionally desirable species. Certainly it is preferable to bare ground. If you don't think so, talk to a superintendent who has successfully eliminated annual bluegrass by chemical means, or lost it for some other reason, and ask him how he begged and prayed that the "lousy miserable good-for-nothing annual bluegrass" would come back and cover up the bare ground. The point being made here is that before you eliminate the annual bluegrass you had better know how much you really have, not how much you tell everyone you have. If annual bluegrass constitutes more than 20 percent of your turf, ask yourself what is going to be in those spots when it dies. If the answer is dead dirt, you may wish to think twice before you eliminate the annual bluegrass.

Before you can maintain annual bluegrass properly, you must first admit that you have it. The three greatest lies told by a golf course superintendent to his fellow superintendents are: "My greens chairman never interferes," "I get everything I ask for," and "I have hardly any annual bluegrass in my greens." First you have to face the facts and admit that you have annual bluegrass greens; then you can use a maintenance, fertility, and pest-control program designed for them and not for creeping bentgrass greens.

Diseases

Annual bluegrass is susceptible to *Sclerotinia* dollar spot, *Rhizoctonia* brown patch, anthracnose, *Helminthosporium* leaf spot, and HAS decline (fig. 11-1). A nitrogen fertility and fungicide treatment schedule for your area can be found in tables 11-3 through 11-6.

Maintenance Programs

Irrigation. Deep, infrequent irrigation in the spring and fall encourages roots to grow downward. Contrary to popular belief, annual bluegrass will root as deeply as will colonial bentgrass, creeping bentgrass, or Kentucky bluegrass in similar soils [129, 160]. Lighter and more frequent waterings may be necessary as root growth becomes shallower in the summer (as it also does on creeping bentgrass). In some areas, syringing during the warmest part of the day may be necessary. As long as good drainage is provided, it is very hard to overwater annual bluegrass.

Mowing Height. Annual bluegrass, like creeping bentgrass, should be mowed to between 1/8 and 5/16 inch; most golf course superintendents prefer 3/16 to 1/4 inch. Mowing

Figure 11-1. Annual bluegrass fairway damaged by HAS decline, with healthy fungicide-treated annual bluegrass approach and green in the background

twice daily in the spring when heavy seedhead production occurs will help to maintain a good putting surface.

Fertility. Annual bluegrass loves nitrogen. More than that, it *requires* nitrogen if it is to thrive, especially during the summer. A nitrogen fertility schedule for your area can be found in tables 11-3 and 11-5. The phosphorus content of the soil should be kept on the high side based on annual soil tests. Just as high phosphorus levels facilitate the encroachment of annual bluegrass into creeping bentgrass and Kentucky bluegrass turfs, so do high levels of phosphorus help to maintain an existing stand of annual bluegrass. The potassium content of the soil should be kept at adequate levels as determined by annual tests (see chapter 7).

Cultural Practices. Vertical mowing to remove graininess is not as necessary with annual bluegrass as it is with creeping bentgrass, but light vertical mowing will help to reduce some of the adverse effects on putting that are caused by heavy seedhead formation in the spring. Brushing or combining also will help to maintain a truer putting surface. Spiking weekly will help to break up surface compaction, and coring one to three times a season, preferably during cool weather, will help to reduce compaction, where it exists, to a depth of 3 inches.

COOL-SEASON GRASSES—TEES

Recommended Species

A seeded creeping bentgrass should be used if any grass other than annual bluegrass is desired on a golf course tee. Penncross creeping bentgrass is the preferred cultivar because of its vigorous growth habit. (Time will tell about Emerald, Penneagle, and other newer grasses.) The reason for using a seed cultivar should be obvious: replacement of divots. The divots can be reseeded where seeded-type creeping bentgrasses have been established.

Penncross tees should receive the same treatment as Penncross greens. They should be cored, vertically mowed, and topdressed. Otherwise, compaction will take place in trafficked areas, and puffiness resulting in scalping during warm weather will occur in areas of the tee that are not extensively used. Tees also should provide firm footing for the golfer; they will not do so unless proper cultural practices are followed. A good preventive fungicide program is necessary to prevent the loss of the Penncross turf to diseases and the subsequent invasion of annual bluegrass. Fungicide schedules for creeping bentgrasses are given in tables 11-2, 11-6, and 11-7.

The Kentucky bluegrasses and the fine-leaf fescues are not suitable for golf greens. Red fescue really isn't suitable for tees either. Kentucky bluegrass is a marginal grass for tees. It usually is rapidly replaced by annual bluegrass, especially when it is mowed to around ½ inch, and most golfers won't stand for tees being mowed to ¾ inch or higher. "Poa" seeds are not commercially available, so if you don't want creeping bentgrass tees because of the extra maintenance and disease-control costs involved, you should plant a blend of the better disease-resistant Kentucky bluegrasses that can tolerate a close mowing height and still compete with annual bluegrass. (Touchdown, Brunswick, and Bensun (A-34) are good choices.) Such Kentucky bluegrasses will fade away slowly when mowed at ½ inch. Touchdown, Brunswick, and Bensun mowed at ¾ inch, coupled with a good preemergence herbicide program to prevent the germination of annual bluegrass, could last for years, especially on tees that are large enough to prevent excessive wear. Planting the cheaper common-type Kentucky bluegrasses would require fungicide treatments for a 3- or 4-year period to prevent the development of bare spots and insure a slow transition from Kentucky bluegrass to annual bluegrass. The cost of fungicide alone would more than offset the seed-price differential between disease-resistant Kentucky bluegrass cultivars and disease-susceptible ones. Annual bluegrass may eventually take over regardless of what you do, but at least you stand a chance of having Kentucky bluegrass tees if you use the proper cultivars mowed at the correct height.

Maintenance Programs

Irrigation. An irrigation program appropriate for creeping bentgrass greens (see p. 135) is also suitable for creeping bentgrass tees, and the same is true for annual bluegrass (see p. 136).

Fertility. The fertility requirements of creeping bentgrass or annual bluegrass tees are the same as those of the greens (see pp. 135-139).

Cultural Practices. Creeping bentgrass tees should receive the same cultural program as creeping bentgrass greens. In addition, the divots, especially on par-3 holes, should be filled periodically throughout the growing season with a soil that contains seed of the grass species you want to have on your tee. If this grass is annual bluegrass, then it should suffice simply to fill the divots with soil.

COOL-SEASON GRASSES—FAIRWAYS

There are five cool-season grasses that often are intentionally used on golf course fairways: creeping bentgrass, colonial bentgrass, Kentucky bluegrass, fine-leaf fescue and perennial ryegrass. Another grass, which is not planted intentionally but makes up 70 to 80 percent of most golf course fairways that are over 10 years old, is annual bluegrass. This is not to say that all fairways consisting of other species are doomed to become annual bluegrass fairways, but it is inevitable that they will unless strict cultural practices are followed.

The four key factors for the survival of Kentucky bluegrass, fine-leaf fescue, and perennial ryegrass are disease control, mowing height, irrigation, and fertility levels. The minimum height of cut for these species is ¾ inch, with 1 to 1½ inch preferred; if they are cut shorter they will not compete with annual bluegrass. (However, you should note that most golfers want the fairways mowed to ½ inch.) Another factor that is important in preventing the invasion of annual bluegrass is the avoidance of overwatering. Overwatering brings on annual bluegrass. The best friend that annual bluegrass has is a golf course superintendent who doesn't know how to operate the automatic watering system properly. Fairways should be kept somewhat dry to allow the more drought-tolerant species to compete with annual bluegrass, and the membership should be warned that the fairways will be harder because of this. As has been noted elsewhere, drainage is as important as the sprinkler heads themselves. Unless good drainage is provided, annual bluegrass will move into the poorly drained areas no matter how little you irrigate. An attempt should be made to keep the phosphorus content of the soil on the low side by fertilizing with carriers that are low in phosphorus. Minimal amounts of nitrogen should be used, since excess nitrogen will favor annual bluegrass over Kentucky bluegrass, fine-leaf fescue, and perennial ryegrass. If you are willing to follow the above program, then the species mentioned above, or cultivars thereof, can be maintained on golf course fairways.

The Bentgrasses

Recommended Species

Colonial bentgrasses can be used as a minor component of mixtures with Kentucky bluegrass or fine-leaf fescues, but by themselves they simply do not make suitable fairway turfs.

Creeping bentgrass can be used as a fairway turf, and it will compete with annual bluegrass when mowed to ½ inch. In order to give the creeping bentgrass a competitive advantage over annual bluegrass, it should be irrigated as little as possible, grown where there is good drainage, and have nitrogen and phosphorus fertility kept at a minimum. The creeping bentgrasses have little disease resistance and are susceptible to *Sclerotinia* dollar spot, *Pythium* blight, *Rhizoctonia* brown patch, *Helminthosporium* leaf spot, *Typhula* blight, *Fusarium* patch, and many other diseases. They must thus be treated heavily with fungicides throughout the year. If creeping bentgrass turfs are not so treated, annual bluegrass will fill in the bare spots and thinned areas left by the various diseases. Furthermore, unless some type of vertical mowing is practiced, creeping bentgrass will become puffy during hot weather and scalping will occur. This will lead to the invasion of annual bluegrass in the scalped areas during the fall. A good preemergence herbicide program should be followed to help prevent the invasion of annual bluegrass. The necessary disease management and cultivation practices will add considerable expense to a maintenance budget—a fact that should be taken into consideration before planting fairways with creeping bentgrass.

Diseases

The same diseases that attack creeping bentgrass on greens and tees also attack it on the fairway. However, many people forget that fact when they put in creeping bentgrass fairways—they forget to multiply the $2,000 fungicide budget for their 2 to 3 acres of greens and tees by a factor large enough (at least 10) to keep their creeping bentgrass fairways disease-free. It should, of course, go without saying that if you don't keep them disease-free then it won't be long before the creeping bentgrass fairways will become "creeping" annual bluegrass fairways. Except in such areas as the bermudagrass-Kentucky bluegrass transition zone where nothing else will grow, or on courses that have large maintenance budgets, you can save yourself a lot of grief by not planting creeping bentgrass fairways. A fungicide schedule for creeping bentgrass fairways is given in table 11-2.

Maintenance Programs

Irrigation. More water is required for creeping bentgrass fairways than for Kentucky bluegrass ones because the former turfgrass is less drought-tolerant than the latter. Still, excess watering should be avoided whenever possible to prevent the invasion of annual bluegrass.

Mowing Height. Creeping bentgrass fairways should be mowed to a height of ⅝ inch or less.

Fertility. Nitrogen levels in the soil should be kept to a minimum. Excessive nitrogen will only increase susceptibility to diseases and environmental stresses, reduce wear tolerance, and increase the amount of thatch. The latter effect could lead to serious scalping problems, and high nitrogen levels will also favor the development of annual bluegrass. Phosphorus concentrations should be kept low, and potassium should be maintained at a concentration determined to be adequate by yearly soil tests. Nitrogen fertility schedules for creeping bentgrass turfs are given in tables 11-1, 11-3, and 11-8.

Cultural Practices. Creeping bentgrass fairways need all the cultural practices that creeping bentgrass greens and tees receive except topdressing, and they really need that—it is just that the cost is prohibitive. Coring should be done two to three times per year, and should be followed by dragging with a heavy steel mat to break up the cores and incorporate the soil into the thatch. The turf should then be swept in order to remove surface debris. Fairways should be vertically mowed two or three times in a season, and this should be followed by sweeping to collect the debris. This practice will help to keep the thatch at a reduced and manageable level; it will also reduce the puffiness associated with bentgrass fairways and prevent scalping during hot weather.

Annual Bluegrass

You can't buy it anywhere. Nobody admits they have it. And yet it makes up 70 to 80 percent of golf course fairways that are over ten years old in the middle and northern regions of the cool-season turfgrass belt. Some people have successfully gotten rid of it, most have not, many have lost their jobs trying to get rid of it, and the smart ones have learned how to live with it. We are talking about "poa"—*Poa annua*, or annual bluegrass.

Annual bluegrass makes a fine fairway turf. It can take a ½ inch mowing height and affords the golfer an upright lie. It does not, as was believed for many years, die from high-temperature stress in the northern and middle regions of the cool-season grass belt. It will die in the summer during periods of heat stress if diseases and insect problems are not controlled.

The basic problem that one encounters in growing annual bluegrass is the lack of information about its cultural requirements and pest problems. It was long treated as a weed, and no research was done on it per se. People therefore tried to adapt management practices appropriate to Kentucky bluegrass and creeping bentgrass to the growing of annual bluegrass. This resulted in two big mistakes. Firstly, anthracnose and the black turfgrass *Ataenius* beetle are not problems on Kentucky bluegrass and creeping bentgrass (at least in the middle and northern regions of the cool-season grassbelt), but they are problems on annual bluegrass (see fig. 11-2). Die-off caused by anthracnose and the *Ataenius* beetle was wrongly attributed to the effects of high temperature. Secondly, although Kentucky bluegrass and creeping bentgrass do well without summer fertilization (in some cases the application of excess nitrogen during the summer actually leads to severe disease problems in these turfgrasses), this is not the case with annual bluegrass. Annual bluegrass requires light applications of nitrogen fertilizer (½ pound per 1000 square feet per month; see tables 11-3 and 11-5) to best survive the summer. More research needs to be done on annual bluegrass and its unique requirements, but to maintain it in the meantime one must stop using cultural and pest-control programs that were developed for Kentucky bluegrass and creeping bentgrass.

Annual bluegrass unfortunately does not confine itself to fairways, where it is acceptable. It also grows on greens and tees. In my opinion it is not a major problem on tees, but it can be a nuisance on greens during certain times of the year. It is a problem on greens in the spring when seedheads form and reduce putting quality, but it is a serious problem only for a few weeks.

Po-San, Dacthal, and Balan notwithstanding, there is not now any satisfactory chemical means of eradicating annual bluegrass or of preventing it from invading a green, tee,

Figure 11–2. Fairway thinned by black turfgrass *Ataenius* beetle. The areas of damage are well defined, whereas damage caused by HAS decline is more general and usually affects the entire fairway.

or fairway. The ultimate solution for greens and tees may be more-aggressive bentgrass that will crowd out the annual bluegrass. For now, the good cultural practices that favor creeping bentgrass over annual bluegrass should be used on lighter soils, and especially on sandy ones. It may be futile to try to prevent invasions by annual bluegrass on the really heavy soils.

Diseases

Annual bluegrass is susceptible to *Sclerotinia* dollar spot, *Helminthosporium* leaf spot, *Rhizoctonia* brown patch, *Pythium* blight, *Corticium* red thread, anthracnose, *Typhula* blight, HAS decline, and *Fusarium* patch. It contracts all of the major diseases that affect creeping bentgrass and is susceptible also to anthracnose and HAS decline. It is the latter disease, and not the heat alone, that kills annual bluegrass during hot weather (see pp. 26-27). Annual bluegrass also has problems with two insect pests. One of these is a small grub called black turfgrass *Ataenius (Ataenius spirtules)*; the other is the turfgrass weevil, which causes annual bluegrass to thin and die during hot weather. For a fungicide treatment schedule, see tables 11-4 and 11-6.

Maintenance Programs

Irrigation. The one thing that will encourage the infestation of Kentucky bluegrass and creeping bentgrass turfs by annual bluegrass is excessive irrigation. The same practice will help to maintain annual bluegrass if good drainage is provided. Heavy, infrequent irrigation in the spring will help to encourage deep root penetration. Light, frequent irrigation, including syringing, may be necessary to maintain annual bluegrass during warm weather.

Mowing Height. Annual bluegrass should be mowed to a height of ½ to ⅝ inch.

Fertility. High rates of application of nitrogen over a season will favor annual bluegrass over most creeping bentgrass and Kentucky bluegrass cultivars. However, excess nitrogen that leads to lush growth should be avoided because it favors the development of disease. High levels of phosphorus (P_2O_5) help to maintain good annual bluegrass fairways. A nitrogen fertility schedule for annual bluegrass is given in tables 11-3 and 11-5.

Cultural Practices. Annual bluegrass fairways require very little cultivation except where calcium arsenate eradication programs have been used, and where chlordane has been used for insect control. Excessive amounts of thatch may have accumulated where these products have been used, and it may require years of coring and vertical mowing to alleviate the problem. Coring once or twice a year should be all the cultivation that is required on annual bluegrass fairways that have no pesticide-induced thatch problem.

The Fine-Leaf Fescues

The fine-leaf fescues will make a turf suitable for unirrigated fairways in cool climates on sandy soils. What other weedy grasses are going to replace them under such a cultural regime? Some broadleaf weed control will have to be practiced, since many of these weeds can survive under such conditions of drought stress, but no other turfgrass species are as suitable as the fine-leaf fescues for unirrigated fairways. It should be kept in mind that we are not talking about soft, lush green fairways. We are talking about fairways that will be almost a soft, lush green in spring and fall, but during the summer months they will be hard and brown. A real artist with an irrigation system may be able to keep them slightly green in the summer, but hardly soft and lush. Attempts to keep them soft and lush will quickly turn a fine-leaf fescue fairway into a not-so-fine-leafed annual bluegrass fairway.

The fine-leaf fescues will compete better with annual bluegrass on lighter soils, especially sandy ones. On the really heavy soils, it may be futile to attempt to keep out annual bluegrass.

Diseases

The fine-leaf fescues are susceptible to *Helminthosporium* leaf spot, net blotch, anthracnose, *Sclerotinia* dollar spot, *Corticium* red thread, and rust.

Maintenance Programs

Irrigation. If fine-leaf fescue fairways are to survive, they must receive as little water as possible. They should be watered only when severe drought stress is evident (when the grass plants show signs of wilt). They should be watered deeply, and not irrigated again until severe drought stress reappears.

Fertility. One of the nice things about fine-leaf fescues is that they will survive very well with the application of as little as 1 pound of actual nitrogen per 1000 square feet per season. If only 1 pound of nitrogen per 1000 square feet is to be applied, the ideal time to apply it is in late summer or early in the fall when the cool weather returns and the grass begins to grow vigorously again.

Cultural Practices. The only cultural practice that should be necessary on a fine-leaf fescue fairway is coring when and where compaction is a problem.

The Kentucky Bluegrasses

Many people who are unhappy with their annual bluegrass fairways want to replace them with Kentucky bluegrass, thinking that all their problems will be solved. What they are in fact doing is trading one set of problems for another. More specifically, they are trading *Sclerotinia* dollar spot, *Helminthosporium* leaf spot, anthracnose, and the black turfgrass *Ataenius* beetle for stripe smut, *Fusarium* blight, *Helminthosporium* melting-out, and bluegrass billbug. This is not to say that annual bluegrass fairways are superior to Kentucky bluegrass fairways. They both have their good and bad points, and they each require a management regimen that should not be imposed on the other species. The main point to be made is that all of your fairway maintenance problems won't be solved by switching from annual bluegrass to Kentucky bluegrass. The Kentucky bluegrass cultivars which have the best chance of surviving as fairway turf are Touchdown, Brunswick, and Bensun. They should be mowed to a minimum height of 1 inch and watered as little as possible.

Diseases

Kentucky bluegrasses are susceptible to *Helminthosporium* melting-out, *Helminthosporium* leaf spot, *Fusarium* blight, stripe smut, *Fusarium* patch, *Typhula* blight, stem rust, and leaf rust.

Maintenance Programs

Irrigation. Kentucky bluegrass fairways should be watered sparingly, and good drainage should be provided.

Mowing Height. Kentucky bluegrass fairways should be mowed to a height of 1 inch or more.

Fertility. Kentucky bluegrass fairways should receive 3 to 4 pounds of actual nitrogen per 1000 square feet per season; the exact amount that should be applied varies with geographic location. Three pounds per 1000 square feet should be applied in parts of the cool-season grassbelt where the growing season is short, and 4 pounds per 1000 square feet should be applied where the growing season is longer. Typical nitrogen fertility programs for each region are given in tables 12-1 and 12-2. There is nothing magical about these programs, and following one of them to the letter will not guarantee you a disease-free fairway. The fertility programs are an attempt to give a new golf course superintendent, or one who is having disease problems, or one who simply is not satisfied with his current nitrogen fertility program, something with which to begin. They are not absolute programs that must be followed exactly.

The programs must be adjusted for soil type, with more nitrogen and more frequent applications thereof necessary on sandy soil than on heavier silt and clay soil. Also, the nitrogen fertility programs for golf courses that are located near large bodies of water, or at higher elevations will need adjustments for climatic variation within the various growing-season zones.

A nitrogen fertility program will work best if the most disease-resistant cultivars that can compete with annual bluegrass at a 1-inch height of cut are used. However, the most dramatic disease reduction may be seen in disease-susceptible cultivars, even though some disease still will be present. The recommended programs are designed not only to supply nitrogen to the grass plant when it is needed, but also to help reduce the severity of *Helminthosporium* melting-out, *Fusarium* blight, and stripe smut, and to manage *Sclerotinia* dollar spot, *Corticium* red thread, and stem and leaf rust.

Cultural Practices. Vertical mowing is normally not required, although coring should be done once or twice a season. Kentucky bluegrass fairways normally will not develop excess thatch unless excessive nitrogen has been used or insecticides have destroyed the earthworm population. Vertical mowing will be required where thatch is a problem, and it will be necessary to collect and dispose of the verdure, mat, and thatch that is removed. These cultural operations should be performed after the annual bluegrass has germinated in the spring and before it begins to germinate in the fall. Making voids in a Kentucky bluegrass turf at the wrong time can allow invasion by annual bluegrass.

Perennial Ryegrass

Perennial ryegrasses have the potential of being a fourth turfgrass species for use in fairway turf; the principal difficulty in so using them is a lack of research. One of the first things that must be done is to determine the differential competitive abilities of the many perennial ryegrass cultivars vis-à-vis other grasses, especially when low mowing heights are used. (Turgeon and Vargas [142] showed that Pennfine perennial ryegrass is more competitive with the Kentucky bluegrasses than is Citation perennial ryegrass. One can extrapolate from these data to predict that Pennfine will be the more competitive with annual bluegrass as well.) More research is needed also on the environmental adaptability, fertility requirements, pest problems, and other cultural requirements of the perennial ryegrasses.

The perennial ryegrasses, at least the vigorous ones, have an advantage over Kentucky bluegrass and creeping bentgrass where overseeding into established annual bluegrass turf is desired. Because of their ability to become established in existing mature turfs, the perennial ryegrasses can be overseeded annually, much as annual bluegrass does naturally. In fact, annual overseeding probably will become a part of perennial ryegrass cultural systems for golf course fairways.

It is becoming more and more evident that one of the failures of Kentucky bluegrass and creeping bentgrass is that the plants simply become old. This is not a very scientific explanation for what happens, but it is similar to people dying of old age. Annual bluegrass turfs continually regenerate themselves from seed as voids in the turf occur, and thus they never really become "old." The only real alternative to annual bluegrass fairways may be annual or semiannual reseeding with perennial ryegrass and a cultural system that favors the perennial ryegrasses over annual bluegrass.*

WARM–SEASON GRASSES—OVERSEEDING

There are two growing seasons for turfgrasses in the southern United States—the warm-grass season and the overseeding season. During the overseeding season, cool-season grass is overseeded into bermudagrass greens, tees, and fairways when they go dormant and discolor in the cool weather. The major diseases of cool-season grasses were discussed earlier: diseases that occur on overseeded grasses will be considered here.

Bermudagrasses are dormant during the fall and winter in most of the southern United States, but golf is played year-round in most of that region. Therefore, the greens, tees, and (sometimes) the fairways are overseeded. Overseeding of greens is done to provide a smooth putting surface, provide green color, and prevent excessive wear of the dormant bermudagrass. On the tees, active growth is required for recovery from injury and also for preventing excessive wear of the dormant bermudagrass. Fairway overseeding is expensive; it usually is used sparingly. Greens are seeded heavily, tees less so, and fairways least heavily of all.

Several grasses, including Italian ryegrass, perennial ryegrass, Kentucky bluegrass, bentgrasses, the fine-leaf fescues, and rough bluegrass, are used to overseed dormant bermudagrass turfs; the most commonly used are the improved turf-type perennial ryegrasses.† Overseeding can be started while the daytime temperatures are still in the 80s, and in some areas such temperatures can be accompanied by high humidity. Frequent irrigation also is used to help establish the overseeded grass. All of the above conditions favor the development of *Pythium* blight (cottony blight), and these diseases can cause severe losses of the young, tender perennial ryegrass seedlings. There also are cold-temperature pythiums that can attack the turf at lower temperatures. When conditions are favorable for the development of *Pythium* blight, the overseeded greens should be treated with Terrazole or chloroneb.

Disease problems also arise if species other than perennial ryegrass are used for overseeding. *Helminthosporium* melting-out and *Fusarium* blight can be problems on the Kentucky bluegrasses, and *Helminthosporium* leaf spot and *Helminthosporium* brown blight can be problems on the fine-leaf fescues and perennial ryegrass, respectively. *Rhizoctonia* brown patch and *Helminthosporium* leaf spot are problems on rough bluegrass, and *Sclerotinia* dollar spot, *Rhizoctonia* brown patch, *Helminthosporium* leaf spot, and *Pythium* blight are problems on overseeded creeping bentgrass.

---

*Perennial ryegrass does not produce rhizomes or stolons and therefore cannot fill in voids left by divots, mechanical injury, or disease. Annual bluegrass will probably fill such voids.

†Typical seeding rates on greens are 2 to 3 pounds per 1000 square feet for creeping bentgrass, 35 to 40 pounds per 1000 square feet for perennial ryegrass, 20 to 25 pounds per 1000 square feet for fine-leaf fescues, and 10 to 12 pounds per 1000 square feet for Kentucky bluegrass. Tees are seeded at ½ to ⅔ of these rates, and fairways at ¼ to ⅓ of them.

Overseeding Bermudagrass Greens

1. Verticut the greens lightly in at least two directions to open up the turf. Be sure to remove debris by mowing at the regularly maintained height of cut.

2. Use only the highest quality seed available, and mixtures or blends of the better turfgrass species and cultivars. Calibrate the seeder to apply the seed at one-half of the regular seeding rate, then apply the seed uniformly in at least two different directions.

3. The seed can be worked into the bermudagrass turf with a drag mat made of either burlap or steel.

4. Topdress lightly with ¼ to ⅛ inch of sand.

5. Drag the top dressing lightly into the turf.

6. Water the greens carefully to prevent any movement of seed. Watering at too heavy a rate will float the seed to the surface and cause uneven seedling establishment.

7. Water the greens daily to keep the moisture content constant during this critical period. A midday application usually is more useful, and greens watered then are not as likely to get *Pythium* blight or damping-off as are greens that are watered at night.

8. Play can continue, but be sure to move the cups daily to cut down on any uneven wear.

9. Grass must be cut high (at least ¼ inch) until seedlings can become established. Be sure that the mower is sharp, and don't use the grass catcher during the first few mowings. Try to mow when the grass is dry.

10. Do not overfertilize with nitrogen at overseeding time because this will tend to encourage unwanted bermudagrass competition and the development of *Pythium* blight. Wait until the seedlings have become established before fertilizing, and water immediately after each fertilizer application.

11. Maintain a constant watch for the development of *Pythium* blight, or apply fungicides on a preventive basis.

WARM–SEASON GRASSES—GREENS

Creeping Bentgrass

The discussion of creeping bentgrasses in the cool-season turfgrass region (pp. 134-136) applies here also. Creeping bentgrasses are used on a permanent basis on golf courses in the northern and middle regions of the warm climatic zone, and as overseeded grasses in the more southerly regions.

Recommended Cultivars

Penncross, Cohansey, and Seaside are good choices for golf course greens. (These recommendations are discussed on p. 134.)

Diseases

Sclerotina dollar spot, *Rhizoctonia* brown patch, *Pythium* blight, *Helminthosporium* leaf spot, and red leaf spot may require fungicide treatment. (See table 11-7 for fungicide recommendations.) It should be kept in mind that *Rhizoctonia* brown patch and *Pythium* blight will be more severe in the warm climatic zone than in the cool-season turfgrass region.

Maintenance Programs

Fertility. The maximum amount of nitrogen that is required in the northern parts of the warm climatic zone is 4 to 5 pounds per 1000 square feet. Farther south, where creeping bentgrass grows for 10 to 12 months a year, the maximum amount of nitrogen that normally is required is 5 to 7 pounds per 1000 square feet. The actual amount of nitrogen that is needed by a given turf will depend upon the texture of the soil. I strongly encourage using nitrogen fertilizer on the basis of "pounds per growing month." However, the less nitrogen that can be used to maintain dense turf, the less severe the major disease problems will be. Adequate levels of phosphorous and potassium, as determined by soil tests, should be maintained (see table 11-8).

Cultural Practices. These are the same as those for cool-season creeping bentgrasses. A well-drained, coarse-textured soil for the root zone is even more critical for creeping bentgrass in the warm climatic zone than it is in the cool-season turfgrass region.

Bermudagrass

The improved fine-leaf bermudagrasses are the preferred turfgrasses for golf course greens in the southern portion of the warm climatic zone where it is simply too hot and humid to maintain creeping bentgrass.

Recommended Cultivars

All fine-leaf bermudagrasses are propagated vegetatively. The cultivars that are best for use on golf course greens are Tifgreen and Tifdwarf. Both have excellent low-temperature hardiness and minimal seedhead formation [4].

Diseases

Spring dead spot (SDS) is potentially the most devastating disease on bermudagrass greens, but fortunately it has seldom been a problem. This is probably because greens receive routine fungicide applications for other diseases. Wilcoxen [159] demonstrated SDS control on fairways with three or four treatments of Daconil 2787 or Actidione-Thiram during the previous season.

Bermudagrass is susceptible also to *Sclerotinia* dollar spot, *Rhizoctonia* brown patch, *Helminthosporium* diseases, and *Pythium* blight. These diseases are not as great a problem as they are on creeping bentgrass, but bermudagrass is susceptible enough that a preventive fungicide program may have to be followed. Bermudagrasses grown in the hot, arid regions have very few turfgrass diseases (see table 11-9).

Maintenance Programs

Mowing Height. The fine-leaf bermudagrasses should be mowed to a height of ⅛ to ¼ inch.

Fertility. Bermudagrass greens, unlike creeping bentgrass greens, don't grow all winter in most areas of the warm climatic zone. As a consequence, the fertility schedule for bermudagrass is different from that for creeping bentgrass (see table 11-10). Nitrogen fertility should be avoided during late summer and early fall to reduce the severity of spring dead spot where it occurs. Phosphorus and potassium should be maintained at adequate levels as determined by soil tests.

Cultural Practices. Bermudagrass greens require the same type of cultural system as do creeping bentgrass greens. This system includes coring to relieve compaction, vertical mowing to remove graininess and thatch, and topdressing to reduce thatch and provide a smooth putting surface. Irrigation should be done as needed to prevent wilt. The quantity of water applied is not as critical as it is with creeping bentgrass greens, where overwatering often leads to the invasion of annual bluegrass. Annual bluegrass behaves as a true winter annual in the warmer parts of the climatic zone, and it will not survive the summer heat. The herbicide Kerb will provide selective control of annual bluegrass in bermudagrass turfs, although proper timing in its application and the use of charcoal may be needed if the greens are overseeded in the winter.

WARM–SEASON GRASSES—TEES

Bermudagrass

Recommended Cultivars

The cultivars Tifway, Tifgreen, Ormond, Santa Anna, and PeeDee are recommended for use on tees.

Diseases

See the discussion of diseases on bermudagrass greens.

Maintenance Programs

Mowing Height. Bermudagrass tees should be mowed to a height of ¼ to ½ inch.
Fertility. The fertility requirements of bermudagrass tees are the same as those of bermudagrass greens.
Cultural Practices. The cultural practices employed for bermudagrass greens should also be applied to bermudagrass tees. In addition, divot holes on the tees should be filled with soil.

Zoysiagrass

Zoysiagrass can be used on tees. However, it is slow to recuperate from damage, and probably should not be planted in areas where intensive use is anticipated. It posesses superior wear tolerance, but openings are slow to heal. On par-3 holes, where irons frequently are used, the zoysiagrass might be replaced by weedy grasses in the bare spots.

Recommended Cultivars

The cultivars FC13521, Emerald, Meyer, and Midwest are recommended for use on tees.

Diseases

Zoysiagrass is susceptible to *Sclerotinia* dollar spot, *Helminthosporium* crown and root rot, rust, and *Rhizoctonia* brown patch.

Maintenance Programs

Fertility. Zoysiagrass tees should receive 2 to 4 pounds of nitrogen per 1000 square feet. For best disease management, the nitrogen should be applied close to the times indicated on table 11-11. Phosphorus and potassium should be maintained at adequate levels as determined by soil tests.

Cultural Practices. Zoysiagrass tees should receive the same cultural practices as do bermudagrass greens, plus filling of divot holes with soil, and possibly even spot plugging.

WARM–SEASON GRASSES—FAIRWAYS

Bermudagrass

Diseases

Bermudagrass fairways are probably the finest fairways off which to play a golf shot. Bermudagrass is the preferred turfgrass species for golf course fairways in the short-dormancy areas of the warm-season grassbelt and, if it were not for spring dead spot (SDS; see fig. 11-3), it would be the choice throughout the climatic zone. But because of spring dead spot many superintendents are looking at the feasibility of zoysiagrass as a fairway turf, at least in the northern part of the warm-season grassbelt and in the transition zone. All the varieties of bermudagrass, with the possible exception of Mid-iron, are suscepti-ble to SDS when they are grown in areas where bermudagrass goes dormant. The longer the dormant period the more serious the SDS problem is. Wilcoxen's work suggests that it may be possible to grow SDS-free bermudagrass if one applies Daconil 2787 or Acti-dione Thiram during the growing season [159]. The cost of such a program would be $6,000 to $10,000 per year. That is a small price to pay for beautiful bermudagrass fairways. It is also a lot cheaper than renovating the fairway every 5 to 6 years. Bermudagrass also is suscepti-

Figure 11–3 Spring dead spot on a golf course tee (Photograph courtesy of Dr. Bill Small)

ble to *Sclerotinia* dollar spot, *Rhizoctonia* brown patch, *Helminthosporium* diseases, and *Pythium* blight. The severity of each disease depends upon the area in which the bermudagrass is grown, but in general disease pressure is greater in the warm humid climatic zones than in the semiarid and arid zones. In comparison to spring dead spot, these diseases can be controlled relatively easily. The times of year when the diseases are most prevalent and when applications of fungicides should be made are given in table 11-9.

Recommended Cultivars

The cultivars Tifway (T-419), Midiron, and U-3 are suitable for use on fairways.

Maintenance Programs

Mowing Height. Bermudagrass fairways should be mowed to a height of ½ to 1 inch.

Fertility. See table 11-10.

Cultural Practices. The cultural program for bermudagrass fairways is the same as that for bermudagrass greens, except topdressing should be omitted because it is too expensive. However, vertical mowing for thatch removal is necessary, especially for some of the more aggressive improved cultivars.

Zoysiagrass

Zoysiagrass may turn out to be the ideal grass species for golf course fairways in the transition zone and in cool regions of the warm-season grassbelt. It has few major diseases at the present time. Many golf course superintendents who have lost their bermudagrass fairways year after year to spring dead spot are trying zoysiagrass on their fairways. At the present time the amount of documented research data is simply too small to allow any conclusions to be drawn.

Zoysiagrass is a slow-growing species. It therefore often is sold to the homeowner on the basis of its requiring less mowing than do other species. This same "good" quality on a homelawn can be an undesirable characteristic on a golf course fairway because zoysiagrass injured mechanically or by disease, or worn by traffic, will be slow to recover. This will leave voids in the turf that may be filled by weeds.

It will take a minimum of 10 years to determine which species, bermudagrass or zoysiagrass, and which cultivars within those species are best adapted for golf course fairways in the northern and middle regions of the warm-season grassbelt and the transition zone.

Zoysiagrass fairways are established vegetatively with either plugs or sprigs (stolons). Sprigs are preferable because they are less expensive to buy and because they can be spread less expensively and more quickly than can plugs. The sprigs should not be completely buried because they will die unless some leaf material remains above the ground. The other important thing to remember when establishing zoysiagrass sprigs is to keep them moist for the first two weeks after establishment. If they become dry they will die.

Diseases

Zoysiagrass is susceptible to *Helminthosporium* crown and root rot, rust, *Rhizoctonia* brown patch, and *Sclerotinia* dollar spot, but the data on the severity of these diseases and on cultivar resistance are sketchy. It would appear at the present time that zoysiagrass rust is the most important disease. As zoysiagrass is more widely grown, more information on the susceptibility of the species to the common turfgrass diseases will become available. See table 11-12 for a fungicide schedule.

Maintenance Programs

Irrigation. Zoysiagrass fairways should be watered infrequently after they are established.

Mowing Height. Zoysiagrass fairways should be mowed to a height of ¾ to 1 inch.

Fertility. The application of 2 to 4 pounds of actual nitrogen per 1000 square feet per season is recommended. See table 11-11.

Cultural Practices. Zoysiagrass can develop a heavy thatch. It will require vertical mowing and coring, with return of the cores, to keep the level of thatch to a minimum.

Buffalograss

Buffalograss is the fine-leaf fescue of the warm-season grasses. Unfortunately, little attempt has been made to develop improved cultivars, as has been done with the fine-leaf fescues. In spite of this, buffalograss is what persists on nonirrigated fairways in the more arid areas of the warm-season grassbelt. Buffalograss requires little water and nitrogen fertility; as a matter of fact, the quickest way to eliminate buffalograss is to irrigate it and fertilize with nitrogen.

Recommended Cultivars

There are no buffalograss cultivars that can be recommended at the present time.

Maintenance Programs

Irrigation. Buffalograss requires little or no supplemental irrigation.

Mowing Height. Buffalograss fairways should be mowed to a height of ¾ to 1 inch.

Fertility. Buffalograss fairways should receive 1 to 2 pounds of nitrogen per 1000 square feet per season.

Cultural Practices. No cultural program has been developed for buffalograss.

(Tables 11-1 through 11-12 follow.)

Table 11-1. Nitrogen Schedule for Creeping Bentgrass Turfs in the Cool Humid Climatic Zone (Zone 1)
(Pounds of actual nitrogen per 1000 square feet)

	Apr.	May	June	July	Aug.	Sept.	Oct.	Nov.	Dec.
Southern region									
High maintenance		½	½	½	½	½			1 (dormant)
Low maintenance		½	½	½		½			1 (dormant)
Diseases	Fusarium patch	Leaf spot	Brown patch	Pythium blight		Leaf spot	Fusarium patch	Typhula blight	
Middle region									
High maintenance			½	½	½	½		1 (dormant)	
Low maintenance			½	½	½	½		1 (dormant)	
Diseases	Fusarium patch		Leaf spot / Brown patch	Pythium blight	Leaf spot		Fusarium patch / Typhula blight		
Northern region									
High maintenance			½	½	½			1 (dormant)	
Low maintenance			½	½	½			1 (dormant)	
Diseases	Fusarium patch		Leaf spot	Brown patch / Pythium blight		Fusarium patch			

Notes: Climatic zones are shown on the map in the Appendix (fig. A-1).

The time period shown for each disease indicates when nitrogen application will make the disease worse and is not necessarily the time when the disease occurs.

This schedule of nitrogen application is designed to help manage *Sclerotinia* dollar spot. It is based on fertilization with water-soluble nitrogen. If insoluble or slow-release nitrogen is used, application can be less frequent, but since the release of nitrogen is affected by many variables (e.g., soil type, soil moisture, organic matter, weather) it is impossible to make up a general schedule.

152

Table 11-2. Fungicide Schedule for Creeping Bentgrass Greens, Tees, and Fairways in the Cool Humid Climatic Zone (Zone 1)

	Mar. 1	Mar. 15	Apr. 1	Apr. 15	May 1	May 15	June 1	June 15	July 1	July 15	Aug. 1	Aug. 15	Sept. 1	Sept. 15	Oct. 1	Oct. 15	Nov. 1	Nov. 15	Dec. 1	Dec. 15	Jan. 1	Jan. 15	Feb. 1	Feb. 15
Southern region																								
High maintenance			NS	NS		S		NS	NS / P	NS S / P	S / P	P	NS	NS	NS	NS	NS	NS						
Low maintenance			NS		NS		S		NS	NS S	NS S		NS		NS		NS							

Diseases (Southern region):
- Fusarium patch — Mar.
- Typhula blight — Mar.
- Leaf spot — May 15–June
- Dollar spot — May 15–June
- Brown patch — June–July
- Pythium blight — July–Aug.
- Leaf spot — Aug.–Sept.
- Dollar spot — Sept.–Oct.
- Fusarium patch — Dec.–Jan.
- Typhula blight — Jan.–Feb.

	Mar. 1	Mar. 15	Apr. 1	Apr. 15	May 1	May 15	June 1	June 15	July 1	July 15	Aug. 1	Aug. 15	Sept. 1	Sept. 15	Oct. 1	Oct. 15	Nov. 1	Nov. 15	Dec. 1	Dec. 15	Jan. 1	Jan. 15	Feb. 1	Feb. 15
Middle region																								
High maintenance				NS	NS	NS	S		NS	NS S / P	S / P		NS	NS	NS	NS	NS							
Low maintenance				NS	NS		S		NS	NS	S		NS		NS	NS								

Diseases (Middle region):
- Fusarium patch — Mar.
- Typhula blight — Mar.
- Leaf spot — June
- Dollar spot — June
- Brown patch — July–Aug.
- Dollar spot — Aug.–Sept.
- Pythium blight — Aug.
- Fusarium patch — Oct.–Nov.
- Typhula blight — Dec.–Jan.

Key: NS = nonsystemic fungicide, S = systemic fungicide (benzimidazole), P = *Pythium* blight fungicide.

Notes: Climatic zones are shown on the map in the Appendix (fig. A-1).

The time period shown for each disease is the time when the disease actually occurs.

Application of *Pythium* blight fungicides may be discontinued if the weather becomes cool, but should be resumed immediately when warm weather returns, especially when the nighttime temperature is above 70 °F.

153

Table 11-2. *Continued*

	Mar. 1	15	Apr. 1	15	May 1	15	June 1	15	July 1	15	Aug. 1	15	Sept. 1	15	Oct. 1	15	Nov. 1	15	Dec. 1	15	Jan. 1	15	Feb. 1	15
Northern region																								
High maintenance					NS	NS			S	NS	S		NS	NS	NS	NS								
Low maintenance					NS				S	NS	S		NS	NS	NS									
Diseases																								
Leaf spot									Leaf spot															
Dollar spot								Dollar spot																
Brown patch											Brown patch													
Fusarium patch			Fusarium patch										Fusarium patch											
Typhula blight			Typhula blight															Typhula blight						

Table 11-3. Nitrogen Schedule for Creeping Bentgrass and Annual Bluegrass in the Cool Oceanic Climatic Zone (Zone 6)
(Pounds of actual nitrogen per 1000 square feet)

	Apr. 1	Apr. 20	May 1	May 20	June 1	June 20	July 1	July 20	Aug. 1	Aug. 20	Sept. 1	Sept. 20
High maintenance	½		½		½		½		½		½	
Low maintenance		½			½				½		½	
Diseases	*Fusarium* patch				Leaf spot			Brown patch			*Fusarium* patch	

Notes: Climatic zones are shown on the map in the Appendix (fig. A-1).

The time period shown for each disease indicates when nitrogen application will make the disease worse and is not necessarily the time when the disease occurs.

This schedule of nitrogen application is designed to help manage *Sclerotinia* dollar spot and anthracnose. It is based on fertilization with water-soluble nitrogen. If insoluble or slow-release nitrogen is used, application can be less frequent, but since the release of nitrogen is affected by many variables (e.g., soil type, soil moisture, organic matter, weather) it is impossible to make up a general schedule.

155

Table 11-4. Fungicide Schedule for Annual Bluegrass Greens, Tees, and Fairways in the Cool Humid Climatic Zone (Zone 1)

	Mar. 15	Apr. 1	Apr. 15	May 1	May 15	June 1	June 15	July 1	July 15	Aug. 1	Aug. 15	Sept. 1	Sept. 15	Oct. 1	Oct. 15	Nov. 1	Nov. 15	Dec. 1	Dec. 15	Jan. 1	Jan. 15
Southern region																					
High maintenance			NS	NS	NS	NS	NS	S P	NS P	S P	P	NS	NS	NS	NS						
Low maintenance						NS	NS	S	NS	S		NS	NS								
Diseases		Fusarium patch		Dollar spot		HAS decline		Brown patch — Pythium blight				Dollar spot									
Middle region																					
High maintenance				NS		NS	NS	S P	S P	S P	S	NS	NS	NS							
Low maintenance							NS	NS	S	NS		NS	NS								
Diseases	Fusarium patch / Typhula blight					Dollar spot — HAS decline		Brown patch — Pythium blight							Fusarium patch		Fusarium patch				Typhula blight

Northern region
High maintenance
Low maintenance

Diseases

NS NS NS NS NS NS S NS NS
        NS NS NS S NS NS
                    P
Fusarium patch
Typhula blight
Dollar spot
HAS decline
Brown patch
Pythium blight
Fusarium patch
Typhula blight

Key: NS = nonsystemic fungicide, S = systemic fungicide (benzimidazole), P = *Pythium* blight fungicide.

Notes: Climatic zones are shown on the map in the Appendix (fig. A-1).

The time period shown for each disease is the time when the disease actually occurs.

Pythium blight fungicides should be applied in the southern region after two continuous days of daytime temperatures greater than 85 °F, high humidity, and nighttime temperatures above 70 °F. In the middle and northern regions the *Pythium* blight fungicides should be applied at the first sign of the disease, and in areas of the golf course where *Pythium* blight is known to occur they should be applied under the same conditions as in the southern region.

157

Table 11-5. Nitrogen Schedule for Annual Bluegrass Greens, Tees, and Fairways in the Cool Humid Climatic Zone (Zone 1) (Pounds of actual nitrogen per 1000 square feet)

	Apr. 1	Apr. 15	May 1	May 15	June 1	June 15	July 1	July 15	Aug. 1	Aug. 15	Sept. 1	Sept. 15	Oct. 1	Oct. 15	Nov. 1	Nov. 15	Dec. 1	Dec. 15
Southern region																		
High maintenance				½		½		½		½		1						1 (dormant)
Low maintenance						½						1						1 (dormant)
Diseases	Fusarium patch →				Brown patch →		Pythium blight →								Fusarium patch →			
Middle region																		
High maintenance						½		½		½		1				1 (dormant)		
Low maintenance						½						1				1 (dormant)		
Diseases	Fusarium patch →				Brown patch →		Pythium blight →						Fusarium patch →					
													Typhula blight →					
Northern region																		
High maintenance						½		½		1					1 (dormant)			
Low maintenance						½				1					1 (dormant)			
Diseases	Fusarium patch →						Brown patch →				Fusarium patch →							
							Pythium blight →						Typhula blight →					

Notes: Climatic zones are shown on the map in the Appendix (fig. A-1).

The time period shown for each disease indicates when nitrogen application will make the disease worse and is not necessarily the time when the disease occurs.

This schedule of nitrogen application is designed to help manage *Sclerotinia* dollar spot and HAS decline. It is based on fertilization with water-soluble nitrogen. If insoluble or slow-release nitrogen is used, application can be less frequent, but since the release of nitrogen is affected by many variables (e.g., soil type, soil moisture, organic matter, weather) it is impossible to make up a general schedule.

Table 11-6. Fungicide Schedule for the Cool Oceanic Climatic Zone (Zone 6)

	Apr. 1	15	May 1	15	June 1	15	July 1	15	Aug. 1	15	Sept. 1	15	Oct. 1	15	Nov. 1	15	Dec. 1	15	Jan. 1	15	Feb. 1	15	Mar. 1	15
Creeping bentgrass and annual bluegrass																								
High maintenance	NS	NS	NS	S		NS	NS	S		NS	NS	NS	S		NS	NS		S	NS	NS	S		NS	NS
Low maintenance		NS		S		NS		S		NS	S			NS		NS		S		NS	NS		S	
Diseases		*Fusarium* patch				Leaf spot					*Fusarium* patch													
						HAS decline																		
Kentucky bluegrass																								
High maintenance	NS	NS	NS	NS			(S)	S		NS	NS	NS	S		NS	NS		NS	NS	NS	NS	NS	NS	NS
Low maintenance		NS		NS				S		NS	NS			NS		NS		NS		NS	NS		NS	NS
Diseases	*Fusarium* patch									Melting-out			*Fusarium* patch											
	Melting-out																							
	Stripe smut*																							
								Fusarium blight																

Key: NS = nonsystemic fungicide, S = systemic fungicide, (S) = systemic fungicide (benzimidazole), (S) = light application of systemic fungicide. In place of heavy applications of systemic fungicide on S dates, the fungicide can be applied lightly on S and (S) dates.

Notes: Climatic zones are shown on the map in the Appendix (fig. A-1).

The time period shown for each disease is the time when the disease actually occurs.

*Stripe smut is a systemic perennial disease which, in my opinion, cannot be managed with chemicals. For systemic fungicides to be effective in managing stripe smut, they must be applied dormantly in the spring and fall or when lateral plant growth begins in the fall, and drenched in immediately. Such treatments are expensive and, depending on the cultivar, may be futile. The best way to manage stripe smut is to plant resistant cultivars.

159

Table 11-7. Fungicide Schedule for Creeping Bentgrass Greens in the Warm Humid Climatic Zone (Zone 3)

	Mar. 1	15	Apr. 1	15	May 1	15	June 1	15	July 1	15	Aug. 1	15	Sept. 1	15	Oct. 1	15	Nov. 1	15
Northern region High maintenance			NS	NS	S	NS	NS	NS P	NS P	NS P	NS P	S P	NS	NS	NS	NS		
Diseases																		

Diseases (Northern region): Dollar spot (Apr.–May); Leaf spot (May–June); Brown patch (June); Pythium blight (June–July); Leaf spot (Aug.–Sept.); Dollar spot (Sept.–Oct.)

	Mar. 1	15	Apr. 1	15	May 1	15	June 1	15	July 1	15	Aug. 1	15	Sept. 1	15	Oct. 1	15	Nov. 1	15
Middle region High maintenance			NS	NS	S	NS	NS P	NS P	NS P	NS P	NS P	S P	NS	NS	NS	NS	NS	
Diseases																		

Diseases (Middle region): Dollar spot (Apr.–May); Leaf spot (May–June); Brown patch (May–June); Pythium blight (June–July); Leaf spot (Sept.); Dollar spot (Sept.–Oct.)

Key: NS = nonsystemic fungicide, S = systemic fungicide (benzimidazole), P = *Pythium* blight fungicide.

Notes: Climatic zones are shown on the map in the Appendix (fig. A-1).

The time period shown for each disease is the time when the disease actually occurs.

Application of *Pythium* blight fungicides may be discontinued if the weather becomes cool, but should be resumed immediately when warm weather returns, especially when the nighttime temperature is above 70 °F.

160

Table 11-8. Nitrogen Schedule for Creeping Bentgrass Greens in the Warm Humid Climatic Zone (Zone 3)
(Pounds of actual nitrogen per 1000 square feet)

	Apr. 1	Apr. 15	May 1	May 15	June 1	June 15	July 1	July 15	Aug. 1	Aug. 15	Sept. 1	Sept. 15	Oct. 1	Oct. 15	Nov. 1	Nov. 15	Dec. 1	Dec. 15	Jan. 1	Jan. 15
Northern region																				
High maintenance		½	½		½		½			½		½	1							1 (dormant)
Low maintenance		½	½		½		½	¼				½								1 (dormant)
Diseases		Leaf spot				Brown patch			Leaf spot											
						Pythium blight														
Middle region																				
High maintenance		½	½		½		½			½		½		1						1 (dormant)
Low maintenance		½	½		½	¼		¼				½								1 (dormant)
Diseases	Leaf spot			Brown patch							Leaf spot									
				Pythium blight																

Notes: Climatic zones are shown on the map in the Appendix (fig. A-1).

The time period shown for each disease indicates when nitrogen application will make the disease worse and is not necessarily the time when the disease occurs.

This schedule of nitrogen application is designed to help manage *Sclerotinia* dollar spot. It is based on fertilization with water-soluble nitrogen. If insoluble or slow-release nitrogen is used, application can be less frequent, but since the release of nitrogen is affected by many variables (e.g., soil type, soil moisture, organic matter, weather) it is impossible to make up a general schedule.

Table 11-9. Fungicide Schedule for Bermudagrass in the Warm Humid Climatic Zone (Zone 3)

	Mar. 15	Apr. 1	Apr. 15	May 1	May 15	June 1	June 15	July 1	July 15	Aug. 1	Aug. 15	Sept. 1	Sept. 15	Oct. 1	Oct. 15	Nov. 1	Nov. 15
Northern region																	
High maintenance		NS	NS	S	S	NS	NS	NS	NS	NS	S	NS		NS	NS		
Low maintenance		NS	NS	S	S	NS	NS	NS	NS	NS	S			NS	NS		
Diseases	Leaf blotch			Dollar spot	Spring dead spot	Brown patch					Dollar spot						
Middle region																	
High maintenance	NS	NS	S	NS	NS	NS	NS	NS	NS	NS	NS	S		NS	NS	NS	
Low maintenance	NS		S	NS	NS	NS	NS	NS	NS	NS	NS	S		NS	NS	NS	
Diseases	Leaf blotch		Dollar spot		Brown patch		Spring dead spot					Dollar spot					
Southern region																	
High maintenance	NS	NS	S	NS	NS	NS	NS	NS	NS	NS	NS	S	S	NS	NS	NS	NS
Low maintenance	NS	NS	S	NS	NS		NS	NS	NS	NS	NS	S	S	NS	NS	NS	NS
Diseases	Leaf blotch		Dollar spot		Brown patch		Spring dead spot						Dollar spot				

Key: NS = nonsystemic fungicide, S = systemic fungicide (benzimidazole).

Notes: Climatic zones are shown on the map in the Appendix (fig. A-1).

The time period shown for each disease is the time when the disease actually occurs.

Table 11-10. Nitrogen Schedule for Bermudagrass Turfs in the Warm Humid Climate Zone (Zone 3)
(Pounds of actual nitrogen per 1000 square feet)

	Mar. 1	Mar. 15	Apr. 1	Apr. 15	May 1	May 15	June 1	June 15	July 1	July 15	Aug. 1	Aug. 15	Sept. 1	Sept. 15	Oct. 1	Oct. 15	Nov. 1	Nov. 15
Northern region																		
High maintenance			½	½	½	½	½	½	½	½								
Low maintenance				½			½			½								
Diseases	Leaf blotch																	
						Brown patch												
								Pythium blight										
												Spring dead spot						
Middle region																		
High maintenance		½	½	½	½	½	½	½	½	½	½							
Low maintenance			½			½				½								
Diseases	Leaf blotch																	
					Brown patch													
							Pythium blight											
												Spring dead spot						
Southern region																		
High maintenance	½	½	½	½	½	½	½	½	½		½							
Low maintenance		½			½			½			½							
Diseases	Leaf blotch																	
				Brown patch														
						Pythium blight												
												Spring dead spot						

Notes: Climatic zones are shown on the map in the Appendix (fig. A-1).

The time period shown for each disease indicates when nitrogen application will make the disease worse and is not necessarily the time when the disease occurs.

This schedule of nitrogen application is designed to help manage *Sclerotinia* dollar spot. It is based on fertilization with water-soluble nitrogen. If insoluble or slow-release nitrogen is used, application can be less frequent, but since the release of nitrogen is affected by many variables (e.g., soil type, soil moisture, organic matter, weather) it is impossible to make up a general schedule.

Table 11-11. Nitrogen Schedule for Zoysiagrass in the Warm Humid Climatic Zone (Zone 3) and the Bermudagrass - Kentucky Bluegrass Transition Zone (Zone 2)
(Pounds of actual nitrogen per 1000 square feet)

	Mar. 1	15	Apr. 1	15	May 1	15	June 1	15	July 1	15	Aug. 1	15	Sept. 1	15	Oct. 1	15	Nov. 1	15
Transition zone																		
High maintenance							½		½		½					½ (dormant)		
Low maintenance							½				½					½ (dormant)		
Diseases				*Helminthosporium*			Brown patch											
Middle region																		
High maintenance					½				½		½		½					
Low maintenance					½				½		½							
Diseases			*Helminthosporium*		Brown patch													
Southern region																		
High maintenance							½		½				½				½ (dormant)	
Low maintenance							½		½				½				½ (dormant)	
Diseases		*Helminthosporium*			Brown patch													

Notes: Climatic zones are shown on the map in the Appendix (fig. A-1).

The time period shown for each disease indicates when nitrogen application will make the disease worse and is not necessarily the time when the disease occurs.

This schedule of nitrogen application is designed to help manage rust and *Sclerotinia* dollar spot. It is based on fertilization with water-soluble nitrogen. If insoluble or slow-release nitrogen is used, application can be less frequent, but since the release of nitrogen is affected by many variables (e.g., soil type, soil moisture, organic matter, weather) it is impossible to make up a general schedule.

164

Table 11-12. Fungicide Schedule for Zoysiagrass in the Warm Humid Climatic Zone (Zone 3) and the Bermudagrass - Kentucky Bluegrass Transition Zone (Zone 2)
(Pounds of actual nitrogen per 1000 square feet)

	Apr. 1	15	May 1	15	June 1	15	July 1	15	Aug. 1	15	Sept. 1	15	Oct. 1	15	Nov. 1	15	Dec. 1	15
Northern region																		
High maintenance		NS	S	NS	NS	NS	NS	NS	NS	NS	S		NS	NS	NS	NS		
Low maintenance		NS		S	NS	NS	NS	NS	NS	NS			NS	NS				
Diseases		Dollar spot	Helminthosporium		Brown patch		Rust				Dollar spot	Helminthosporium						
Middle region																		
High maintenance	NS	S	NS	NS	NS	NS	NS	NS	NS	S	S	NS	NS	NS	NS			
Low maintenance	NS		S	NS	NS	NS	NS	NS	NS			NS	NS	NS	NS			
Diseases	Dollar spot	Helminthosporium		Brown patch		Rust					Dollar spot		Helminthosporium					
Southern region																		
High maintenance	S		NS	NS	NS	NS	NS	NS	NS	NS	S		S	NS	NS			
Low maintenance	S		NS	NS	NS	NS	NS	NS			S		NS	NS				
Diseases	Dollar spot	Helminthosporium		Brown patch		Rust					Dollar spot		Helminthosporium					

Key: NS = nonsystemic fungicide, S = systemic fungicide (benzimidazole).

Notes: Climatic zones are shown on the map in the Appendix (fig. A-1).

The time period shown for each disease is the time when the disease actually occurs.

165

chapter twelve

DISEASE MANAGEMENT STRATEGIES FOR HOME-LAWN GRASSES

COOL-SEASON GRASSES

This chapter will deal with the advantages and disadvantages of the various lawn grasses and the cultural practices and chemical controls necessary to maintain them. The adaptability of some turfgrass species to shade will be discussed also.

The Kentucky bluegrasses and the fine-leaf fescues are the most important home-lawn grasses in the cool-season turfgrass region. The bentgrasses (creeping and colonial) are too disease-prone and require too much maintenance to be desirable home-lawn turfgrasses. The perennial ryegrasses are undesirable in many areas because of their lack of winter hardiness, their susceptibility to disease, and their poor mowability where rotary mowers are used.

The Kentucky Bluegrasses

Both universities and private industry have devoted more effort to the improvement of the Kentucky bluegrasses than to the improvement of any other turfgrass species. As a result, there are many fine improved Kentucky bluegrass cultivars from which to choose. Unfortunately, there are many poor ones also. I will attempt here to separate the good from the bad and the ugly. It may be that some people will be unhappy with this chapter because their particular cultivar either was not mentioned or was not recommended for use. But in the long run, the facts about the various cultivars will become known anyway. I hope that they will become known sooner because of this chapter, and that this knowledge will save a lot of homeowners the grief of sodding or seeding the wrong cultivar and then trying to make the best of an impossible situation.

Environmental Adaptation

The Kentucky bluegrasses have the widest adaptation of all the cool-season turfgrass species. The diversity arises partially from the numerous cultivars, which give a broad genetic base from which to choose. Kentucky bluegrass can be grown in all parts of the cool-season turfgrass belt. It does best when grown in full sunlight, but certain cultivars can survive in the shade.

Cultivars

Kentucky bluegrass cultivars are generally put into two categories, the "improved types" and the "common types." In general, the "improved types" are those cultivars which have been bred or selected for resistance to *Helminthosporium* melting-out; the "common types" are those cultivars that have little or no such resistance. The first "improved" cultivar was Merion, which was discovered by Joe Vallentine on the Merion golf course in Pennsylvania. This discovery was really the beginning of the Kentucky bluegrass era for home lawns, and Merion has been widely used for many years. It started the sod industry on its way, because sod growers needed a grass that they could raise without chemical sprays. A list of improved and common-type Kentucky bluegrasses, with recommendations, is given in chapter 9.

The Kentucky bluegrasses, particularly Merion, were found to have other disease problems after the *Helminthosporium*-resistant cultivars became established. Diseases that once were considered to be of minor importance suddenly became major problems, and a new disease, *Fusarium* blight (fig. 12-1) was discovered. It is likely that stripe smut (and later flag smut), stem rust, and powdery mildew became problems because Merion is a single strain (common really is many different strains combined into a single cultivar.) The fact that Merion is a single strain with a narrow genetic base allowed these three pathogens (which are composed of many different genotypes called races) to attack it. Those races which could attack Merion eventually became the dominant ones in the population, and they parasitized Merion wherever it was grown. It became obvious that Merion had no horizontal resistance to these pathogens, and as a consequence powdery mildew became a problem in the shade, stem rust became a problem under conditions of low fertility or where long periods of cool fall weather occurred, and stripe smut, like *Fusarium* blight, became a problem everywhere (see fig. 12-2).

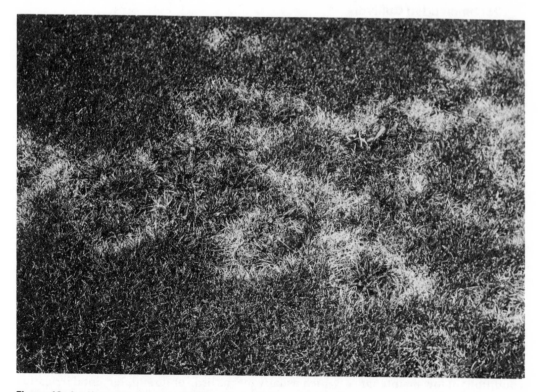

Figure 12–1.   Kentucky bluegrass turf infected with *Fusarium* blight

Figure 12–2.   Merion Kentucky bluegrass turf infected with stripe smut

Recommended Cultivars

Today there are three major diseases of Kentucky bluegrasses: *Helminthosporium* melting-out, *Fusarium* blight, and stripe smut. In order to have a lawn that can be sustained at a high level of quality, a cultivar that has resistance to all three diseases should be used whenever possible. Resistance to only one or two of them will result in an unsatisfactory lawn, because any one of the three major diseases is capable of destroying an entire lawn or making it so unattractive that you'll wish you had planted corn. At least then you would have had something to harvest.

In order to obtain the most disease-free lawn possible, you should use one of the following grass cultivars.

Adelphi	Touchdown
Majestic	Edmundi
Baron	Victa
Parade	Brunswick
Cheri	

A blend of three or four of these cultivars should be used for best results. They are resistant to *Helminthosporium* melting-out and are believed to be resistant to *Fusarium* blight. It also should be possible to avoid serious problems with stripe smut by using a blend of these cultivars. They won't remain disease-resistant forever, but for now these cultivars are the most disease-resistant available.

Do the common-type Kentucky bluegrasses have a place? The answer is very definitely yes! They will do much better than the improved types when grown under conditions of low maintenance, which usually means little or no supplemental irrigation or nitrogen. This is not to say that a common-type Kentucky bluegrass lawn will look as nice as the high-maintenance lawn; it will not, and it may eventually be taken over by weeds. It simply means that it will look better for a longer period of time under conditions of low maintenance than will the improved Kentucky bluegrass cultivars.

Maintenance Programs

Fertility. According to the literature, the "improved" Kentucky bluegrass cultivars require 3 to 6 pounds of nitrogen per 1000 square feet per season—approximately ½ to 1 pound per 1000 square feet per growing month. This much nitrogen will do for a lawn what "Typhoid Mary" did for typhoid—cause an epidemic! Two to 3 pounds per 1000 square feet per season is plenty in northern areas, and 3 to 4 pounds per 1000 square feet per season is enough in the southern part of the cool-season turfgrass region where clippings are returned to the turf. Correct use of nitrogen fertilizer isn't simply a matter of applying ½ pound per 1000 square feet per growing month, because timing of nitrogen fertility and disease development are very important. Stated simply, most nitrogen should be applied in the late summer and fall. For more detailed information on when to apply nitrogen, see tables 12-1 and 12-2.

Conforming to this late-summer-and-fall schedule for applying nitrogen fertilizer will be the single hardest thing for a homeowner to do. It is easy to get out in the spring and work on a lawn after being cooped-up all winter. Even mowing the lawn doesn't seem too bad. But try to get the average homeowner to apply most of his nitrogen in the late summer when he is thinking about vacation, or in the fall when he is so sick of mowing the lawn that he is praying for a frost. Try to convince him to apply more nitrogen to encourage growth to continue into the fall. Late summer, fall, and dormant application are the only way to go if the homeowner wants a minimal amount of disease problems.

Applying most of the nitrogen in the spring and early summer will lead to serious problems with *Fusarium* blight, *Helminthosporium* melting-out, and stripe smut. Turgeon and Meyer [141] have demonstrated an increase in *Fusarium* blight with high spring nitrogen fertility, and Vargas and Detweiler have made similar observations about *Helminthosporium* melting-out. High levels of nitrogen in early summer and midsummer have led to increased loss of stripe-smut-infected turf. Late summer, fall, and dormant applications will help to reduce the severity of these diseases. Such a nitrogen fertility schedule also will reduce the severity of red thread and rust, which are problems on slow-growing turf in the fall.

There is one other aspect of home-lawn fertility programs that must be explored. It is called commercial lawn care. For the most part, commercial firms do an outstanding job. One problem is the timing involved in the application of preemergence and postemergence herbicides, because commercial applicators believe that these should be applied in the spring. Two pounds of the total 4 pounds of nitrogen applied annually usually are applied in the spring, the third is applied in midsummer, and the last is applied in late summer or early fall. Of course the timing problem always arises when one tries to combine two separate operations (nitrogen fertility and weed control) into one. The ideal times for both may not always coincide. In the long run, everyone would be more satisfied if the commercial lawn-care operators would separate the two operations and apply the nitrogen according to the schedule in table 12-1, even though following that schedule would entail an increase in costs. For what good is a well-fertilized lawn that is marred by disease? The people treating the lawn aren't happy, the homeowner isn't happy, and even if he rationalizes it all by saying "It is a disease problem—I can't do anything about it," the homeowner eventually will become so disgusted with his lawn that he will stop the service with some remark like "It looked better before," or "Why spend the money if it is going to look like this?"

Table 12-1. Nitrogen Schedule for Kentucky Bluegrass Turfs in the Cool Humid Climatic Zone (Zone 1)
(Pounds of actual nitrogen per 1000 square feet)

	Apr. 1	15	May 1	15	June 1	15	July 1	15	Aug. 1	15	Sept. 1	15	Oct. 1	15	Nov. 1	15	Dec. 1	15
Southern region																		
High maintenance				½	½		½		½			1					1 (dormant)	
Low maintenance					½							1					1 (dormant)	
Diseases	Melting-out ———		———															
			Fusarium blight ———															
					Stripe smut ———													
Middle region																		
High maintenance					½		½		½		1				1 (dormant)			
Low maintenance					½						1				1 (dormant)			
Diseases	Melting-out ———		———															
			Fusarium blight ———															
					Stripe smut ———		———											
Northern region																		
High maintenance					½		½			1						1 (dormant)		
Low maintenance					½					1						1 (dormant)		
Diseases			Melting-out ———															
			Fusarium blight ———															
								Stripe smut ———										

Notes: Climatic zones are shown on the map in the Appendix (fig. A-1).

The time period shown for each disease indicates when nitrogen application will make the disease worse and is not necessarily the time when the disease occurs.

This schedule of nitrogen application is designed to help manage *Sclerotinia* dollar spot, *Corticium* red thread, and rust. It is based on fertilization with water-soluble nitrogen. If insoluble or slow-release nitrogen is used, application can be less frequent, but since the release of nitrogen is affected by many variables (e.g., soil type, soil moisture, organic matter, weather) it is impossible to make up a general schedule.

Table 12-2. Nitrogen Schedule for Kentucky Bluegrass in the Cool Oceanic Climatic Zone (Zone 6) (Pounds of actual nitrogen per 1000 square feet)

	Mar. 20	Apr. 10	May 1	May 20	June 10	July 1	July 20	Aug. 10	Sept. 1	Sept. 20	Oct. 10	Nov. 1	Dec. 20
High maintenance				½	½	½	½	½	½		½		1 (dormant)
Low maintenance				½	½	½	½		½		½		1 (dormant)
Diseases	*Fusarium* patch / Melting-out / *Fusarium* blight				Stripe smut				*Fusarium* patch / Melting-out				

Notes: Climatic zones are shown on the map in the Appendix (fig. A-1).

The time period shown for each disease indicates when nitrogen application will make the disease worse and is not necessarily the time when the disease occurs.

This schedule of nitrogen application is designed to help manage *Sclerotinia* dollar spot, *Corticium* red thread, and rust. It is based on fertilization with water-soluble nitrogen. If insoluble or slow-release nitrogen is used, application can be less frequent, but since the release of nitrogen is affected by many variables (e.g., soil type, soil moisture, organic matter, weather) it is impossible to make up a general schedule.

This discussion reminds me of the time I was giving a talk to a commercial lawn-applicators group. I suggested the above-mentioned treatment schedule, much to the dismay of some of the people in attendance. One of them nervously stood up to try to "clarify" for the others what I had "really" said. He stated something to the effect of, "Dr. Vargas, you are talking only about fertility in relation to diseases," to which I answered with a smirk, "Yes, only in relation to diseases!" With a sigh of relief, he turned to the audience and said, "I hope you all understand that he is talking only about diseases." I said, "Yep, if you aren't worried about diseases there is no need to follow my schedule." Since my sarcastic remarks obviously went over his head, he sat down content that he had saved the day and that things would go on as they always had.

To me the issue is like having your car painted, and having someone advising you to apply rust proofing before you drive it through the salt of the first winter, only to have someone else stand up and say, "But you are talking only about preventing rust." What good is a nicely painted car that is rusted out? What good is a well-fertilized lawn that is marred by disease? Yes, all I was talking about was preventing diseases—also known as "how you can have a lawn that you can be proud of."

Collecting Clippings to Prevent Thatch.   This theory should rank with such fairy tales as *Peter Pan, Goldilocks and the Three Bears,* and *Cinderella.* God alone probably knows who started the rumor, but few have spread as fast and as thoroughly. Good experimental data recently have disproved the theory that clippings are a major contributor to thatch development, but common sense should have disproved the theory long ago. Few areas have the thatch problem that a golf course green has, and yet clippings are removed there all the time! Collecting the clippings just removes valuable nitrogen and potassium. An additional 1 to 2 pounds of nitrogen per 1000 square feet, as well as supplemental potassium, will have to be added each season where the clippings are removed. Thatch is composed primarily of rhizomes, stolons, leaf sheaths, and roots, which you don't mow. What you do mow is the leaf blades, which are composed of materials that are broken down readily by microorganisms. The other plant parts have a high cellulose and lignin content, are therefore not readily broken down by microorganisms, and consequently contribute to the development of thatch.

Does Thatch Cause Disease?   Many people say that thatch causes disease, but there is little evidence that it actually does so. The available evidence suggests that the excess nitrogen that comes from returning the clippings is probably more responsible for an increase in a disease problem than is the thatch per se. Turfs that are maintained in thatch are more susceptible to drought than are turfs that are maintained in soils, and consequently diseases like *Fusarium* blight and stripe smut will be more severe under the former conditions. This explanation differs from the inoculum potential theory, which suggests that the fungus grows as a saprophyte in the thatch and builds up large amounts of inoculum that can attack the plant under the proper conditions.

Removal of the clippings for a crown or root rot disease like *Fusarium* blight has little effect on inoculum levels. There are enough airborne spores of the fungi that cause *Helminthosporium* melting–out, rust, powdery mildew, and smut to negate what little could be done by removing clippings. The perfect example again is golf course greens, where clippings are always removed—there are as many disease problems on golf course greens as there are anywhere else.

Should you dethatch your lawn? The answer to that question depends on how much weight you have gained during the winter. If you gained a lot of weight, the exercise of running the power rake might be good for you. On the other hand, if you are too far out of shape it might kill you! But it will do nothing for your thatch problem. You will remove the winter-killed grass, which would break down anyway, but you will not remove the thatch or correct a thatch problem. Where severe thatch exists the lawn should be cored (aerated) and the soil in the cores returned to help facilitate thatch breakdown. It may be necessary to repeat this operation several times where severe thatch problems exist.

Maintenance Programs

Mowing Height.   Mow to a height of 2 to 3 inches (note: *not* ½ to 1 inch). You are not going to putt, chip, or drive off your lawn. Since the ideal height of cut for the survival of Kentucky bluegrass is 2 to 3 inches, mow it to that height.

Fertility.   Kentucky bluegrass lawns require 3 to 4 pounds of nitrogen per 1000 square feet per season. See table 12-1 for a fertility schedule.

Dethatching.   Coring should be practiced where thatch is a problem.

Irrigation.   Water only when grass begins to show drought stress. Infrequent deep waterings are best for minimizing the incidence of wilt.

Kentucky Bluegrass Lawns with Existing Disease Problems

The fertility schedule in tables 12-1 and 12-2 should be followed in order to minimize the three major disease problems of Kentucky bluegrass turfs: *Helminthosporium* melting-out, *Fusarium* blight, and stripe smut. High levels of nitrogen in the early spring will increase the severity of *Helminthosporium* melting-out, high levels in the early and late spring will increase the amount of *Fusarium* blight, and high levels of nitrogen in the early summer and midsummer will increase the amount of turf lost to stripe smut.

Helminthosporium **Melting-out.**   The recommended treatment for *Helminthosporium* melting-out is a fungicide spray program that begins in the fall, coincident with the start of cool, wet weather (temperature below 70 °F). One of the fungicides recommended in chapter 6 should be used. A treatment with one of the PCNB products listed there should be made after the last mowing in the fall. The PCNB products are the only ones that give protection over the entire winter and spring without having to be reapplied. The PCNB products tend to be phytotoxic when used in warm weather, so other fungicides (e.g., chlorothalonil, mancozeb, iprodione, or anilazine) should be applied in the spring until the warm weather of summer arrives. Reducing spring fertility and raising the mowing height also will help. A fungicide program for the control of *Helminthosporium* melting-out can be very time consuming and costly, so "do it right the first time" and plant a *Helminthosporium*-resistant cultivar.

Fusarium **Blight.**   It was noted in chapter 2 that the symptoms of *Fusarium* blight appear when the infected plants are under drought stress. Light, frequent irrigation during dry periods will help to suppress the development of symptoms. Heavy, infrequent irrigation is of little use because the infected plants have short roots. *Fusarium*-blight-infected turf needs no more than 20 minutes of irrigation, but it needs it daily during warm weather and every two to three days during cool, dry weather. The ideal time for irrigation is the warmest part of the day. A word of caution: A 10,000-square-foot lawn infected with *Fusarium* blight cannot be irrigated adequately with one dinky little sprinkler!

Chemical management can be obtained with any of the benzimidazole systemic fungicides (benomyl, thiophanate-methyl, or thiophanate-ethyl) if they are applied properly. This means irrigating the area the night before the fungicide is applied and drenching-in the systemic fungicide before it has a chance to dry on the foliage. *Fusarium* blight is a crown and root rot problem, and the fungicide should be applied to the affected parts of the plants. The benzimidazole systemic fungicides will be translocated upward,

Table 12-3. Fungicide Schedule for Kentucky Bluegrass Turfs in the Cool Humid Climatic Zone (Zone 1)

	Mar. 1	15	Apr. 1	15	May 1	15	June 1	15	July 1	15	Aug. 1	15	Sept. 1	15	Oct. 1	15	Nov. 1	15	Dec. 1	15	Jan. 1	15
Southern region																						
High maintenance		NS	NS	NS	NS	NS		S	(S)	S	(S)			NS	NS	NS	NS	NS				
Low maintenance				NS		NS										NS						
Diseases		Stripe smut* / Melting-out						Fusarium blight								Melting-out						
Middle region																						
High maintenance			NS	NS	NS	NS			S	(S)	S		NS	NS	NS	NS						
Low maintenance					NS	NS					S			NS		NS						
Diseases		Stripe smut*		Melting-out					Fusarium blight							Melting-out						
Northern region																						
High maintenance				NS	NS	NS		NS	(S)	S	S	S	NS	NS	NS	NS						
Low maintenance						NS	NS				S	S				NS						
Diseases		Stripe smut*			Melting-out				Fusarium blight						Melting-out							

Key: NS = nonsystemic fungicide, S = systemic fungicide (benzimidazole), (S) = light application of systemic fungicide. In place of heavy application of systemic fungicide on S dates, the fungicide can be applied lightly on S and (S) dates.

Notes: Climatic zones are shown on the map in the Appendix (fig. A-1).

The time period shown for each disease is the time when the disease actually occurs.

*Stripe smut is a systemic perennial disease which, in my opinion, cannot be managed with chemicals. For systemic fungicides to be effective in managing stripe smut, they must be applied dormantly in the spring and fall or when lateral plant growth begins in the fall, and drenched in immediately. Such treatments are expensive and, depending on the cultivar, may be futile. The best way to manage stripe smut is to plant resistant cultivars.

Table 12-4. Fungicide Schedule for Kentucky Bluegrass in the Bermudagrass - Kentucky Bluegrass Transition Zone (Zone 2)

	Apr. 1	15	May 1	15	June 1	15	July 1	15	Aug. 1	15	Sept. 1	15	Oct. 1	15	Nov. 1	15	Dec. 1	15
High maintenance	NS	NS	NS			S (S)	S	(S)	(S)					NS	NS			
Low maintenance		NS	NS				S							NS	NS			
Diseases	Melting-out				Fusarium blight								Melting-out					
	Stripe smut*																	

Key: NS = nonsystemic fungicide, S = systemic fungicide (benzimidazole), (S) = light application of systemic fungicide. In place of heavy applications of systemic fungicide on S dates, the fungicide can be applied lightly on S and (S) dates.

Notes: Climatic zones are shown on the map in the Appendix (fig. A-1).

The time period shown for each disease is the time when the disease actually occurs.

*Stripe smut is a systemic perennial disease which, in my opinion, cannot be managed with chemicals. For systemic fungicides to be effective in managing stripe smut, they must be applied dormantly in the spring and fall or when lateral plant growth begins in the fall, and drenched in immediately. Such treatments are expensive and, depending on the cultivar, may be futile. The best way to manage stripe smut is to plant resistant cultivars.

but they are not translocated downward. This treatment is very expensive, and because of the expense many people assume that one treatment will cure their problem forever. It won't, and retreatment will be necessary every year in order to prevent the problem from recurring.

Resistance to the benzimidazole systemic fungicides by some strains of the *Fusarium* fungi that cause *Fusarium* blight has been reported [120, 128]. This means that the benzimidazole systemic fungicides probably will lose their effectiveness in treating *Fusarium* blight. (The development of resistance by the *Fusarium* fungi was not unexpected; it has been reported for every other major pathogen against which the benzimidazoles have been used [78].)

Smiley and Craven [117] found that the experimental fungicides fernarinol and iprodione would suppress symptoms of *Fusarium* blight caused by the benzimidazole-resistant strains of *Fusarium roseum*. If one or all of these compounds receive full registration, there will be an alternative to the benzimidazole fungicides for the control of *Fusarium* blight.

Stripe Smut. Having stripe smut in your lawn is a little like having a serious case of diabetes; you can live with it provided you maintain a proper diet and take good care of yourself. A turfgrass plant infected with stripe smut is infected for life; all plants arising from that infected mother plant will be infected. Stripe smut is a systemic disease that may remain dormant in the crown of the plant during the warm weather of summer or the cold weather of fall. Or it can spread up the veins of the leaves, eventually rupturing them and releasing many black spores that may attack other plants. But whether the spores are visible or not, the plant is always in a weakened condition, and the first stress to which it is subjected may kill it. The most common stress is summer drought. Many people who take good care of their lawns and water them religiously while they are home go away on vacation and forget them. If a healthy lawn of Kentucky bluegrass is not irrigated, it simply will go dormant and revive when water is applied again. However, if a lawn is infected with stripe smut and the same thing is allowed to happen, instead of going dormant it will go dead! It is, therefore, important that one not let a lawn infected with stripe smut dry out.

Stripe smut can be managed (really, arrested) with high concentrations (4 to 8 ounces per 1000 square feet) of the benzimidazole systemic fungicides. The best results are obtained when the systemic fungicides are applied as drenches when the grass is dormant [69]. However, applying the systemic fungicides in this manner increases the incidence of *Helminthosporium* melting-out in the spring. Even resistant cultivars like Merion become susceptible to *Helminthosporium* melting-out after such treatments. This means that the stripe-smut treatment must be accompanied by a *Helminthosporium* treatment. The PCNBs are the only fungicides that give the long-term *Helminthosporium* control required when the benzimidazole systemic fungicides are used as dormant applications to control stripe smut [70].

Applications of the benzimidazole systemic fungicides in the late spring and early fall are also effective against stripe smut if they are applied when the grass is growing actively. Avoid applying them when grass growth is beginning to slow down because of warm weather. While these treatments are not as effective as are dormant applications, they do minimize *Helminthosporium* problems [145]. But what is the bottom line? The bottom line is that these are merely stopgap measures. The systemic fungicides, no matter when they are applied, don't eradicate the disease—it comes back every year. Resistance to the benzimidazole systemic fungicides by every major pathogen on which they have been used has been reported [78], and resistance to the systemic fungicides will occur in the smuts also. You may obtain 2 or 3 years of control with the benzimidazole systemic fungicides if you apply them yearly. But what do you do when resistance develops? The first choice should be the renovation of the lawn and its reestablishment with a blend of resistant cultivars (see fig. 12-3). Short of this, you should follow the fertility program given in tables 12-1 and 12-2. That program stresses applying most of the nitrogen in the late summer and fall, and adhering to this regimen, along with diligently irrigating the lawn and not allowing it to undergo drought stress, should prevent the death of the lawn.

Rusts. In most areas the rusts can be managed adequately with nitrogen fertility. Rust is usually not a problem if enough nitrogen is applied that the turfgrass is mowed at least once a week. However, cold not lack of nitrogen, is responsible for the slow growth of turfgrass in some coastal and northern areas. In these areas a maneb, mancozeb, zineb, or cycloheximide fungicide should be used in the fall of the year. Two or three applications 7 to 10 days apart will be necessary to control the rust.

Corticium **Red Thread.** Red thread, like rust, can be controlled in most areas with adequate levels of nitrogen. A fungicide must be used in far-northern and coastal areas where the slow growth is due to cool weather and not to inadequate amounts of nitrogen. The benzimidazole systemic fungicides and chlorothalonil will control the disease. The benzimidazole systemic fungicides should be applied with chlorothalonil, or alternated with it, to try to delay the development of resistance.

Powdery Mildew. Powdery mildew is a problem primarily in the shade. It will occur in open areas during falls that have many days of overcast weather. It is not a serious prob-

Figure 12–3. Renovation and reseeding, with a commercial seeder, of a lawn infected with *Fusarium* blight and stripe smut

lem when it occurs in open areas, but it is a serious problem in the shade. The benzimidazole systemic fungicides will give economically feasible management, but resistance usually develops during the second season. Karathane and cycloheximide can be used, but they must be put on almost weekly from early summer until the snow flies, which makes them impractical for most homeowners to use. There may someday be Kentucky bluegrass cultivars that have both shade tolerance and resistance to powdery mildew and *Helminthosporium* melting-out in the shade. As things stand now, Glade is shade-tolerant and has resistance to powdery mildew, but it lacks resistance to *Helminthosporium*, Nugget is resistant to *Helminthosporium* melting-out, but it lacks resistance to powdery mildew and is susceptible to *Fusarium* blight. Bensun (Warren's A-34) appears to have resistance to both *Helminthosporium* melting-out and powdery mildew, but it is susceptible to *Fusarium* blight. Bensun Kentucky bluegrass may be the best choice for planting in moist, dense shade in the northern areas of the cool-season grassbelt, and the improved cultivars of *Poa trivialis* may be the best choices in the middle and southern regions. The fine-leaf fescues will do well in open shade, but *Helminthosporium* leaf spot and powdery mildew will destroy them in dense, moist shade.

Fairy Rings.   Fairy rings are not a problem of the grass as much as they are a problem of the soil. The fungi that cause fairy ring grow on organic matter in the soil or thatch. They release nitrogen as they grow, and the nitrogen in turn causes the zone of stimulation (darker, taller grass) to form outside of the main body of the fungus. The turf is usually yellow, wilting, or dead where the main body of the fungus is growing in the thatch (see fig. 12-4). The yellow color develops because the fungus interferes with nutrient uptake. Wilting and death of the grass occurs when the body (mycelium) of the fungus

Figure 12–4.   Kentucky bluegrass sod field heavily infested with *Tricholoma* fairy ring

prevents moisture from reaching the root system. The only way to get rid of the fungus is physically to remove the soil that contains it. This can be accomplished by digging out the soil and sod from an area that is one foot deep and extends one foot beyond the fairy ring. The excised material then is replaced by healthy soil and sod. If the fairy ring covers a large area, you may wish to remove the sod, till the area, and have it fumigated with methyl bromide. (Methyl bromide is a deadly gas and should be applied only by experienced personnel.) There is a lot written about drilling holes and dumping this or that fungicide down the holes to kill the fairy ring. It won't work.

Cold-Temperature Brown Patch. The importance of cold-temperature brown patch has been underestimated, and the true effect of this disease on the maintenance of high-quality Kentucky bluegrass is not known. The main reason for this state of affairs is that cold-temperature brown patch often has been confused with *Fusarium* blight (see fig. 12-5). Now that the disease has been correctly identified, it should be possible to develop methods of controlling it.

Fine-Leaf Fescue

There are four species of fine-leaf fescue that commonly are referred to as red fescue. These are *Festuca rubra* L. subspecies *commutata* Gaud (chewings fescue), *Festuca rubra* L. subspecies rubra (spreading red fescue), *Festuca rubra* L. subspecies *trichophylla* (creeping red fescue), and *Festuca longifolia* Thuill (hard fescue). Because of their susceptibility to *Helminthosporium* leaf spot and other diseases, the fine-leaf fescues are used mostly on low-maintenance home lawns, either by themselves or in mixtures with the common-

Figure 12–5. Cold-temperature brown patch in a Kentucky bluegrass lawn

type Kentucky bluegrasses. The fescues are especially well adapted to sandy soil, and they will survive nicely on one pound of nitrogen per square feet per season. The fine-leaf fescues do well also in areas of open shade; in fact, they often do better there than they do under conditions of full sunlight. In the southern part of the cool-season climatic region, open shade is the only environment in which they will survive.

Attempts have been made to select and improve the fine-leaf fescues in order to make them more desirable turfgrasses. Most of the selecting has been done so far on the basis of such agronomic characteristics as color, texture, and creeping habit, and very little selection has been done on the basis of resistance to disease. However, there are now some programs for breeding and selecting fine-leaf fescues for resistance to disease, and better cultivars should be available in the future.

Helminthosporium leaf spot is assumed by most researchers to be the most important disease of the fine-leaf fescues in most areas today, and it could be the limiting factor in the use of these turfgrasses in home lawns. It may be, though, that everyone is looking for resistance to *Helminthosporium* leaf spot and forgetting about the other known diseases of the fine-leaf fescues—diseases such as *Corticium* red thread, rust, *Fusarium* patch, anthracnose, and *Sclerotinia* dollar spot. These are diseases mainly of slow-growing or low-maintenance turf, and the fine-leaf fescues will remain green and compete with weeds when grown under low-maintenance conditions. It is necessary that a lawn grass have resistance to *Helminthosporium* leaf spot, but why go through the screening processes looking just for resistance to that disease, only to have to start all over again because the leaf-spot-resistant fine-leaf fescue is destroyed by *Corticium* red thread, anthracnose, dollar spot, or rust?

If cultivars that are resistant to the major diseases are found, the fine-leaf fescues could be the home-lawn turfgrasses of the future. They will become more desirable as resources like water and fertilizer become less available and more expensive.

Maintenance Programs

Mowing Height.   The fine-leaf fescues should be mowed to a height of 2 to 3 inches.

Fertility.   The fine-leaf fescues require no more than 1 to 3 pounds of nitrogen per 1000 square feet per season, and the less nitrogen that is applied the better. Other nutrients (mainly phosphorous and potassium) should be added as the need for them is established by soil tests.

Irrigation.   Irrigate as infrequently as possible; the fine-leaf fescues have excellent drought tolerance. The two quickest ways to destroy a fine-leaf fescue are overwatering and overfertilizing it.

Recommended Cultivars

No one cultivar is perfect, and not enough good information is available to recommend blends. Listed below are the best of a very poor lot.

Pennlawn—Susceptible to *Helminthosporium* leaf spot, anthracnose, *Corticium* red
  thread, and rust.
Wintergreen—Susceptible to *Helminthosporium* leaf spot; rust resistant.
C-26—Best available resistance to *Helminthosporium* leaf spot, but not truly resistant.
Dawson—Susceptible to *Sclerotinia* dollar spot, anthracnose, and *Helminthosporium*
  leaf spot; not recommended.

See table 10-2 for information on other fine-leaf fescue cultivars.

Perennial Ryegrasses

The improved perennial ryegrasses have improved mowability. That is, they mow better than the old "common" type, which mows like baling wire, but they still don't mow like the Kentucky bluegrasses and fine-leaf fescues. They still look bad in midsummer if they are mowed with a reel mower, but they look terrible if mowed with a dull rotary mower. Perhaps the shabbiness could be tolerated if the improved perennial ryegrasses had any excellent disease resistances and good turf density, but they don't. It is another case of a turfgrass being developed for an agronomic characteristic with little regard for susceptibility to disease. Besides the lack of mowing quality and the poor disease resistance, many of the perennial ryegrasses lack cold-hardiness; simply stated, they winter-kill. The perennial ryegrasses may someday be an acceptable turfgrass species for home lawns, but that someday isn't here yet. More breeding or selecting for better mowing quality, greater winter hardiness, and better disease control are needed before they can be recommended. For more information on specific disease problems, see chapter 9. Because I consider it futile to try to maintain perennial ryegrass, I won't discuss lawn-disease control and maintenance practices. Furthermore, even if I wanted to discuss them, it would be impossible because the necessary research has not yet been done. I find the lack of research amazing when the grass is being so widely recommended, but in light of the history of turfgrass, the situation is not surprising!

Creeping Bentgrass

If you don't have a creeping bentgrass lawn, don't plant one unless you have enough money to hire a professional landscaper to take care of it, or enough time and money to take care of it yourself. If you want a nice-looking bentgrass lawn you must treat it like a golf course green. This means that in addition to mowing, irrigating, and fertilizing, you must also topdress and verticut. If creeping bentgrass is not topdressed and verticut, it will become thatchy and puffy and it will scalp in the summer. It also will be susceptible to *Helminthosporium* leaf spot, *Sclerotinia* dollar spot, *Rhizoctonia* brown patch, *Pythium* blight, and the snow molds. For a maintenance schedule and disease-control program, see the discussion of golf course greens in chapter 11.

Tall Fescue

Tall fescue is grown in general-use areas (roadsides and parks) and on home lawns, especially in the Kentucky bluegrass–bermudagrass transition zone. The Kentucky bluegrasses and bermudagrasses are the preferred species in this region, but if proper care is not taken of them they will die, and broadleaf weeds and weedy grasses will take over. Tall fescue is therefore the preferred turfgrass species for low-maintenance areas. Kentucky 31 and Alta are the best cultivars available. More work needs to be done on breeding and selecting new tall fescue cultivars.

Maintenance Programs

Tall fescue requires the application of 1 to 3 pounds of nitrogen per 1000 square feet per year. Phosphorus and potassium should be added as the need for them is established by soil tests.

Mow to a height of 2 to 3 inches.

Water as little as possible; overwatering will eliminate the tall fescue. The species is extremely drought-tolerant.

Diseases

Tall fescue is susceptible to *Helminthosporium* net blotch, *Rhizoctonia* brown patch, and rust and to other diseases which may have to be controlled if they become severe.

Poa trivialis (Rough Bluegrass)

Normally considered to be a weed when it occurs in high-quality lawns, *Poa trivialis* does have a place as a turfgrass in dense, moist shade, especially in the middle and southern regions of the cool climatic zone. Very few other turfgrass species or cultivars will survive in heavily shaded areas. Rough bluegrass has been reported to be susceptible to *Helminthosporium* leaf spot, rust, stripe smut, *Rhizoctonia* brown patch, *Ophiobolus* patch, *Fusarium* patch, and *Typhula* blight. The real truth of the matter is that it has not been grown widely or in high-quality turfgrass areas enough to know what its important and unimportant disease problems are.

Maintenance Programs

Irrigate it! It grows best when it is kept moist.

It can be mowed as low as ½ inch, but a height of 2 to 3 inches is preferable.

Apply 1 to 3 pounds of nitrogen per 1000 square feet per season. The less nitrogen applied, the better. P_2O_5 + K_2O should be added when need for them is established by soil tests.

Zoysiagrass

Zoysiagrass is a fine warm-season turfgrass, but it turns brown at the first frost and remains so until late spring or early summer. If you want a lawn that is green for 2 to 5 months, then zoysiagrass is what you are looking for; but if you want a lawn that is green for the entire growing season, then zoysiagrass isn't for you. Zoysiagrass is discussed elsewhere as a desirable turfgrass species for warm-season lawns (see p. 185).

WARM-SEASON GRASSES

Dealing with home-lawn diseases of warm-season grasses is not as easy as dealing with home-lawn diseases of cool-season grasses. Firstly, most cool-season lawns are composed of Kentucky bluegrass. Secondly, more information is available on the disease resistance and susceptibility of cool-season cultivars. Warm-season home lawns are composed of many different species, for example, bermudagrass, centipedegrass, bahiagrass, St. Augustinegrass, and zoysiagrass. It is too early to tell, from the point of view either of plant pathology or agronomy, which grass is the superior one or which cultivar of the superior species is to be preferred. It may even turn out that one species is best for the hot, humid regions and another is best for the hot, arid regions.

Bermudagrass

The limiting factor in the use of bermudagrass on home lawns (or anywhere for that matter) is a devastating disease called spring dead spot (SDS; see fig. 12-6). The cause of SDS is still unknown. It is a problem on bermudagrass everywhere but in the most southern regions of the warm climatic zone, where bermudagrass has a short (1 to 2 month) dormant period or no dormant period at all. The longer the dormant period, the more serious SDS becomes.

Figure 12–6. Spring dead spot (SDS) on bermudagrass lawn (Photograph courtesy of Dr. R. V. Sturgeon)

The bermudagrasses, especially the "improved" cultivar, are notorious thatch producers and usually require some kind of mechanical dethatching yearly. Since most homeowners don't own the necessary equipment, either it must be rented or the homeowner must pay someone to do the job. This is an expense that a homeowner should take into account before establishing a bermudagrass lawn.

Steve Wilcoxen [159] demonstrated on his golf course fairway the control of SDS with spring and summer application of chlorothalonil and cycloheximide plus thiram. These fungicides were applied during either April and May, June and July, or August and September. All three protocols were equally effective in managing SDS. Homeowners who have bermudagrass lawns may wish to try a similar schedule, applying one of the fungicides on a weekly basis for 2 months. The management program is expensive, but so is replacing a lawn.

There are indications that a new bermudagrass cultivar, Midiron, has some resistance to SDS. Midiron has excellent low-temperature hardiness, which may account for its resistance to SDS, but it is simply too soon to make a judgment. Limiting the application of nitrogen in late summer and early fall will help to reduce the severity of SDS.

Rhizoctonia brown patch, *Helminthosporium*, and *Sclerotinia* dollar spot are serious problems on bermudagrass in the humid regions of the warm climatic zone. To prevent severe loss of grass, a preventive fungicide such as PCNB, chlorthalonil, or mancozeb must be applied on a 10-to-14-day schedule.

St. Augustinegrass

St. Augustinegrass decline (SAD; see fig. 12-7) is the most serious of the diseases that attack St. Augustinegrass in Texas, New Mexico, and Louisiana. It is a viral disease, and

Figure 12–7. Foliar symptoms of St. Augustinegrass decline virus (SAD) on a St. Augustinegrass blade (Photograph courtesy of Dr. Bobby G. Joyner)

there is no chemical control for it once a plant becomes infected. SAD is transmitted mechanically by mowing; once it occurs in a small area of a turf it usually is spread very rapidly throughout the entire turf area by the mowers. However, it may take 3 to 5 years before the turf is badly thinned if it is maintained at a high cultural intensity. Toler and Walla at Texas A & M University, in cooperation with the Florida Agricultural Experiment Station, screened 250 St. Augustinegrass lines and found a selection that was resistant to SAD [137]. This cultivar, which they named Floratam, also has a resistance to chinch bugs and is more tolerant of some strains of *Rhizoctonia solani* than is Texas common.

Gray leaf spot, which is caused by *Piricularia grisea,* is also a serious problem on St. Augustinegrass, especially on newly sprigged areas or where the grass is succulent and growing rapidly because of nitrogen fertilization. The disease is most serious at temperatures between 70 and 80 °F (spring and fall) under conditions of high humidity. Irrigation during the daytime (to allow the foliage to dry more rapidly) and avoidance of high nitrogen fertility during the warm months will aid in reducing the severity of disease. Mancozeb, chlorothalonil, or anilazine can be used on a 7-to-10-day schedule to manage the disease. *Rhizoctonia* brown patch (fig. 12-8), which is caused by *Rhizoctonia solani,* is a problem on St. Augustinegrass during the spring and early fall when the temperatures are between 75 and 90 °F and humidity is high. The disease is most severe during rainy periods when nocturnal temperatures remain high, and on poorly drained soils. High nitrogen fertility and shade increase the severity of *Rhizoctonia* brown patch, as they do with gray leaf spot. Brown patch can be controlled by applying any of many fungicides (e.g., chlorothalonil, cycloheximide-thiram, or mancozeb) at 7-to-10-day intervals.

St. Augustinegrass is one of the preferred species for home lawns and general turf in the southern portions of the warm humid climatic zone, especially along the Gulf Coast in Florida. Floratam has excellent resistance to SAD and chinch bugs, either one of which will destroy St. Augustinegrass, but it lacks good agronomic characteristics. Also, it does

Figure 12–8. *Rhizoctonia* brown patch on St. Augustinegrass

well only in the warmer areas of the St. Augustinegrass growing region because it lacks low-temperature hardiness. Other cultivars are being developed under the aegis of Texas A & M University; it is to be hoped that they will become available soon. Avoidance of excess nitrogen fertility in the spring and early fall should help to reduce the severity of gray leaf spot and *Rhizoctonia* brown patch.

Zoysiagrass

Zoysiagrass is the most disease-resistant of all the warm-season turfgrasses that are in widespread use. It is the most cold-temperature-tolerant of all the warm-season grasses that are being grown from the midregions of the cool climatic zone to the southern regions of the warm-season grass belt. While zoysiagrass will grow in the cool climatic zone, it is not recommended for use there because it discolors (turns brown) with the coming of cool weather in the late summer or early fall and doesn't green-up until the warm weather of summer comes again. However, it is an excellent turfgrass for lawns in the warm-season grass regions where rust is not a severe problem.

Zoysiagrass is susceptible to *Rhizoctonia* brown patch and rust. *Rhizoctonia* brown patch can be a severe problem during periods of hot, humid weather when the temperatures remain between 75 and 90 °F. The avoidance of excess nitrogen just before and during this period will aid in reducing the severity of disease. Zoysiagrass is a slow-growing turfgrass, which is fine, especially if you are not fanatic about mowing, but the slow growth rate makes rust a more severe problem on zoysiagrass than it is on most other grass species. Zoysiagrass' slow growth rate precludes in most cases the use of nitrogen fertility to manage rust. A fungicide program using chlorothalonil or mancozeb on a 7-to-10-day basis will be necessary.

Recommended Cultivars

Meyer and Midwest are two improved zoysiagrass cultivars that have good low-temperature hardiness.

Centipedegrass and Bahiagrass

Centipedegrass and bahiagrass are used on low-maintenance turf areas; hence little is known about their disease problems, nor is much concern given them. This situation may change, and more information may be forthcoming, especially about bahiagrass. Bahiagrass rapidly is replacing St. Augustinegrass in Florida, where chinch bug and SAD have destroyed many St. Augustinegrass lawns.

chapter thirteen

ATHLETIC FIELDS AND SPORTS TURF—DO IT RIGHT THE FIRST TIME

SOIL

To say that you start from the bottom when building an athletic field is an understatement. If it isn't built with the proper soil and drainage, no matter what is done to the top it will always look like a disaster area. This means that in most places one can't simply push the native soils around until a field with a crown is obtained and expect the result to be a satisfactory sports field unless the site is fortunate enough to be composed of a sandy loam, loamy sand, or pure sand soil. If the site is not composed of one of these desirable soil types, remove the native soil to a depth of 18 inches and replace it with sand. Sand is the ideal medium for growing turf, provided that you have adequate water, but it is tough to convince most people of this. They always want to mess it up with peat moss, organic matter, or clay. Such practices are like pouring salt, pepper, or sugar into a vintage wine to give it flavor. It doesn't need any flavor; it is beautiful by itself and so is sand! There is even an all-sand athletic field that you can buy called PAT (Prescription Athletic Turf). For more details, see reference 24.

Why not use silt or clay? Because sports fields are subjected to compaction more than are most other turf areas. Sand will not compact like silt and clay, even when it is wet. The soil structure of a clay or silt will be destroyed by a few football or soccer games in the rain, and a compaction problem will be present. Slicing and coring will help to alleviate the problem, but the next time that the field is played on in the rain the compaction problem will return.

Should a sports turf be seeded or sodded? The answer to that question is, unequivocally, *seeded*. It is the difference between real hair and a wig. If you pull and tug at real hair, it won't come out because it's rooted in your scalp. If you pull and tug on a wig, it will come off because the hair is rooted only in the wig. Mineral sod is no better than muck sod; neither will root properly and a tearing problem will result. The tearing occurs at the interface between the soil and sod layers. The roots of the turfgrass will enter the second layer during the wet conditions of early spring, but with the advent of warm weather and drying of the upper portion of the turf the roots will withdraw back into the top layer. Top dressing with sand will only move the layering problem down unless the layer of foreign soil reaches a depth of at least 6 inches. (This assumes that the field below the sod was sand; otherwise there will be a problem with three layers.) While sod may be fine for a home-lawn turf, it isn't tolerable on an athletic field where the turf is subjected to tearing.

The layering problem can be eliminated from a sand field by coring and top dressing with sand, but if the maintenance program is really to be effective the cores must be removed. Doing this two or three times a year for 3 or 4 years should remove enough of the soil layer to provide a satisfactory turf. A golf-green-type coring unit should be used because it removes more cores per square inch than do fairway-type units. But think of all the aggravation that could have been avoided if things had been done correctly in the first place!

Soilless (washed) sod is another alternative. This is sod that has had the soil removed by several washing operations. It should provide a good playing surface because the undesirable aspect of sod, the soil and subsequent layering problem, has been removed. It may be more expensive to use, but the playability of the field will be far superior to that of one which was established using unwashed sod.

In its first season of use, the turf on a soilless-sod athletic field will not look as dense prior to the first game as would ordinary sod with soil. But what really counts is the root structure. The soilless sod will have a superior root system, and in subsequent years it will look far better on top, as well as on the bottom, when compared to a field established from sod with soil.

TURFGRASS SPECIES—NORTHERN

Once the proper soil—either sand or a loamy sand—has been used, the next problem is to select the proper turfgrass species or cultivars. There is nothing better than Kentucky bluegrass for an elite athletic field with the budget to maintain it properly. The improved Kentucky bluegrass cultivars, which have resistance to the three major diseases (*Helminthosporium* melting-out, *Fusarium* blight, and stripe smut), should be used on such elite fields. These cultivars include Touchdown, Majestic, Adelphi, Parade, Baron, Victa, Cheri, Brunswick, and Edmundi. Time and effort must be put into watering, fertilizing, mowing, and other maintenance practices if a first-class field is desired. If the proper care is not given to an elite field of Kentucky bluegrasses, they will soon be replaced by less desirable weedy grasses.

Better wear tolerance can be obtained on fields that will not receive the care that is necessary to maintain a Kentucky bluegrass turf by mixing one or two of the common Kentucky bluegrasses, or Baron, Cheri, Victa, Touchdown, or Parade, with an improved perennial ryegrass such as Yorktown II, Derby, Diplomat, Omega, or Pennfine, or an improved tall fescue such as Kentucky 31, Alta, Goar, Kenwell, or Fawn. The field will not look as good as a first-class field of elite Kentucky bluegrass, but it should provide a good playing surface. It may be necessary to apply fungicides for disease control during portions of the growing season (see fig. 13-1). In the transition zone, tall fescue, by itself or in a mixture with common Kentucky bluegrass or perennial ryegrass, will give adequate cover under low-maintenance conditions.

Most athletic fields are overwatered, which usually leads to invasion of the turf by creeping bentgrass and annual bluegrass. This has happened on many sand fields, but it should not have occurred there because sand affords the ideal system for culturally controlling annual bluegrass through drought stress. However, most field superintendents insist on keeping the fields moist during the entire growing season. Even football fields that aren't going to be played on until fall are heavily watered all summer long. The end result of such practices usually is the encroachment of annual bluegrass and creeping bentgrass.

Figure 13-1. Brown blight *(Helminthosporium siccans)* thinning a new seeding of perennial ryegrass

There is nothing wrong with annual bluegrass on an athletic field or golf course fairway as long as it is managed as annual bluegrass and not as if it were Kentucky bluegrass, but if you want to avoid having it, a stringent irrigation program should be followed. For maintenance, fertility, and fungicide programs for annual bluegrass, see chapter 11.

TURFGRASS SPECIES—SOUTHERN

Bermudagrass is ideal for southern athletic fields. Unfortunately, it goes dormant during the football season. Overseeding with an improved perennial ryegrass will give protection to the dormant bermudagrass and add recuperative potential during the playing season. Because of their cold-hardiness, Tufcote and Midiron are preferred varieties for the transition zone and the northern portions of the warm-season grassbelt.

Spring dead spot (SDS) must be controlled on bermudagrass athletic fields, even if the fields are dormant when football games are played. Also, scars left by SDS certainly will mar the appearance of an athletic field used for such sports as baseball, softball, and soccer that are played when the bermudagrass is actively growing. For disease-control recommendations, see chapter 11. Other diseases, such as the *Helminthosporium* diseases and *Rhizoctonia* brown patch, should be treated as they occur. See table 11-9 for a treatment schedule.

FERTILITY

The amount of nitrogen required will depend on the type of soil, the amount of rainfall or supplemental irrigation, whether the clippings are removed or returned, and the turfgrass species or cultivar that was used. Sandy soils will require more nitrogen than will the heavier silt and clay soils. More nitrogen will be needed if the clippings are removed than if they are returned. If the clippings are returned, 3 to 4 pounds of nitrogen per 1000 square feet per season will be needed on the elite Kentucky bluegrasses. If the clippings are removed, 4 to 6 pounds of nitrogen per 1000 square feet per season will be needed, depending on your location. On sand athletic fields, light, frequent applications of nitrogen (¼ to ½ pounds of actual nitrogen per 1000 square feet per application) are the ideal way to fertilize.

Low-maintenance athletic fields require 1 to 3 pounds of nitrogen per 1000 square feet each season; the exact amount depends on the location and whether the clippings are collected or returned. See the fertility recommendations for common Kentucky bluegrasses in chapter 12.

Phosphorus and potassium concentrations should be checked with a yearly soil test, and the amounts of these important nutrients should be maintained at adequate levels.

CULTIVATION

Northern Areas

Athletic fields constructed of sand should require only dormant reseeding of bare or thin spots after the football season in the fall or in the early spring. Athletic fields on loam, silt, or clay will require coring, spiking and slicing to help to correct compaction problems.

Southern Areas

Athletic fields on sand will probably require respprigging of bermudagrass in bare spots. This can be done in the spring. Those athletic fields on loam, silt, or clay will require coring, spiking and slicing to help to correct compaction problems.

APPENDIX

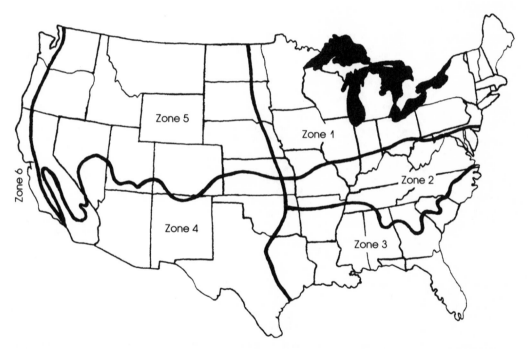

Figure A-1. The six climatic zones referred to in the nitrogen and fungicide schedules given in chapters 11 and 12

Zone 1—Cool humid climatic zone
Zone 2—Bermudagrass–Kentucky bluegrass transition zone
Zone 3—Warm humid climatic zone
Zone 4—Warm arid climatic zone
Zone 5—Cool arid climatic zone
Zone 6—Cool oceanic climatic zone

Disease	Causal Agent	Hosts	Cultural Control	Chemical Control
Anthracnose	*Colletotrichum graminicola*	Annual bluegrass Fine-leaf fescue Kentucky bluegrass Perennial ryegrass	Adequate nitrogen. Cool grass by syringing.	Thiram, maneb plus zinc sulfate, chlorothalonil, benomyl, thiophanate-methyl, thiophanate-ethyl, thiaphanate-methyl + mancozeb.
Brown patch	*Rhizoctonia solani*	All major turfgrass species	Reduce nitrogen. Remove "dew." Increase air movement.	Mancozeb, maneb plus zinc sulfate, chlorothalonil, anilazine, cycloheximide + thiram, cycloheximide, benomyl, thiophanate-methyl, thiophanate-ethyl, thiram, thiophanate-methyl + maneb, cadmium compounds, thiophanate + thiram, PCNB, iprodione.
Copper spot	*Gloeocercospora sorghi*	Creeping bentgrass	None.	Cadmium compounds, chlorothalonil, anilazine, thiophanate-methyl, benomyl, thiophanate-ethyl.
Dollar spot	*Sclerotinia homoeocarpa*	Annual bluegrass Bahiagrass Bermudagrass Centipedegrass Colonial bentgrass Creeping bentgrass Fine-leaf fescues Kentucky bluegrass Perennial ryegrass St. Augustinegrass Zoysiagrass	Increase nitrogen. Remove "dew."	Benomyl, thiophanate-ethyl, thiophanate-methyl, chlorothalonil, anilazine, cycloheximide + thiram, cycloheximide + PCNB, cadmium compounds, thiophanate + thiram, thiram, thiabendazole, benomyl, thiophanate-methyl, iprodione, thiophanate-methyl plus maneb.
Fading-out (*Curvularia – Helminthosporium* Complex)	*Curvularia* spp.	Canada bluegrass Creeping bentgrass Kentucky bluegrass *Poa trivialis* Spreading fescue	Cool grass by syringing.	Chlorothalonil, cycloheximide + PCNB, cycloheximide, cycloheximide + thiram.
Fairy ring	Many fungi, mostly in the class *Basidiomycetes*	All turf areas	Removal of infested sod and soil. Replacing with clean soil and reseed or sod.	Soil fumigants: methyl bromide, chloropicrin, vapam. Vorlex.
Fusarium blight	*Fusarium roseum* and *F. tricinctum,* sometimes in combination with nematodes	Kentucky bluegrass Centipedegrass	Light, frequent waterings during dry periods. Fungicides *must* be drenched to be effective.	Benomyl, thiophanate-methyl, thiophanate-ethyl
Gray leaf spot	*Piricularia grisea*	St. Augustinegrass	Reduce nitrogen. Daytime watering.	Cycloheximide + thiram, chlorothalonil, mancozeb, anilazine, zineb

Disease	Causal Agent	Hosts	Cultural Control	Chemical Control
Helminthosporium Diseases				
Brown blight	*H. siccans*	Ryegrass	Remove clippings.	Mancozeb,
Leaf blotch	*H. cynodontis*	Bermudagrass	Raise cutting	chlorothalonil,
Leaf spot	*H. sorokinianum*	Bentgrass, Fine-leaf fescue, Kentucky bluegrass	height. Plant resistant cultivars. Reduce nitrogen.	cycloheximide, anilazine, maneb plus zinc sulfate,
Melting-out	*H. vagans*	Kentucky bluegrass		cycloheximide
Net-blotch	*H. dictyoides*	Fescue		+ thiram,
Red leaf spot	*H. erythrospilum*	Creeping bentgrass		cycloheximide
Stem and Crown Necrosis	*H. spiciferum*	Bermudagrass		+ PCNB, iprodione.
Zonate eye spot	*H. giganteum*	Bermudagrass		
Ophiobolus patch	*Ophiobolus graminis*	Annual bluegrass Colonial bentgrass Creeping bentgrass Kentucky bluegrass Tall fescue Velvet bentgrass	Reduce soil pH. Avoid liming. Use acidic fertilizers. Sulfur, phosphorus.	None.
Powdery mildew	*Erysiphe graminis*	Bermudagrass Fine-leaf fescue Kentucky bluegrass Red top	Reduce shade. Plant resistant species.	Benomyl, cycloheximide, dinocap.
Pythium blight (cottony blight)	*Pythium* spp.		Improve soil drainage. Increase air circulation.	Chloroneb, etridiazol.
Red thread (Pink patch)	*Corticium fuciforme*	Annual bluegrass Creeping bentgrass Fine-leaf fescue Kentucky bluegrass Perennial ryegrass	Increase nitrogen	Chlorothalonil, thiophanate-ethyl, cycloheximide + thiram, thiophanate + thiram.
The Rusts				
Bermudagrass rust	*Puccinia cynodontis*	Bermudagrass	Fertilize with nitrogen.	Maneb plus zinc sulfate, cycloheximide
Crown rust	*P. coronata*	Perennial ryegrass Tall fescue Fine-leaf fescue		cycloheximide, + thiram, chlorothalonil, zineb,
Leaf rust	*P. brachypodii*	Kentucky bluegrass		mancozeb.
Stem rust	*P. graminis*	Kentucky bluegrass		
Stripe rust	*P. striiformis*	Kentucky bluegrass		
Zoysiagrass rust	*P. zoysia*	Zoysiagrass		
Slime mold	*Mucilago spongiosa* *Physarum cinereum*	All grasses; the molds live as saprophytes on them.	Remove by brushing or with sharp spray of water from a hose.	Not necessary.
The Smuts				
Stripe smut	*Ustilago striiformis*	Kentucky bluegrass	Reduce summer nitrogen fertility.	Benomyl, thiophanate-ethyl,
Flag smut	*Urocystis agropyri*	Creeping bentgrass Colonial bentgrass		thiophanate-methyl, PCNB.
The Snow Molds				
Typhula blight	*Typhula* spp.	Annual bluegrass	Avoid early fall nitrogen fertility that leads to lush growth.	Mercury compds, PCNB products,
Fusarium patch	*Fusarium nivale*	Colonial bentgrass		chloroneb. These
Sclerotinia borealis	*S. borealis*	Creeping bentgrass Fine-leaf fescues		products in combination will
LTB	not identified	Kentucky bluegrass Perennial ryegrass Tall fescue Velvet bentgrass		control snow mold complexes. Mancozeb will control *Fusarium* patch where repeat applications can be made.

Disease	Causal Agent	Hosts	Cultural Control	Chemical Control
Spring dead spot	Unknown	Bermudagrass	Avoid late summer nitrogen. Reduce thatch.	Chlorothalonil, cyclo- heximide + thiram, may be tried.
Yellow tufts	*Sclerophthora macrospora*	Annual bluegrass Creeping bentgrass Kentucky bluegrass	Iron sulfate.	None.

All agricultural chemicals recommended for use in this chart should be applied in accordance with the direc-tions on the manufacturer's label as registered under the Federal Insecticide, Fungicide, and Rodenticide Act. Mention of a trademark or proprietary product does not constitute a guarantee or warranty of the prod-uct by the author or the publisher and does not imply approval to the exclusion of other products that may also be suitable.

REFERENCES

1. Alexander, P. M. 1969. Anthracnose—Serious disease problem. *USGA Green Section Record* 7(5):8-9.

2. Bean, G. A. and R. D. Wilcoxson. 1964. Pathogenicity of three species of Helminthosporium on roots of bluegrass. *Phytopathology* 54:1084-1985.

3. Beard, J. B. 1966. Fungicide and fertilizer applications as they affect Typhula snow mold control on turf. *Quart. Bull. Mich. Agric. Exp. Sta.* 49:221-228.

4. Beard, J. B. 1973. *Turfgrass: Science and culture.* Prentice-Hall, Englewood Cliffs, N.J., p. 658.

5. Beard, J. B. 1976. Turfgrass Wear. *Mich. Turfgrass Conf. Proc.* 5:68-72.

6. Beard, J. B., P. E. Rieke, A. J. Turgeon, and J. M. Vargas, Jr. 1978. Annual Bluegrass (*Poa annua* L.): Description, adaptation, culture and control. *Mich. State Univ. Agric. Exp. Sta. Res. Rep.* No. 352, 31 pp.

7. Beard, J. B., J. M. Vargas, Jr., and P. E. Rieke. 1973. Influence of the nitrogen fertility level on Tricholoma fairy ring development in Merion Kentucky bluegrass (*Poa pratensis* L.). *Agron. J.* 65:994-995.

8. Bell, A. A., and L. R. Krusberg. 1964. Occurrence and control of a nematode of the genus *Hypsoperine* on zoysia and bermudagrass in Maryland. *Plant Dis. Reptr.* 48:721-722.

9. Bird, G. W., and J. M. Vargas, Jr. 1976. Diagnosis and control of nematode problems on turfgrass. *Mich. State Univ. Ext. Bull.* E-940, 4 pp.

10. Bloom, J. R., and H. B. Couch. 1960. Influence of environment on disease of turfgrasses. I. Effect of nutrition, pH, and soil moisture on Rhizoctonia brown patch. *Phytopathology* 50:532-535.

11. Britton, M. P. 1957. Bluegrass rust studies. *Proc. 1957 Midwest Reg. Turf Conf.*, pp. 78-79.

12. Britton, M. P. 1969. Turfgrass diseases. In *Turfgrass Sci.*, ASA Monogr. Ser., No. 14, pp. 288-335.

13. Brown, Guy E., H. Cole, Jr., and R. R. Nelson. 1972. Pathogenicity of *Curvularia* spp. to turfgrass. *Plant Dis. Reptr.* 56(1):59-63.

14. Christie, J. R. 1959. *Plant nematodes—Their binomics and control.* Univ. Fla. Agric. Exp. Sta., Gainesville, p. 256.

15. Christie, J. R., J. M. Good, Jr., and G. C. Nutter. 1954. Nematodes associated with injury to turf. *Proc. Soil Sci. Soc. Fla.* 14:167-169.

16. Colbaugh, P. F., and R. M. Endo. 1974. Drought stress: An important factor stimulating the development of *Helminthosporium sativum* on Kentucky bluegrass. *Proc. Second Int. Turfgrass Res. Conf.*, pp. 328-334.

17. Cole, H., B. Taylor, and J. Duich. 1968. Evidence of differing tolerance to fungicides among isolates of *Sclerotinia homeocarpa. Phytopathology* 56:683-686.

18. Couch, H. B. 1973. *Diseases of turfgrasses, 2nd ed.* Robert E. Krieger, Huntington, N.Y., p. 348.

19. Couch, H. B., and E. R. Bedford. 1966. Fusarium blight of turfgrasses. *Phytopathology* 56:781-786.

20. Couch, H. B., and J. R. Bloom. 1960. Influence of environment on diseases of turfgrasses. II. Effect of nutrition, pH, and soil moisture on Sclerotinia dollar spot. *Phytopathology* 50:761-763.

21. Coursen, B. W., and W. R. Jenkins. 1958. Host-parasite relationships of the pin nematode, *Paratylenchus projectus,* on tobacco and on fescue (Abstr.). *Phytopathology* 48:460.

22. Coursen, B. W., R. W. Rhode, and W. R. Jenkins. 1958. Additions to the host lists of the nematodes, *Paratylenchus projectus* and *Trichidorus christiei. Plant Dis. Reptr.* 42:456-460.

23. Courtney, W. D., and H. B. Howell. 1952. Investigations on bentgrass nematode *Anguina agrostis* (Steinbuch 1799) Filipjev 1936. *Plant Dis. Reptr.* 36:75-83.

24. Daniel, W. H., R. P. Freeborg, and M. J. Robey. 1974. Prescription athletic turf system. *Proc. Second Internat. Turfgrass Res. Conf.,* pp. 277-280.

25. Davidse, L. C. 1973. Antimitotic activity of methyl benzimidazole-2-yl carbamate (MBC) in *Aspergillus nidulans. Pestic. Biochem. Physiol.* 3:317-325.

26. Davidson, R. M., Jr., and R. L. Goss. 1972. Effects of P, S, N, lime, Chlordane, and fungicides on Ophiobolus patch disease of turf. *Plant Dis. Reptr.* 56:565-567.

27. Dickson, W. K., and C. R. Funk. 1976. Regional test of Kentucky bluegrass varieties, blends and mixtures at New Brunswick, New Jersey. *Rutgers Turfgrass Proc.,* pp. 92-97.

28. DiEdwardo, A. A. 1963. Pathogenicity and host-parasite relationships of nematodes on turf in Florida. *Fla. Agric. Exp. Sta. Ann. Rep.,* p. 109.

29. DiEdwardo, A. A., and V. G. Perry. 1964. *Heterodera leuceilyma* N.SP. *(Nemata: Heteroderidae)* a severe pathogen of St. Augustinegrass in Florida. *Fla. Agric. Exp. Sta. Bull.,* No. 687, pp. 1-35.

30. "Distribution of plant-parasitic nematodes in the South." 1960. Report of the USDA Regional Project S-19. *Southern Cooperative Ser. Bull.,* No. 74.

31. Duell, R. W., and R. M. Schmit. 1974. Grass varieties for roadsides. *Proc. Second Int. Turfgrass Res. Conf.,* pp. 541-550.

32. Ellis, M. B. 1971. *Dematiaceous Hyphomycetes.* Commonwealth Mycological Institute, Kew, Surrey, England, 607 pp.

33. Ellis, M. B. 1976. *More Dematiaceous Hyphomycetes.* Commonwealth Mycological Institute, Kew, Surrey, England, 507 pp.

34. Endo, R. M. 1961. Turfgrass diseases in southern California. *Plant Dis. Reptr.* 45:869-873; see also *Calif. Turfgrass Cult.* 10(3):22.

35. Endo, R. M. 1963. Influence of temperature on rate of growth of five fungus pathogens of turfgrass and on rate of disease spread. *Phytopathology* 53:857-861.

36. Endo, R. M., and P. F. Colbaugh. 1974. Fusarium blight of Kentucky bluegrass in California. *Proc. Second Int. Turfgrass Res. Conf.,* pp. 325-327.

37. Endo, R. M., and I. Malca. 1965. Morphological and cytohistological responses of primary roots of bentgrass to *Sclerotinia homeocarpa* and D-Galactose. *Phytopathology* 55:781-789.

38. Endo, R. M., I. Malca, and E. M. Krausman. 1964. Degeneration of the apical meristem and apex of bentgrass roots by a fungal toxin. *Phytopathology* 54:1175-1176.

39. Feder, W. A., and J. Feldmesser. 1957. Additions to the host list of *Radopholus similia,* the burrowing nematode. *Plant Dis. Reptr.* 41:33.

40. Filer, T. H., Jr. 1965. Damage to turfgrasses caused by cyanogenic compounds produced by *Marasmius oreades,* a fairy ring fungus. *Plant Dis. Reptr.* 49:571-574.

41. Filer, T. H., Jr. 1966. Effect on grass and cereal seedlings of hydrogen cyanide produced by mycelium and sporophores of *Marasmius oreades. Plant Dis. Reptr.* 50:264-266.

42. Filer, T. H., Jr. 1966. Red thread found on Bermuda grass. *Plant Dis. Reptr.* 50:525-526.

43. Freeman, T. E. 1964. Influence of nitrogen on severity of *Piricularia grisea* infection of St. Augustinegrass. *Phytopathology* 54:1187-1189.

44. Freeman, T. E. 1965. Rust of *Zoysia* spp. in Florida. *Plant Dis. Reptr.* 49:382.

45. Freeman, T. E. 1969. Diseases of turfgrasses in warm-humid regions. *Proc. First Int. Turfgrass Res. Conf.*, pp. 340-345.

46. Fulton, D. E., H. Cole, Jr., and P. E. Nelson. 1974. Fusarium blight symptoms on seedling and mature Merion Kentucky bluegrass plants inoculated with *Fusarium roseum* and *Fusarium tricinctum*. *Phytopathology* 64:354-357.

47. Gaskin, T. A. 1965. Varietal reaction of Kentucky bluegrass to Septoria leaf spot *(Septoria macropoda)*. *Plant Dis. Reptr.* 49:802.

48. Gaskin, T. A. 1966. Evidence for physiologic races of stripe smut *(Ustilago striiformis)* attacking Kentucky bluegrass. *Plant Dis. Reptr.* 40:430-431.

49. Good, J. M., A. E. Steele, and T. J. Ratcliffe. 1959. Occurrence of plant parasitic nematodes in Georgia turf nurseries. *Plant Dis. Reptr.* 43:236-238.

50. Goss, R. L. 1969. Some inter-relationships between nutrition and turfgrass diseases. *Proc. First Int. Turfgrass Res. Conf.*, pp. 351-361.

51. Goss, R. L., and C. J. Gould. 1964. Nitrogen, phosphorus, sulfur and pests. *Proc. Mich. Turfgrass Conf.* 3:75-77.

52. Gould, C. J. 1973. Ophiobolus patch: Bane to bentgrass. *Golf Superintendent* 41(3):44-46.

53. Gould, C. J., R. L. Goss, and M. Eglitis. 1961. Ophiobolus patch disease of turf in western Washington. *Plant Disease Reptr.* 45:296-297.

54. Hardison, J. R. 1963. Commercial control of *Puccinia striiformis* and other rusts in seed crops of *Poa pratensis* by nickel fungicides. *Phytopathology* 53:209-216.

55. Heald, C. M. 1969. Histopathology of 'Tifdwarf' bermuda grass infected with *Meloidogyne graminis* (Sledge and Golfden) Whitehead. *J. Nematol.* 1(1):9-10.

56. Heald, C. M., and G. W. Burton. 1968. Effect of organic and inorganic nitrogen on nematode populations on turf. *Plant Dis. Reptr.* 52:46-48.

57. Heald, C. M., and V. G. Perry. 1969. Nematodes and other pests. In *Turfgrass Sci.*, ASA Monogr. Ser., No. 140, pp. 358-369.

58. Healy, M. J., M. P. Britton, and J. D. Butler. 1965. Stripe smut damage on 'Pennlu' creeping bentgrass. *Plant Dis. Reptr.* 49:710.

59. Hearn, J. H. 1943. *Rhizoctonia solani* Kuhn and the brown patch disease of grass. *Proc. Texas Acad. Sci.* 26:41-42.

60. Hendrix, F. F., Jr., W. A. Campbell, and J. B. Moncrief. 1970. Pythium species associated with golf turfgrasses in the south and southeast. *Plant Dis. Reptr.* 54(5):419-421.

61. Hodges, C. F. 1969. Morphological differences in Kentucky bluegrass infected by stripe smut. *Plant Dis. Reptr.* 53:967-968.

62. Hodges, C. F., and M. P. Britton. 1969. Infection of Merion bluegrass, *Poa pratensis*, by stripe smut, *Ustilago striiformis*. *Phytopathology* 59:301-304.

63. Hodges, F., and J. P. Madsen. 1978. The competitive and synergistic interactions of *Drechslera sorokiniana* and *Curvularia geniculata* on leaf spot development on *Poa pratensis*. *Can. J. Bot.* 56(10);1240-1247.

64. Hodges, C. F., and D. P. Taylor. 1965. Morphology and pathological histology of bentgrass roots infected by a member of the *Meloidogyne incognita* group. *Nematologica* 11:40.

65. Hodges, C. F., and D. P. Taylor. 1966. Host-parasite interactions of a root-knot nematode and creeping bentgrass, *Agrostis palustris*. *Phytopathology* 56:88-91.

66. Howard, F. L. 1953. Helminthosporium-Curvularia blights of turf and their cure. *Golf Course Reptr.* 21(2):5-9.

67. Howard, F. L., and M. E. Davies. 1953. *Curvularia* 'fading out' of turfgrasses (Abstr.). *Phytopathology* 43:109.

68. Howard, F. L., J. B. Roswell, and H. L. Keil. 1951. Fungus diseases of turfgrasses. *Univ. R. I. Agric. Exp. Sta. Bull.*, No. 308.

69. Jackson, N. 1970. Evaluation of some chemicals for control of stripe smut in Kentucky bluegrass turf. *Plant Dis. Reptr.* 54:168-170.

70. Jackson, N., and J. M. Fenstermacher. 1974. Fungicidal control of stripe smut and melting-out with consequent maintenance of sward density in 'Merion' Kentucky bluegrass turf. *Plant Dis. Reptr.* 48(6):573-576.

71. Jackson, N., and P. H. Dernoeden. 1980. *Sclerophthora macrospora:* The incitant of yellow tuft of turfgrasses. *Plant Diseases* 64:915-916.

72. Jackson, N., and J. D. Smith. 1965. Fungal diseases of turf grasses. In *Sports Turf Res. Inst. Publ.*, 2nd ed., pp. 1-97.

73. Joyner, B. G., R. E. Partyka, and P. O. Larsen. 1977. *Rhizoctonia* brown patch of Kentucky bluegrass. *Plant Dis. Reptr.* 61:749-752.

74. Kelsheimer, E. G., and Amegda J. Overman. 1953. Notes on some ecto-parasitic nematodes found attacking lawns in the Tampa Bay area. *Proc. Fla. State Hort.* 66:301-303.

75. Kozelnicky, G. M. 1974. Updating 20 years of research: spring dead spot on bermudagrass. *USGA Green Sect. Rec.* 12(3)12-15.

76. Kozelnicky, G. M., and W. N. Garrett. 1966. The occurrence of zoysia rust in Georgia. *Plant Dis. Reptr.* 50:839.

77. Kreitlow, K. W., F. V. Juska, and R. T. Haard. 1965. A rust on *Zoysia japonica* new to North America. *Plant Dis. Reptr.* 49:185-186.

78. Lacy, M. L., and J. M. Vargas, Jr. 1977. Resistance of Fungi to Fungicides, pp. 239-256. In H. von R. Wegler (ed.), *Chemie de Pflanzenschutz-und Schadlings bekämpfungsmittel*, Vol. 4. Springer-Verlag, Berlin.

79. Larsen, P. O. 1979. Leaf blight and crown rot of Toronto creeping bentgrass. *Greens Sect. Rec.* 17:5-7.

80. Laughlin, C. W., and J. M. Vargas, Jr. 1970. Bentgrass nematode control. *Fungicide and Nematicide Tests* 26:152.

81. Laughlin, C. W., and J. M. Vargas, Jr. 1972. Influence of benomyl on the control of *Tylenchorhynchus dubius* with selected nonfumigant nematicides. *Plant Dis. Reptr.* 56:546-548.

82. Laughlin, C. W., and J. M. Vargas, Jr. 1972. Pathogenic potential of *Tylenchorhynchus dubius* on selected turfgrasses. *J. Nematol.* 4:277-289.

83. Laughlin, C. W., and J. M. Vargas, Jr. 1972. *Results of 1972 Fungicide-Nematicide Tests* 27:164-165.

84. Lebeau, J. B. 1964. Control of snow mold by regulating winter soil temperature. *Phytopathology* 54:693-696.

85. Lebeau, J. B., and C. E. Logsdon. 1958. Snow mold of forage crops in Alaska and Yukon. *Phytopathology* 48:148-150.

86. Loegering, W. Q., D. A. Sleper, James M. Johnson, and K. H. Asay. 1976. Rating general resistance on a single-plant basis. *Phytopathology* 65:1445-1448.

87. Lucas, L. T. 1976. Chemical control of spring dead spot. *Proc. Am. Phytopathol. Soc.* 3:339.

88. McCoy, N. L., R. W. Toler, and J. Amador. 1969. St. Augustine Decline (SAD)—A virus disease of St. Augustinegrass. *Plant Dis. Reptr.* 53:955-958.

89. McCoy, R. E., and H. C. Young, Jr. 1968. Bermudagrass thatch decomposition in relation to spring dead spot (Abstr.). *Phytopathology* 58:401.

90. Madison, J. H. 1971. *Practical Turfgrass Management.* Van Nostrand-Reinhold, New York, p. 466.

91. Mai, W. F., H. W. Crittenden, and W. R. Jenkins. 1960. Distribution of stylet-bearing nematodes in the northeastern United States. Report of the Technical Committee of the NE Regional Project, NE-34. *N.J. Agric. Exp. Sta. Bull.*, p. 795.

92. Meyer, W. A., and A. J. Turgeon. 1975. Control of red leaf spot on 'Toronto' creeping bentgrass. *Plant Dis. Reptr.* 59(8):642-645.

93. Mirza, K., and V. G. Perry. 1967. Histopathology of St. Augustinegrass roots infected by *Hypsoperine graminis* Sledge and Golden. *Nematologica* 13:146-147.

94. Monteith, J., Jr., and A. S. Dahl. 1932. Turf diseases and their control. *USGA Green Sect. Bull.* 12(4):87-187.

95. Mueller, W. C., N. Jackson, and J. M. Fenstermacher. 1974. Occurrence of *Sclerophthora macrospora* in turfgrass affected with yellow tuft. *Plant Dis. Reptr.* 58:848-850.

96. Northeastern Regional Turfgrass Evaluation of Kentucky Bluegrasses (*Poa pratensis* L.) 1968-1973. 1979. Report of the NE-57 Technical Research Committee. NE Regional Research Publication, *Penn. State Univ. Bull.*, No. 814, pp. 1-59.

97. Parris, G. K. 1957. Screening Mississippi soils for plant parasitic nematodes. *Plant Dis. Reptr.* 41:705.

98. Perry, V. G. 1953. The awl nematode *Dolichodorus heterocephalus*, a devastating plant parasite. *Proc. Helminthol. Soc. Wash.* 20(1):21-27.

99. Perry, V. G. 1958. A disease of Kentucky blue grass incited by certain spiral nematodes. *Phytopathology* 48:397.

100. Perry, V. G., H. M. Darling, and G. Thorne. 1959. Anatomy taxonomy and control of certain spiral nematodes attacking bluegrass in Wisconsin. *Univ. Wis. Agric. Exp. Sta. Res. Bull.*, No. 207.

101. Perry, V. G., and K. M. Maur. 1968. The pseudo-knot nematode of turf grasses. *Florida Turf* 1(1):3-8.

102. Powell, W. M. 1964. The occurrence of *Tylenchorhynchus maximus* in Georgia. *Plant Dis. Reptr.* 48:70-71.

103. Remsberg, Ruth E. 1940. The snow molds of grains and grasses caused by *Typhula itoana* and *Typhula idahoensis*. *Phytopathology* 30:178-180.

104. Rhoades, H. L. 1962. Effects of sting and stubby-root nematodes on St. Augustinegrass. *Plant Dis. Reptr.* 46:424-427.

105. Rhoades, H. L. 1962. Effects of sting and stubby-root nematodes on St. Augustinegrass. *Proc. Univ. Fla. Turf-Grass Manage. Conf.* 10:28-29.

106. Rhoades, H. L. 1965. Parasitism and pathogenicity of *Trichodorus proximus* to St. Augustinegrass. *Plant Dis. Reptr.* 49:259-262.

107. Riffle, J. W. 1964. Root-knot nematode on African Bermuda grass in New Mexico. *Plant Dis. Reptr.* 48:964-965.

108. Riggs, R. D., J. L. Dale, and M. L. Hamblen. 1962. Reaction on Bermuda grass varieties and lines to root-knot nematodes. *Phytopathology* 52:587-588.

109. Rivers, J. E., and A. A. DiEdwardo. 1963. The effect of sting (*Belonolaimus longicaudatus*) and lance (*Hoplolaimus coronatus*) nematodes on bermudagrass. *Proc. Univ. Fla. Turf-Grass Manage. Conf.* 11:150-151.

110. Rowell, J. B. 1951. Observation on the pathogenicity of *Rhizoctonia solani* on bentgrass. *Plant Dis. Reptr.* 35:240-242.

111. Sanders, P. L. 1978. Uptake, translocation, and efficacy of triadimefon in control of turfgrass pathogens. *Phytopathology* 68:1482-1487.

112. Sanders, P. L., L. L. Burpee, H. Cole, Jr., and J. M. Duich. 1978. Control of fungal pathogens of turfgrass with the experimental iprodione fungicide RP 26019. *Plant Dis. Reptr.* 62:549-553.

113. Schoevers, T.A.C. 1937. Some observations of turf diseases in Holland. *J. Bd. Green Res.* 5(16):23-26.

114. Shearman, R. C., and P. E. Rieke. 1972. How to interpret soil test results for turfgrasses. *42nd Ann. Mich. Turfgrass Conf. Proc.* 1:93-96.

115. Sledge, E. B. 1960. Studies on Meloidogyne spp. on grass. *State Plant Board Fla.* 14:108-110.

116. Smiley, R. W. 1979. *In vitro* effects of Fusarium blight controlling fungicides on pathogens of *Poa pratensis*. *Soil Biol. Biochem.*

117. Smiley, R. W., and M. M. Craven. 1977. Control of benzimidazole-tolerant *Fusarium roseum* on Kentucky bluegrass. *Plant Dis. Reptr.* 61:484-488.

118. Smiley, R. W., and M. M. Craven. 1978. Fusarium species in soil and crowns of *Poa pratensis* treated with fungicides. *Soil Biol Biochem.*

119. Smiley, R. W., and M. M. Craven. 1978. Is Fusarium blight of Kentucky bluegrass an abiotic disease? *Agron. Abstr.*

120. Smiley, R. W., and R. J. Howard. 1976. Tolerance to benzimidazole-derivation fungicides by *Fusarium roseum* on Kentucky bluegrass turf. *Plant Dis. Reptr.* 60:91-94.

121. Smith, J. D. 1954. A disease of *Poa annua, J. Sports Turf Res. Inst.* 8(29):344-353.

122. Smith, J. D. 1955. Fungi and turf disease. 5. Dollar spot disease. *J. Sports Turf Res. Inst.* 9:34-59.

123. Smith, J. D. 1956. Fungi and turf diseases. 6. Ophiobolus patch. *J. Sports Turf Res. Inst.* 9:180-202.

124. Smith, J. D. 1959. The effect of lime application on the occurrence of *Fusarium* patch disease on forced *Poa annua* turf. *J. Sports Turf. Res. Inst.* 9(34):467-470.

125. Smith, J. D. 1974. Snow molds of turfgrasses in Saskatchewan. *Proc. Second Int. Turfgrass Res. Conf.*, pp. 313-324.

126. Smithson, H., L. B. Loring, and H. J. Jensen. 1963. The "grass-root-gall nematode" found on annual bluegrass roots in Oregon. *Plant Dis. Reptr.* 47:440-441.

127. Somerville, A. M., Jr., V. G. Young, Jr., and J. L. Carnes. 1957. Occurrence of plant parasitic nematodes in soil and root samples from declining plants in several states. *Plant Dis. Reptr.* 41:187-191.

128. Somerville, R. W., and R. J. Howard. 1976. Tolerance to benzimidazole-derivation fungicides by *Fusarium roseum* on Kentucky bluegrass turf. *Plant Dis. Reptr.* 60:91-94.

129. Spraque, H. B., and G. W. Burton. 1937. Annual bluegrass (*Poa annua* L.) and its requirement for growth. *N.J. Agric. Exp. Sta. Bull.*, No. 630, pp. 1-24.

130. Stienstra, W. C. 1978. Snow molds on Minnesota golf greens. *Third Int. Turfgrass Res. Conf.* 3:271-274.

131. Sturgeon, R. V., and K. E. Jackson. 1978. Role of soil fungicides and nematicides in maintaining bermudagrass (*Cynodon dactylon*) and creeping bentgrass (*Agrostis palustris*) turf. *Proc. Third Int. Turfgrass Res. Conf.* 3:293-300.

132. Subirats, F. J., and R. L. Self. 1972. Fusarium blight of centipede grass. *Plant Dis. Reptr.* 56:42-44.

133. Tarjan, A. C. 1964. Rejuvenation of nematized centipedegrass turf with chemical drenches. *Proc. Fla. State Hort. Soc.* 77:456-461.

134. Tarjan, A. C., and M. H. Ferguson. 1951. Observations of nematodes in yellow tuft of bentgrass. *USGA J. and Turf Manage.* 4(2):28-30.

135. Tarjan, A. C., and S. W. Hart. 1955. Occurrence of yellow tuft of bentgrass in Rhode Island. *Plant Dis. Reptr.* 39:185.

136. Taylor, D. P., M. P. Britton, and H. Carol Hechler. 1963. Occurrence of plant parasitic nematodes in Illinois golf greens. *Plant Dis. Reptr.* 47:134-135.

137. Toler, R. W., and W. J. Walla. 1976. *Turf Diseases TAES Prog. Rep. RP-3375C*, 30 pp.

138. Troll, J., and R. A. Rohde. 1965. Pathogenicity of the nematodes *Pratylenchus penetrans* and *Tylenchorhynchus claytoni* on turfgrasses (Abstr.). *Phytopathology* 56:1285.

139. Troll, J., and A. C. Tarjan. 1954. Widespread occurrence of root parasitic nematodes in golf course greens in Rhode Island. *Plant Dis. Reptr.* 38:342-344.

140. Turgeon, A. J. 1975. Turfgrass variety evaluation results: 1975. *Ill. Turfgrass Conf. Proc.* 16:28-32.

141. Turgeon, A. J., and W. A. Meyer. 1974. Effects of mowing height and fertilization level on disease incidence in five Kentucky bluegrasses. *Plant Dis. Reptr.* 58:514-516.

142. Turgeon, A. J., and J. M. Vargas, Jr. 1980. An approach to turfgrass cultivar evaluation. *Proc. Third Int. Turfgrass Conf.* 3:19-30.

143. Vaartnous, H., and C. R. Elliott. 1969. Snowmolds on lawns and lawngrasses in northwest Canada. *Plant Dis. Reptr.* 53:891-894.

144. Van der Plank, J. E. 1968. *Plant diseases: Epidemics and control.* Academic Press, New York.

145. Vargas, J. M., Jr. 1972. Evaluation of four systemic fungicides for control of stripe smut in 'Merion' Kentucky bluegrass turf. *Plant Dis. Reptr.* 56:334-336.

146. Vargas, J. M., Jr. 1976. Disease poses threat to annual bluegrass. *Golf Superintendent* 44:42-45.

147. Vargas, J. M., Jr. 1976. Major Disease in Sod Production. *Ill. Turfgrass Conf.* 16:70-71.

148. Vargas, J. M., Jr., J. B. Beard, and K. T. Payne. 1972. The comparative incidence of Typhula blight and Fusarium patch on 56 Kentucky bluegrass cultivars. *Plant Dis. Reptr.* 56:32-34.

149. Vargas, J. M., Jr., and R. Detweiler. 1976. Anthracnose. *46th Ann. Mich. Turfgrass Conf. Proc.* 5:27-28.

150. Vargas, J. M., Jr., and R. Detweiler. 1976. Turfgrass disease research report. *Mich. Turfgrass Conf. Proc.* 5:7-23.

151. Vargas, J. M., Jr., R. Detweiler, and J. Hyde. 1977. Anthracnose fertility-fungicide interactions. *Mich. Turfgrass Conf. Proc.* 6:3-12.

152. Vargas, J. M., Jr., and C. W. Laughlin. 1972. The role of *Tylenchorhynchus dubius* in the development of Fusarium blight. *Phytopathology* 62:1311-1314.

153. Vargas, J. M., Jr., K. T. Payne, A. J. Turgeon and R. Detweiler. 1980. Turfgrass disease-resistance-selection, development and use. *Proc. Turfgrass Disease Symp.*, Columbus, Ohio, June 1979.

154. Vargas, J. M., Jr., and A. J. Turgeon. 1975. Translocation of C^{14} labelled chloroneb in three turfgrass species. *Can. J. Plant Sci.* 55:85-88.

155. Vargas, J. M., Jr., and A. J. Turgeon. 1978. The principles of blending Kentucky bluegrass cultivars for disease resistance. *Proc. Third Int. Turfgrass Res. Conf.* 3:45-54.

156. Vargas, J. M., Jr., H. C. Young, and E. E. Saari. 1967. The effect of light and temperature on urediospore germination infection and disease development of *Puccinia cynodontis*, and isolation of pathogenic races. *Phytopathology* 57:405-409.

157. Wadsworth, D. F., and H. C. Young, Jr. 1960. Spring dead spot of bermudagrass. *Plant Dis. Reptr.* 44:516-518.

158. Weiling, J. L., S. G. Jensen, and R. I. Hamilton. 1957. *Helminthosporium sativum*, a destructive pathogen of bluegrass. *Phytopathology* 47:744-746.

159. Wilcoxen, S. N. 1976. The complex nature of spring dead spot. *Golf Superintendent* 44:36-38.

160. Wilkinson, J. F., and D. T. Duff. 1972. Rooting of *Poa annua* L. *Poa pratensis* L. and *Agrostis palustris* Huds. at three soil bulk densities. *Agron. J.* 64:66-68.

INDEX